Escape From Death Valley

Escape From Death Valley

As Told by
WILLIAM LEWIS MANLY
and Other '49ers

Researched, Edited, and Annotated by
LEROY & JEAN JOHNSON

Reno & Las Vegas : University of Nevada Press

University of Nevada Press, Reno, Nevada 89557 USA
© LeRoy and Jean Johnson 1987. All rights reserved
Book design by Dave Comstock
Printed in the United States of America

*The paper used in this book meets the requirements of American
Standard for Information Sciences—Permanence of Paper for Printed Library Materials,
ANSI Z39.48-1984. The binding was sewn for strength and durability*

Library of Congress Cataloging-in-Publication Data

Escape from Death Valley.

Bibliography: p.
Includes index.
1. Death Valley (Calif. and Nev.)—History.
2. Death Valley (Calif. and Nev.)—Description and travel. 3.
Manley, William Lewis, b. 1820—Journeys—Death Valley (Calif.
and Nev.) 4. Overland journeys to the Pacific. I. Manly, William Lewis, b. 1820. II. Johnson, LeRoy C. III. Johnson, Jean,
1937–   .
F868.D2E73   1987   917.94'87   86-11430
ISBN 0-87417-120-2 (alk. paper)
ISBN 0-87417-108-3 (pbk. : alk. paper)

Second printing, 1987.

To Clara and Ezra

Contents

Illustrations and Maps

This story is not meant to be sensational, but a plain, unvarnished tale of truth. . . . Perhaps in days to come it may be of even more interest than now.

William Lewis Manly
Death Valley in '49

Foreword

Some years ago, LeRoy and Jean Johnson came to me to discuss their research project with respect to the adventures of Manly and Rogers and other participants in the great Death Valley episode of the California gold rush drama. They soon convinced me they came well qualified and sincerely dedicated to pursuance of the task.

As they recounted to me some of their earlier investigative hikes into the region, they reminded me of an Easter vacation my artist friend Aim Morhardt of Bishop, California, and I spent searching out the route Manly and Rogers had followed easterly across the Panamint Range on their return to the Long Camp in Death Valley when they brought sorely needed relief to the Bennett-Arcan party.

Memories of that Easter experience convinced me the Johnsons had taken on a long, tortuous, and tiring challenge if they were to trace the many trails of the Death Valley pioneers. It also struck me that they were entering into a limitless field of literary research that they would have to complete to supplement their endless desert and mountain hikes.

It was a tremendous undertaking for that small family. After scanning their final manuscript, I was led to exclaim by quoting, in part, from a sonnet of mine titled "Dream of a Climber."

> The cliffs and shales of mountains barred their way
> when, young at heart, they struggled through the dawn.
> And where their bodies lagged their souls moved on
> toward thunder-heads and summits bleak and gray
> and, as they labored through the long, long day,
> they braved the crags that creviced canyons spawn and won
>   the crest . . .

Manly has been quoted as saying in his famous book *Death Valley in '49*, "This story is not meant to be entertaining, but a plain, unvarnished tale of truth . . . perhaps in days to come it may be of even more interest than now." Future historians may use the same reference to this book so carefully researched by LeRoy and Jean Johnson.

As I counseled the Johnsons when they first visited me, "Believe Manly," I can now counsel all future researchers, "Believe the Johnsons."

ARDIS MANLY WALKER
Kernville, California

Preface

For many years LeRoy wanted to take an extended desert hike. When we read William Lewis Manly's *Death Valley in '49*, LeRoy said, "Aha! That's the trip I want to take—from Death Valley to the site of the Rancho San Francisco at Castaic Junction." Manly's story had all the elements of an adventure. In the winter of 1849–50, on the way to the California gold fields, two selfless and heroic young men came close to death in their struggle to save men, women, and children who were lost in the vastness of the Great American Desert. LeRoy wanted to follow the trails of the valiant young men, William Lewis Manly and John Haney Rogers, who hiked 270 miles from Death Valley to the Rancho San Francisco to find horses and food for the nearly starving emigrants stranded in the valley.

After Manly and Rogers returned to the eight remaining members of the Bennett-Arcan wagon train still in Death Valley, they all emerged from their seemingly interminable desert ordeal emaciated and destitute but with pride and dignity intact. As E. I. Edwards said, it is "one of the most vividly romantic exploits ever recorded." Tracing Manly and Rogers's footsteps was a journey worth attempting.

As a Boy Scout LeRoy spent a good deal of time hiking in the desert. He had climbed from the depths of Death Valley to the top of Telescope Peak and had hiked across the valley from Aguereberry Point to Furnace Creek Ranch. Supposedly all he needed to do in preparation for his 270-mile trek over the Manly-Rogers trail was to search the Death Valley literature to find a description of the route. But the more he read, the more confused he became. Historians such as Carl I. Wheat and Dr. John E. Wolff disagreed on the route. Whose interpretation was LeRoy to believe? The date for the trek was already set; no more time remained for reading. LeRoy and Dr. Richard Bush, a backpacking companion, started the long hike on January 14, 1973, knowing they might not be following Manly and Rogers's exact footsteps. The hike was a story in itself, but it was only the first chapter in what became a lengthy research project conducted on the ground, in the air, and through libraries from Washington, D.C., to California.

LeRoy's long hike was rewarding in many ways. It allowed us to establish time-distance relationships along the route where Manly's firsthand accounts did not provide any and to confirm the ones he did provide. LeRoy and Dick accomplished this by camping at or near the same places as did Manly and Rogers, and thus traveled the same distances in the same time frames. For instance, there was the question of how many miles two men could logically cover in one day. If LeRoy and Dick covered a certain distance in one day, they could believe Manly when he said he and Rogers did the same. By hiking at the same time of year, they discovered certain phenomena, such as thin sheets of ice suspended above the ground, in the same areas where Manly and Rogers found them 123 years earlier. Most importantly, the trip gave us a deep appreciation for the magnitude of the physical effort and selfless privations Manly and Rogers endured as they covered the terrible distance not once but three times.

After the long hike, LeRoy became more determined (some say obsessed) than ever to solve the riddle of the route (or routes). As a reader at The Bancroft and Huntington libraries and the National Archives, he had access to most of the pertinent literature. Historians and Death Valley experts were most generous with their time and interest. Others asked necessary and pointed questions or suggested alternatives to be considered. Researching the route became a family passion that consumed our vacations for over thirteen years.

Because LeRoy is a trained researcher, his approach to solving the riddle of the routes differs from that of some historians. It would not do for us to hike a canyon only once. Oh, no! We hiked every canyon and many of the ridges on both sides of the Panamint Range between Pleasant Canyon and Goler Wash, every canyon and canyon branch on both sides of the Slate Range in the Manly Pass area, and every canyon in the Argus Range between Wilson and Burro canyons. Some were hiked five times. Only in this thorough way could we confidently say a particular canyon fit Manly's descriptions better than any other canyon.

There are two reasons we wrote this book. First, to document our observations and conclusions as to the routes Manly, Rogers, and the Bennett and Arcan families used to get into and out of Death Valley during the winter of 1849–50. Second, to present for the first time since 1888 the California desert portion of "From Vermont to California," Manly's serialized account of his journey west during the gold rush (part II, with our analyses in the notes). This account differs in several important ways from his well-known book *Death Valley in '49*, published six years later. We expand upon these differences in part I, which also includes a discussion of the method we used to locate the routes, a thorough literature review, some of our adventures while researching the routes, and a synopsis of the routes. Part III is John Rogers's (Rodgers) short newspaper account of the trip from Hobble Creek to Los Angeles. Part IV is an excerpt of Louis Nusbaumer's journal that supplements Manly's account, and part V includes letters written by Reverend James Welsh Brier that relate specifically to the Manly-Rogers routes.

We have two groups of readers in mind—those who enjoy their history in the comfort of an armchair, and the hikers and scholars who want to know not only where the trails are but how we came to our conclusions. A few of our interpretations are at variance with some currently espoused, but our notes and references explain our rationale.

By knowing just where this small group of lost emigrants camped, what canyons they passed through, and what springs they found, we can bridge the gap of time and touch our historical roots. We can all take pride in and marvel at the accomplishments of these hardy emigrants as they exemplified the strong, independent, and compassionate spirit characteristic of America's pioneers. Because much of Death Valley and portions of the California desert are virtually unchanged since 1850, one can walk where the '49ers walked, see what they saw, and experience some of the sensations they felt. But in order to do this we have to know just where they traveled. That is why we bring you this intensely felt narrative by William Lewis Manly and why we researched his footsteps so thoroughly. To guide the reader through the labyrinth of desert canyons and mountain ranges, we include detailed maps to delineate the route. We use brackets in quoted material to insert modern place names, corrections, or comments. Our notes explain the reasoning behind our conclusions, the sources of our data, and supplementary information.

Manly spelled his name *Manley* with the *e* throughout the publication of "From Vermont to California," as well as on the copyright page and in the text of *Death Valley in '49*. However, the title page of *Death Valley in '49* and his personal letters are signed *Manly* without the *e*. Henry S. Manley (1965:28), a Manley family historian, says the name should be spelled with an *e*. But, because *Manly* is the commonly recognized spelling, we use it in our narrative and notes. Family names are left as spelled in original documents. John Rogers's name is spelled *Rodgers* in the byline of his newspaper account, the only example of that spelling we found. Manly and Rogers consistently spell *Arcane* with the *e*; but on the family tombstones it is spelled *Arcan,* so we spell it *Arcan* in our writing. (In Manly's day, the pronunciation was with the long *a;* Moody called him R. Kane.) We have retained Manly's original punctuation and spelling in excerpts from his letters and in "From Vermont to California," except in rare cases where the error was obviously typographical. The editor of the *Santa Clara Valley* corrected Manly's "whares" and "thars," which are found throughout his letters. We also keep the original spelling and punctuation in Reverend and Mrs. Brier's letters, but break them up into paragraphs for clarity and add spaces where periods were omitted. In our text and notes we use the correct name *Rancho San Francisco* rather than *San Francisquito* as used by most '49ers and historians (see note 61).

Nusbaumer's journal posed special problems. Some pages are missing, and there are smudged words and significant changes in penmanship as well as English words or abbreviations inserted into his German text. He consistently used brackets to add afterthoughts or points of clarification. We changed his brackets to parentheses because we use brackets throughout the book to insert our own comments. Illegible or missing words and phrases are indicated by the word *illegible* in brackets. Nusbaumer spelled Anton Schlögel's name three different ways, so we settled on *Schlögel*.

Literature is cited by author/year/page except for maps and documents in the Jayhawker and Palmer collections at the Henry J. Huntington Library, San Marino, California. The Jayhawker Collection has 1,105 numbered pieces spanning 1849 to 1938; each has a JA number. Material from the Palmer Collection is cited by HM numbers. U.S. Geological Survey maps are cited by quadrangle name/state/scale/year. The USGS maps are not listed in the bibliography, but older maps are cited by author and date.

Acknowledgments

We give special thanks to three husband and wife teams who have given us encouragement, ground support, shelter, and intellectual challenge during the course of our research. Matt and Rosemary Ryan, also known as Mr. and Mrs. Death Valley, have unselfishly hauled us to remote canyons, shared their many years of firsthand experiences in Death Valley, and gently nudged us away from the brink when we were about to go over an intellectual cliff. But they allowed us to wander into a mental box canyon knowing we would finally backtrack and find the right way. Ardis and Gayle Walker shared their home, their wisdom, and their extensive library with us. Ardis, a noted California scholar, author, and poet, advised us to *"Believe Manly. When in doubt, believe Manly,"* a maxim that guided us throughout our research. The original edition of Manly's book that they gave us was a constant inspiration when we became discouraged. It is the one in which Ardis discovered the Manly map now on display in the Death Valley Museum. Mary and Paul DeDecker also shared their home, remote camping spots, and library with us, and have helped us realize the importance of sharing our outdoor experiences with our children. As a prominent California botanist, Mary has helped us identify desert plants.

Our parents, Curt and Pearl Johnson and Ezra and Clara Hornibrook, gave continued support with their interest and active participation in our trips. Without Ezra's ground support on our "long hike" and during repeated ventures through the Death Valley area, we could not have researched this book. To our many hiking companions, especially Dick Bush, owner of Madroño Vineyards, who hiked "the long hike," and Fred Camphausen, owner of Mountain High Ltd., who was our official escort on several trips into the Naval Weapons Center, China Lake, we extend special thanks for sharing many desert trails. And to George Marks, co-founder of Sierra Design, we give special thanks for equipping the long hike.

We sincerely acknowledge the cooperation of Dr. James Hart and the Council of The Bancroft Library for allowing us to retranslate the Nusbaumer journal, and to the library staff we extend our sincere appreciation for their assistance. We thank Barbara Johnson for retranslating the journal and Clyde and Gela Hunt, who checked it. We owe special thanks to Virginia Rust and her staff at the Huntington Library for guiding us through the Jayhawker and Palmer collections and many of the rare documents in the library's care. To the staff of the National Park Service, particularly Pete Sanchez, and members of the Death Valley '49ers we extend our appreciation for the help they gave us. And we thank Francis M. Wheat, Carl I. Wheat's son, for his cooperation in permitting us to use material from his father's collection.

Finally, our heartfelt thanks to Eric and Mark, our sons, who were in on every phase of the research, for their questions and their help in finding the answers.

Part I

Our Analysis of the Manly-Rogers Routes

1. Manly and Rogers's route down the Green River from Wyoming (a) to Utah (b), and their trek to Hobble Creek, south of Provo, Utah.

2. Approximate route of the Bennett-Arcan Party from Hobble Creek, Utah, to the Rancho San Francisco near Saugus, in southern California.

Historical Background

The westward migration over the Oregon Trail was already under way when the cry of "Gold!" added the final impetus to complete the nation's dream of manifest destiny. James Marshall's chance discovery of gold on January 24, 1848, at Sutter's Mill on the American River set into motion a mass migration unparalleled in history. Prior to 1849, about 15,000 people had migrated to Oregon and Alta California via overland routes, and another 4,600, mostly Mormons, went as far west as Salt Lake Valley, where they settled and established their New Zion. However, in 1849, the first year of the gold rush, 25,000 people migrated overland to California. The emigrants went for different reasons; some to find new land to settle, others to seek a quick and easy fortune, and still others to find new horizons and adventure.

Several wagon trains arrived at Salt Lake City too late in the fall of 1849 to attempt a Sierra Nevada crossing. The fate of the Donner party and Frémont's disastrous fourth expedition were still fresh in their minds. The Mormons encouraged the emigrants to take a southern route via the Old Spanish Trail to Pueblo de Los Angeles and then north to the gold fields—a route traversed so far by only one wagon. The advantages of the route were a lack of snow, no major mountain ranges to cross, and a guide who had traveled the route before. The disadvantage pointed out by Captain Hunt, their guide, was a scarcity of water and forage for the animals. He warned the emigrants they would lose some of their cattle along the way, but the unknown dangers of the southern route outweighed the known dangers of a late Sierra Nevada crossing. Over one hundred wagons started south from the rendezvous on Hobble Creek south of Provo, Utah. Some wagons belonged to families such as the Bennetts, Arcans, Moodys, Skinners, Wades, and Briers. Other wagons were shared by groups of single men such as the Jayhawkers who had bound themselves together with oaths of allegiance for mutual protection. Still others were miscellaneous individuals drawn together at Salt Lake. The train included Dutch, German, French; Catholic, Protestant, Mormon; black, white; young and old—a truly American composite.

After a month of arduous travel south from Hobble Creek, dissension in the train reached its highest point near what is now

Enterprise, Utah. Some packers who had overtaken the train had with them a map, apparently drawn by a mountain man named Elijah (called Barney) Ward, showing a route that would cut 300 to 500 miles from their journey to the gold fields, a route due west with water holes along the base of a mountain range. Adding credence to this map was one drawn by Frémont's cartographer in 1848 showing a mountain range running east and west that Frémont thought to be the southern boundary of the Great Basin. But Frémont's map also labeled this extensive area with the warning "Unexplored." The train divided, and all but seven wagons headed directly west into unknown territory.

After three days of easy travel westward up Shoal Creek, they encountered Beaver Dam Wash, a long, deep chasm that stopped the oxen in their tracks. Here at "Mountain Misery" about seventy-five wagons turned back to follow Hunt's train along the Old Spanish Trail. The Bennett, Arcan, Wade, and Brier families, all with women and young children, decided to cast their lot with the adventurous single men who were determined to follow the questionable cutoff sketched on the Barney Ward map. They detoured north around the chasm and continued west.

The train splintered into smaller and smaller groups as the going became more difficult. Near Papoose Dry Lake in southwestern Nevada, the Jayhawker group, the Brier family, and the Georgia-Mississippi boys headed due west, while another group composed of at least seven wagons (which we call the Bennett-Arcan train) turned south.

William Lewis Manly, the central figure of this book, scouted for this latter, loosely knit group. Asabel (Asahel) and Sarah Bennett had two wagons and three young children: George, 8; Melissa, a year younger; and Martha, 4. In addition to the family members, there were two wagon drivers plus Lewis Manly and John Rogers. Manly and the Bennetts came from southwestern Wisconsin, and Rogers was from Tennessee. The Arcans, from Chicago, also had two wagons and two drivers in addition to the family members— John (Jean) Baptiste Arcan, his pregnant wife Abigail, and their 2-year-old son Charlie. The Earhart brothers and a grown son had a wagon, as did Anton Schlögel. Other unnamed men probably traveled with them. Another wagon was shared by Captain Culverwell, Louis Nusbaumer, Mr. Hadapp, Mr. Fish, Mr. Isham, and Mr. Smith, a black man. The Wade family traveled a day or so behind the others with their two wagons (some say one) and were not considered part of the train. Their party included Harry and Mary Wade, four children, and a driver. More details on the families are found in the introductions to parts II, III, IV, and V and in the epilogue.

Food was already in short supply before the emigrants reached the Amargosa Desert east of Death Valley. One traveler was so desperate that he stole meat intended for the Bennett and Arcan children. Water became more valuable than gold. Manly and John Rogers, who crossed the plains together, scouted the route ahead and searched for precious springs. When they returned from one of their trips they found Sarah Bennett and Abigail Arcan in heartrending distress.

> The four children were crying for water but there was not a drop to give them, and none could be reached before sometime next day. The mothers were nearly crazy, for they expected the children would choke with thirst and die in their arms, and would rather perish themselves than suffer the agony of seeing their little ones gasp and slowly die. They reproached themselves as being the cause of all this trouble. For the love of gold they had left homes where hunger had never come, and often in sleep dreamed of the bounteous tables of their old homes only to be woefully disappointed in the morning. There was great gladness when John Rogers and I appeared in the camp and gave the mothers full canteens of water for themselves and little ones, and there were tears of joy and thankfulness upon their cheeks as they blessed us over and over again [Manly 1894:129].

When the members of the Bennett-Arcan train finally reached Death Valley and discovered they could not get over the Panamint Range with their wagons, they asked Manly and Rogers to go on foot to find and return with food to eat and horses for the women and children to ride. We let Manly tell his story from the Amargosa Desert onward in part II.

Manly and Rogers had faced other perils together. They first met at Council Bluffs, Iowa, where Manly was hired as a wagon driver for a small train organized by a Mr. Dallas. Manly had planned to travel with his friends the Bennetts, but they left unexpectedly for the California gold fields while he was away purchasing a Winnebago Indian pony. Both Manly and Rogers drove wagons across the plains, but as they crossed the Rocky Mountains, the drivers learned they were to be let go in Salt Lake City for the winter with no prospects for work and no chance to get through to the gold fields. They had to look out for themselves, so they decided to float down the Green River to the Pacific Ocean. After losing their boat, building canoes out of logs, and racing rapids with nearly disastrous results, five of the seven would-be sailors took the advice of the Ute chief Walkara (Wakara, Wahara), and left the river to travel cross-country toward Salt Lake City. But before reaching Salt Lake, they came across the rendezvous of wagons preparing for the journey south to Los Angeles. Quite by accident, Manly found the Bennett wagons and in them all the gear and money he had left with the

Bennetts in Mineral Point, Wisconsin. Manly was better off than his fellow Green River friends, who had only the clothes on their backs. He bought flour and bacon for them and gave them all his money "for they might need some, and I did not." By the time the large wagon train reached the cutoff, Rogers was also a member of the Bennett party.

Manly and Rogers were physically quite different. William Lewis Manly was 29 years old, short (about 5 feet 8 inches tall) and fair. John Haney Rogers, age 24 or 25, was a big man with a dark complexion who stood over 6 feet 2 inches tall. Manly came from a family-oriented, strict New England background; Rogers came from Tennessee, and although we know nothing about his upbringing or his family, his dedication and sacrifice on behalf of the Bennett-Arcan families attest to his personal values. Both men had confidence in their abilities, having already tested their strength in the forests and wilderness across a great continent. They also shared strong convictions and faith in themselves.

We often call these stalwart men "the boys," a term used by Asabel Bennett, who exclaimed, "The boys have come. The boys have come!" when Manly and Rogers returned to Death Valley after a perilous 500-mile trek to find provisions for the destitute families.

The subject of this book is the route of the Bennett-Arcan wagon train from Ash Meadows to the western side of Death Valley, and from there the trails used by Manly and Rogers as they crossed the mountains and deserts to find and return with provisions and then to guide the Bennett-Arcan families to safety.

Research Method

Our research on the Manly-Rogers trails through the California deserts did not start out as a family affair, but it ended up that way. A family joke was that our boys, Eric and Mark, did not know they could vacation somewhere other than Death Valley until they were old enough to have cars of their own. Although LeRoy did his longest (270 miles) and hardest (he almost didn't make it) hiking in the company of other men, most of and research was done by our family. Eric was 10 when we started our research in 1972; fortunately, our desert experiences were such that when he was 13 he decided to hike the full 130-mile length of the Death Valley National Monument. Mark was 8 when we started our desert hiking, and by the time he was in the fourth grade he had climbed Telescope and Sentinel peaks and twice crossed the Slate Range over Manly Pass.

Our experiences in and about Death Valley have ranged from wonderful to life threatening in temperatures from well below freezing to 112° F. In the name of research we (usually LeRoy) sampled every water source we found, some of them fouled by wild burros, and others salty and full of minerals. Our boys hunted Easter eggs in Furnace Creek Wash and found Easter candy speared on yucca spines in Etcheron Valley near Carricut Lake in the Argus Range. Eric celebrated birthdays on a pile of tremendous rocks near the sandy Trona golf course and in a miner's cabin in Pleasant Canyon, Panamint Range. The boys watched Mojave rattlesnakes in a courting ritual and shared their dinner with a shy desert kit fox; Eric was bitten by the brown recluse spider, and Mark caught tarantulas and desert lizards in deep desert canyons. They also helped us with time-distance relationships and were instrumental in three most important discoveries. Through it all, they kept a detached attitude and therefore acted as a leveling agent to our sometimes obsessive involvement with the research.

The most enjoyable part of our research was collecting the data and reaching tentative conclusions. The most difficult part was the necessity to rethink and reinterpret the data and to search the literature for helpful nuggets of information. The conflicting information found in the literature led to mental hair pulling and frustration, and it was only after we spent a great deal of time with all the applicable literature and many days of hiking that we felt comfortable at last with our conclusions.

Since we were not getting the results we wanted by hiking bits and pieces of the desert with Manly's book *Death Valley in '49* in hand, we settled on an organized way to search for the routes. Because LeRoy is a scientist and Jean a musician, a formal structure was natural to both of us. First we decided that what we were doing was research. A scientist once defined research as "the manner in which we solve knotty problems in our attempt to push back the frontiers of human ignorance" (Leedy 1980:4). Webster gives a more definitive description of research: "Critical and exhaustive investigation or experimentation having for its aim the discovery of new facts and their correct interpretation, the revision of accepted conclusions, theories, or laws, in the light of newly discovered facts." (*Webster's New International Dictionary*, 1939). Our research was concerned more with reexamining accepted conclusions and interpreting old facts than with the discovery of new facts.

A common approach to solving problems or searching for truth in most disciplines is the *scientific method*. It is a systematic search consisting of a general set of steps that researchers throughout the world use to solve problems, although not every researcher uses exactly the same number or sequence of steps.

Using the scientific method did not diminish the fun and excitement of our research, nor did it reduce our personal involvement. The challenge one finds while putting together a jigsaw puzzle or searching for hidden treasure was still there. The opportunity to imagine what it was like way-back-then and to simulate the hardships and joys the original participants experienced is still available, especially in the desert, where there are great expanses basically unchanged in the past 200 years. In short, the scientific method provided an excellent framework on which to organize our findings and the procedures we used to carry out our historical research.

We used the following steps in our study of the Manly-Rogers trails into and out of Death Valley.

1. Identify the main problem and break it down into subproblems.
2. Review the literature.
3. Choose a method or procedure for collecting data.
4. Formulate hypotheses (logical assumptions) to be tested.
5. Collect data about the chosen hypotheses.
6. Interpret the data.
7. Make tentative conclusions and piece together the subproblems.
8. Reexamine the tentative conclusions and form final conclusions. Redo steps 4, 5, 6, and 7 if necessary.
9. Present or publish the procedures and findings.

Identify the Problem

Our first step was to identify the main problem. Simply stated, it was: *What route or routes did Manly and Rogers use during their heroic rescue mission?* We divided the problem into three parts: (1) What route did Manly and Rogers take from Death Valley to the Rancho San Francisco (at Castaic Junction near Newhall) in their mission to secure horses and provisions? (2) What route did they use to return to Death Valley? (3) What route did they use to leave the valley when they led the Bennett and Arcan families to the Rancho San Francisco?

We divided each part of the main problem into subproblems. Valleys became subproblems, as did mountain ranges, and some of the mountain ranges were divided into east-side and west-side subproblems. Thus, we disaggregated the problem into segments we could handle more easily. Each subproblem had to be systematically researched and carefully analyzed before the complete problem could be solved. This was analogous to piecing together a complex puzzle, and, as with many an old puzzle handed down over time, some pieces were missing.

Review the Literature

The next step was to review the literature to become familiar with Death Valley history. We needed to see what information was available and what conclusions others had made. We first divided the literary sources into two groups: (1) primary sources—firsthand accounts of the 1849 emigrants, subsequent early explorers, and miners; and (2) secondary sources—all other references.

We had to rely heavily on the literature for clues to the routes since physical evidence of the emigrants' passing has long since been scoured away by wind and rain. The charred remnants of their wagons and abandoned belongings have vanished. Today the only vestiges of the sojourn of the '49ers in the Death Valley region are two rocks inscribed by William B. Rood (probably chiseled twenty years later when he returned as a prospector) and an "1849" inscription of dubious date in Marble Canyon. Unlike the terrain along the Old Spanish Trail, none of the landmarks in the Death Valley area had previously been seen by white men or women; thus, those who kept journals could not record place names to help guide us along their footsteps. Fortunately, both Manly and James Brier returned to the Panamint Range years later and used some of the names still used today.

The literature review was much more difficult than we had expected; numerous conflicts among the various accounts forced us to choose some pieces of information and reject others. We came to realize that a comprehensive search and analysis of this large body of literature was needed, both the firsthand information and later interpretations, to determine which was of value. Some literature not cited in the text was included in the bibliography to help other researchers when they enter the labyrinth of Death Valley literature.

There are four extant firsthand accounts from the group of about thirty men, women, and children who turned south into Death Valley; two accounts written by William Lewis Manly, one by John Haney Rogers, and one by Louis Nusbaumer.

Manly kept a diary beginning in March 1849, that continued throughout his long journey to California from Mineral Point, Wisconsin, through his return to Mineral Point in February 1851. He used it as a reference to write a 300-page letter to his parents in which he told of his experiences during the overland journey to the gold fields and his return via the Isthmus of Panama. After he finished his long letter in the spring of 1851, Manly visited an old trapping partner, Robert McCloud, who persuaded him to return to California. The letter, which Manly (1894:439) requested not be published because he felt it was "ungrammatical and the spelling so incorrect that it would be no credit to me," was read and reread by his parents and friends. This first narrative of Manly's sojourn to California was reduced to ashes when his parents' home burned. And the diary? It, too, was destroyed in the fire (JA 612).

Manly said he dictated an account to one of Hubert Bancroft's scribes in 1884, but it has never been found. The first published account of Manly's heroic trek was gleaned from him by a reporter for an article published in the San Jose newspaper the *Pioneer*, April 21 and 28, 1877. It is reprinted in *The Jayhawkers' Oath and Other Sketches*, edited by Arthur Woodward. We classify this as a second-hand account because Manly did not write it, and it is unlikely he reviewed the article before it was published.

Probably the most important account in all the early Death Valley literature is the one Manly wrote from 1887 through early 1890, the California desert portion of which is reprinted in part II. In a letter (JA 644) dated January 27, 1889, written to be read at the yearly Jayhawker reunion, Manly said:

> My good friends . . . I may tell you here that I got a fall one year ago last July which distroyed me for work for the balance of my life   I have got so I can walk about but my back will always be weak. After this accident I was persuaded to write out such an account of our & my trip across the plains as I could remember   I commenced to please my friends but found it a verry hard dificult job after 38 years have passed along   it has been published here in a horticultural magazine called the Santa [Clara] Valley   a full page each month 4 [3] columns in a page & Feb & Mch bring us out to Los Angeles   this has been to me unpleasant work. [Spelling, capitalization, and punctuation in all quotes are original unless otherwise stated.]

The first issue of "From Vermont to California" was published in June 1887, and the account ran monthly through July 1890. It began, "I was born in St. Albans, Vt. in 1820," but Manly's name did not appear as the author, nor was it mentioned in the text. However, from the third issue on, the articles were by-lined "W. L. Manley" (spelled with the *e*). Of the thirty-eight issues, thirty-three are housed in The Bancroft Library, University of California, Berkeley. Burr Belden, noted Death Valley historian, searched for years for the five missing issues; we continued the search and have found one of them. The first missing issue covered the trek across the Nevada desert to the Ash Meadows area. The eleven consecutive issues covering the trek from Ash Meadows, Nevada, to Los Angeles are reprinted for the first time in part II.

We prefer this serialized version of Manly's exploits to his better-known book, *Death Valley in '49*, published in 1894. The spontaneous flow of words written under the pressure of a monthly deadline is more representative of Manly's true feelings, reflections, and memories. Burr Belden shared our opinion. He wrote us in 1973 that "From Vermont to California" was "primarily Manly himself, and not what had rubbed off from others—which in my mind somewhat diminished the value of the book."

To refresh his memory and to get more information for his writing, Manly began a lively correspondence with other '49ers, and he traveled about to obtain their stories. From these conversations sprang the articles collected by Arthur Woodward in *The Jayhawkers' Oath and Other Sketches*. Thus, Manly's published accounts were not merely an old man's memories, but were based on several trips over the area, on conversations with contemporaries, and on two accounts he wrote before 1887—his diary and his long letter.

Death Valley in '49 (sometimes referred to as "the book" or the 1894 account) has been the most accessible version of Manly's accounts. E. I. Edwards (1962b:85) says, "Manly's book is the cornerstone of Death Valley's literary structure." Charles F. Lummis (1897:116), editor of *The Land of Sunshine*, reviewed the book, calling it "one of the most interesting books of the season." However, he added that it was "printed by 'blacksmiths' who have disfigured its every page with misspellings and letters upside down. . . . Pity it is that a narrative of so much worth historically should have fallen to the tough mercies of (let us hope) the most incompetent printers in California. San Jose. The Pacific Tree and Vine Co., $2.00."

Manly apparently felt the need for help in writing his book. He wrote to Jayhawker John Colton, March 16, 1890 (JA 617):

> I have been by many asked to put it in book form but . . . all
> would look better if it was writen as it would have been done by
> a person who had som ability in that particular way   when I

study over this trip I can see whare much is left out but too late
to put in [the serialized version] so I have to let it go as Ed Doty
says with much left out   so if you get the naration please excuse
the uneducated backwoods writer.

California historian Lawrence Clark Powell said in a conversation with E. I. Edwards, "I am certain that the old man he was in
1894 could not alone have written such a powerful narrative. There
is a wide gap between it and the shorter pieces and the letters
written at the same period" (Powell 1971:41). Edwards concurred.
He showed a letter to Powell that suggested a Mr. Munn "assisted
Manly in the preparation of the manuscript for *Death Valley in '49*"
(Powell 1971:42). Powell tried unsuccessfully to confirm or refute
this possibility.

Another writing assistant was suggested to Powell in a letter
from Mrs. Lillie M. Kirkgaard (1971), who had been head of the Fine
Arts and California Department of the Pasadena Public Library for
many years. She said Miss Helen E. Harley wrote the book for
Manly when she was 17 years old. Miss Harley's father, editor for a
northern California newspaper, had tutored her in journalism. Mrs.
Kirkgaard said a friend of Manly's approached Miss Harley about
writing Manly's experiences, which she proceeded to do. Miss Harley told Mrs. Kirkgaard about her dealings with Manly; how he
often "came with scribbled notes on grease spotted paper bags and
would sometimes break into uncontrolled weeping during his reminiscences. Not only did she have to organize scribbled notes but had
to get him emotionally organized for coherence." On August 25,
1975, Mrs. Kirkgaard told us Miss Harley "was very disappointed to
not have been given credit for the book."

Powell (1971:34) felt "the general form and style are the same in
the two versions," but we feel there are distinct differences. Powell
may have come to his conclusion by comparing the last few months
(May 1889 through May 1890) of the serialized account to the last 110
pages of the book, which are almost verbatim. Only now and then is
a sentence or paragraph left out of the book or a single word
changed. This is in marked contrast to the differences found from
the beginnings of the accounts through Manly's arrival in Los Angeles and the interviews with Jayhawkers and other '49ers.

After carefully comparing the two accounts, we conclude the
writing assistant was a lady—quite possibly Miss Harley. An example of differences between the two accounts is the description of
soil texture along a trail across the Mojave Desert—the trail used by
Indians on their horse-stealing raids into the coastal regions of
California. In the June 1888 issue of "From Vermont to California,"
Manly wrote "the ground was very soft and light as snuff." In his
book (Manly 1894:165) this was changed to "dirt finer than the finest

flour"—a decidedly feminine touch. In the same issue, Manly correctly ascribed the death of many horses and cattle to the "long dry road," whereas the book suggests "poison water" or a mysterious unknown agent (Manly 1894:165). And the accurate description of coyotes in the San Gabriel Mountains in the 1888 account was changed to wolves by 1894 when the book was published.

A good example of the more elaborate writing found in Manly's book is the memorable discovery of fresh water in Soledad Canyon after Manly and Rogers's arduous tramp over the desert. In 1888, Manly wrote, "about sundown we came to another canyon that joined ours and in it we found a beautiful little babbling brook. Here we made our camp and had some good wood and water." In *Death Valley in '49* (p. 169), this was rewritten:

> We followed down the ravine for many miles, and when this came out into a larger one, we were greatly pleased at the prospect, for down the latter came a beautiful little running brook of clear pure water, singing as it danced over the stones, a happy song and telling us to drink and drink again, and you may be sure we did drink, for it had been months and months since we had had such water, pure, sweet, free from the terrible alkali and stagnant taste that had been in almost every drop we had seen.

One direct reference to an editor is found in Manly's book (1894:367) in the introduction to Erkson's narrative: "The following was dictated to the editor of this book." And in a letter to John Colton on April 4, 1894 (JA 624), Manly wrote, "I have spent more than 3 years getting it together & in proper shape for the printer I had to have one assistant because I am not able to do such work & have it grammatical." A possibility is that Mr. Munn assisted Manly with the technical layout and Miss Harley reworked the 1887 to 1889 serialized text with help from Manly's dictation and additional notes. For some reason, either lack of time or Miss Harley no longer being able to work on the book, from page 390 on, *Death Valley in '49* is virtually identical to "From Vermont to California."

Death Valley in '49 was started in 1890 and took three years to complete. Manly was concerned over the amount of money it was going to cost him to publish it, and after its publication his letters expressed worry about making back the money he had invested. The original and facsimiles have three charming illustrations apparently drawn by Manly specifically for the book. In August 1894 (HM 50802), he wrote Palmer:

> I never tried before to make a picture on paper until I made up my mind to show my friends the sunken valley so much talked of & writen about—I should have put in more sketches but they would make my Book too expensive to reach all—I had 4 sketch-

es on Green River that would have been good for some to look at
as they read along—the sketches in my book are only to show
the reader how we worked our way from *purgatory to heaven* . . .
Rogers myself & the 2 little children you can see on the ox is all
that is now left.

There are five subsequent editions of Manly's book. All our
citations are to the original 1894 edition, a facsimile of which is
readily available in the Chalfant Press paperback edition.

The third surviving firsthand account is John Rogers's short
narrative in the *Merced Star*, April 26, 1894, written when John was
about 71 years old (part III of this volume). It differs from Manly's
accounts in a number of details, some adding to and some con-
tradicting Manly. The account is chronological in only a general
way, more a collage of memories than a report of daily actions and
events. Therefore, historians must be careful how they use it. Its
primary value lies in corroborating other accounts. If Rogers mentions an incident, it happened—however, not necessarily where,
when, or with whom he mentions it.

The fourth extant account is Louis Nusbaumer's journal.
Thanks to the Nusbaumer family, it is now preserved in The Bancroft Library. It was written in German with occasional English
phrases and abbreviations such as "100 mls" and "Hurrah for California." We are fortunate he decided to keep detailed entries from
the Ash Meadows area onward through Death Valley. Although the
entries tell what he did on each day, the differences in penmanship
and the changes from pen to pencil indicate that several "daily"
entries were written at one time. We had translated the portion of
his journal that helps with our analysis of the Manly-Rogers routes
(part IV of this volume).

Others who wrote firsthand accounts were members of the
Brier family, the Jayhawkers, and the Georgia-Mississippi boys,
who moved north in Death Valley. Two journals written by
Jayhawkers survive and are housed in the Huntington Library. Asa
Haynes's original diary contains concise entries of mileages and
direction, but almost no descriptions of camps or terrain. He made
two copies of his first entries in the same notebook, and there are
discrepancies between them. A typed copy of Sheldon Young's log
is more descriptive, but his mileages are not always reliable. Hafen
and Hafen (1954b:62) say, "Young's mileages are frequently too
large." Young's original log was apparently lost, but we still consider the copy a firsthand account, although with reservations—there
is no proof of the copy's accuracy.

In addition to Haynes's and Young's journals there are letters
by Reverend James Welsh Brier, newspaper articles based on Juliet
Brier's memories, newspaper articles by John Wells Brier, and rem-

iniscences by Edward Coker, Thomas Shannon, Dow Stephens, and J. B. Colton. There are also numerous letters by other Jayhawkers in the Jayhawker Collection. They are not all equal in value or reliability and should not be weighted equally as evidence to support a hypothesis. For example, of those who left accounts, only Manly and James Brier returned to the Death Valley area, and thus refreshed their memories by retracing their footsteps. For this reason, we invest more trust in their accounts than in those of others who had been there only once and under trying conditions. Manly returned to rescue the Bennett-Arcan families in 1850 and returned again to rescue Charles Alvord in 1860. James Brier retraced his 1850 route from Indian Wells east to the Panamint Range as a miners' guide in spring 1873. He said on January 17, 1876 (JA 70), that from Indian Wells Spring "to Death Valley (as it is now called) every rod of the way looked as familiar to me as though I been there but a day before."

There are numerous discrepancies among the various accounts left by the emigrants who passed through Death Valley. One reason is that reporters and editors sometimes modified the accounts for publication—they were more interested in a dramatic story than in documenting historical events.

Mrs. Brier's two newspaper interviews are vignettes of memory and not necessarily in chronological order. John Brier said in 1908 (JA 87), "it gives her the most excruciating agony of mind to attempt a recital of events connected with our journey. Besides, those events are so mingled and confused in her memory, that her testimony is practically worthless." However, we can consider certain details to be reliable. For instance, the details of Christmas at Travertine Springs are probably correct; certain special days remain clear in a mother's memory.

John Brier, age 6 when he crossed the desert, wrote two accounts for newspaper publication. He remembered "the events stamped on the memory of a very small boy" (JA 88), although his memory was reinforced by his parents' retelling of the experience. His reputation as a fine orator, a man of words, is particularly obvious in his florid 1911 account. Although he was in the Nevada-California desert in 1849, we consider his accounts secondhand because he related mostly what his parents told him. Consequently he mixed up or misplaced certain locations and facts.

In 1916, Jayhawker L. Dow Stephens, 89 years old at the time, wrote *Life Sketches of a Jayhawker of '49*. Keeping in mind the natural drawbacks of being written so many years after the fact, it is a good firsthand account. It sheds little light on the Manly-Rogers routes, but is helpful in tracing the Jayhawkers through the deserts. He incorrectly said that Fish and Isham died in Death Valley, but in the 1870s the name Death Valley was loosely applied to the entire region where the emigrants witnessed their greatest suffering—Death Valley, Panamint Valley, Searles Valley, and the mountains in between. Wheeler (1872:16) said it was "one of the most desolate regions upon the face of the earth . . . [and] this entire section is known in common parlance . . . as 'Death Valley,' while the 'Death Valley proper' should be limited to that remarkable depression which, at its lowest surface, falls beneath the level of the ocean." Stephens was speaking "in common parlance" when he said Fish and Isham died in Death Valley. All other firsthand accounts clearly document that Fish and Isham died west of Death Valley.

Edward Coker conveyed his reminiscences to Manly in 1892 (Manly 1894:373); since it was retold by Manly, we consider it a secondary source. Coker's account is full of inaccuracies and causes more trouble than help.

Thomas Shannon and other Jayhawkers wrote letters, now housed in the Huntington Library, to be read at the annual Jayhawker reunion, but they are only slightly helpful in shedding light on the Manly-Rogers routes.

Another secondary source is Mrs. Edward Burrell's newspaper article (in Woodward 1949b:157–165), which gives sketchy details of the Wades' trip as they followed the Bennett-Arcan wagon train into the southern reaches of Death Valley. It sheds no light on the routes used by Manly and Rogers.

Some primary sources have been reprinted in the last few years. For example, some of Manly's articles and some written by Jayhawkers are reprinted in *The Jayhawkers' Oath,* edited by Arthur Woodward. Margaret Long (1950) includes Sheldon Young's log, part of Nusbaumer's journal, Mrs. Brier's 1898 article, and John Colton's interview in her *Shadow of the Arrow.* Burr Belden's *Death Valley Heroine* contains both of Mrs. Brier's reports. Ellenbecker's *Jayhawkers of Death Valley* gives us the third copy of Asa Haynes's brief diary. Whenever possible we checked these reprints against the originals. We found, for example, that George Miller's (1919) story about William B. Rood was reprinted by Harold and Lucile Weight (1959), but we could not use the reprint because of editorial changes. Minor changes and corrections have been added to all but the facsimile editions of Manly's *Death Valley in '49.* E. I. Edwards lists the location of most of the early published Death Valley literature in his excellent "descriptive bibliography," *The Enduring Desert.*

One of the biggest hindrances to the solution of just where the Manly-Rogers routes crossed the desert was caused by the many contradictions among the firsthand accounts. For instance, there are several differences between Manly's accounts and John Rogers's account, between Mrs. Brier's two versions, and between Coker's reminiscences and those of the Reverend and Mrs. Brier.

Even more frustrating are the contradictions between sources *by the same person.* This problem is most obvious in Manly's and James Brier's accounts. Because Manly's 1888 and 1894 accounts are by far our most important sources of information, it is disconcerting to reject one of Manly's statements and accept another on the same subject. Some of the differences between Manly's 1888 and his 1894 account were corrections, omissions, or editorial changes (made by his writing assistant) for style or dramatization. But some of the inconsistencies are major. For instance, one small phrase in the 1888 account was the clue that led us to conclude that Manly and Rogers used more than one route. *"We had to try a new pass* in the last range, for the way we came over could not be crossed by a dog, let alone our horses. *We tried a canyon further south.* This was all new to us" (emphasis added). Obviously, the boys ascended the west side of the Panamints in a canyon *south* of the one in which they descended on their way out for provisions. This information was not in Manly's book.

Other conflicts concern camps mentioned in Manly's 1888 account and not mentioned in 1894—and vice versa. Sometimes information is left out of both accounts, as in the case of the missing camp between the floor of Death Valley and Arrastre Spring when the families left the valley. We discuss this missing camp later.

Manly gave four different numbers in four different accounts to describe how many days it took to travel from Death Valley to the Rancho San Francisco with the families. He said it took seventeen days in his 1877 account (in Woodward 1949b:18), twenty-one days in an article written April 15, 1895, in the *Pioneer* (in Woodward 1949b:52), twenty-two days in his book (1894:266), and twenty-five days at the end of his 1888 account. To compound the problem, we are not sure if he was counting days from the long camp at Bennetts Well or after leaving the valley proper.

Manly's 1877 article that appeared in the *Pioneer* had a number of errors in it. For instance, Manly was born April 4, 1820, not 1821; he married Miss Mary Jane Woods in 1862, not 1861; he remained in Moore's Flat, California, until 1859, not 1869; he was near Mineral Point, Wisconsin, in 1851, not 1852; he rescued Alvord in the Panamints during the winter of 1860–61, not 1862. Decisions must be made about which data to use and which to reject. Considerable controversy about such decisions has already occurred and will probably continue, although we have tried our best to come to the most logical conclusions based on all the data now available.

In addition to the '49er accounts, we reviewed the pertinent literature to see what others have done in the same area of study to test their hypotheses and to provide insight into possible new solutions. The escape routes of the Bennett-Arcan party and the Jayhawker-Brier groups from Death Valley have fascinated historians for over a century, and they have arrived at varied conclusions as to which routes were taken. Theoretically, reviewing the literature should have been easy, but in reality the more we read, the more questions arose—conflicts became more apparent. After testing the hypotheses of most historians, we found we could not always rely on their interpretations and conclusions.

Chalfant, in *Death Valley, The Facts*, retells the Death Valley '49ers' story so broadly that it provides little help to the researcher. In addition, he creates the myth that "the mesquite trees . . . were laden with nutritious seed pods which to them [the emigrants] meant nothing" (Chalfant 1930:38 & 1936:39). However, the emigrants could not use the pods because they mature and fall to the ground in July and were either eaten by rodents or gathered by Indians. Pods remaining on the trees were riddled by insects and were of little value. He goes on to interject another myth into the literature. Based on Manly's comment (1894:205) that when the boys returned to the long camp in Death Valley they "took a seat under the wagon, the only shady place," Chalfant (1936:41) concludes the long camp was not at Bennetts Well, because the "numerous mesquite trees, some of venerable age" around the well would have provided shade. But mesquite trees are leafless in the winter and provide little protection from the sun. Both these myths have been repeated so often in the Death Valley literature that they are unfortunately accepted as facts (e.g., Fairbanks 1932; Federal Writers' Project 1939:41; Southworth 1978:99).

Dr. John E. Wolff (1931) explained his analysis of the route in a 29-page pamphlet that included a map and twelve photographs. As a retired geologist, he spent many days hiking and analyzing the terrain of the Panamint mountains and the Slate Range. He was the first to publish an analysis of the Manly-Rogers route and was responsible for naming Manly Peak, Manly Pass, and Manly Fall by submitting his suggestions to the U.S. Geographic Board. However, his treatment of the route has not been widely accepted. Part of the problem lies in the obscurity of Wolff's work, possibly because it was not laced with titillating hearsay about old ox shoes along trails or purported quotes from local residents. Dr. Wolff apparently worked without the benefit of the Jayhawker Collection or Manly's "From Vermont to California." Working only with Manly's book, a pair of legs, and his scientific mind, he correctly traced the escape route of the Bennett-Arcan party from Arrastre Spring on the eastern side of the Panamint Range to Wilson Canyon in the Argus Range (but his map shows that the Bennett-Arcan families detoured to Searles Lake, which they did not do; only Manly and Rogers went to the lake on their first trip out). Dr. Wolff made no attempt to differentiate between Manly and Rogers's route for provisions and the families' exit route, nor did he carry the route farther west.

Eight years later, Carl I. Wheat (1939b) published "Trailing the

Forty-Niners Through Death Valley." This article was reprinted as a 37-page booklet with five photographs and two maps. Wheat became a close friend of T. R. Goodwin, then superintendent of Death Valley National Monument. Numerous letters between Wheat and Goodwin deal with the Manly-Rogers and the Jayhawker routes. These letters are valuable references in that they reveal the extent to which Wheat relied on secondhand information for determining the routes. Hearsay information sometimes led him astray in his interpretation of the routes. For example, he says (1939b:104n30) of Manly Pass in the Slate Range that "the pass in question is reported to the writer by an old prospector who lives near Anvil Spring to be impassable for animals." But the Death Valley Encampment trail riders have crossed the pass with horses several times. Thus, on the basis of an old prospector's word, Wheat rejected Manly Pass as a possible route over the Slate Range. "They-went-that-a-way" statements must be considered hearsay and weighed carefully, particularly statements by Indians of bygone years. Jedediah Smith (1977:64) once wrote, "It is a general characteristic of Indians to answer your questions in a manner that they think will please you but without any regard to the truth." Glasscock (1940:25) reported a similar observation in connection with Indian George being "always willing to oblige his white friends" with what they wanted to hear.

Modern historians have been confused by the seemingly credible story "Hungry Bill Talks" (Wheat 1939a), most easily accessible in *Death Valley Tales*. In this story the body of a man with a broken leg and a bullet hole in his head was discovered on the eastern approach to Towne Pass after the '49ers left the area. Apparently, after the young man broke his leg, one of his companions ended his suffering by shooting him in the head. Hungry Bill, a Death Valley resident, was the brother-in-law of Indian George (Boyles 1940:6), who claimed to have seen the '49ers when he was a young boy. As the story continues, Hungry Bill showed Wheat a locket found on the dead man that contained a photograph of a lovely young lady. This story is often cited as true, but a letter from John W. Beck (1939) to Carl I. Wheat shows that the report was fictitious. The "Hungry Bill Talks" article was written as fiction, but writers looking for a dramatic story have perpetuated it as fact. The importance of Wheat's work lies in the excellent and extensive literature documentation in his footnotes.

Another problem with the secondary source material is that subsequent authors have assumed that interpretations in more recently published material are somehow better than previous ones. For instance, Margaret Long is more accurate and intuitive in her first edition of *Shadow of the Arrow* (1941) than in her second edition (1950), which incorporates new and presumably better information. She did an excellent job of historical research, including extensive literature review and on-the-ground work. She was able to investigate areas that are off limits to civilians today. Her second edition, the most accessible of the two, includes additional information based on interviews with miners and prospectors as well as literature available after her first edition was submitted for publication. Unfortunately, she changed several of her conclusions based on this additional secondhand information and diluted her fine research with hearsay.

John Southworth also has two editions of his book *Death Valley in 1849* (1978); the second one (1980) was expanded after additional interpretation. His book is enjoyable to read, but there are several inaccuracies. For instance, he says Dr. Wolff did not originate the names for Manly Fall and Manly Pass because they were already on the "Searles Lake topographic quadrangle map, 1915 edition" (Southworth 1978 [1980]:114). However, these place names are *not* on the 1915 topographic map—they were approved by the U.S. Geographic Board in 1932. Southworth (1978:99) perpetuates Chalfant's myth (1936:39) that "the mesquite trees . . . were laden with nutritious seed pods." These and other inaccuracies detract from Southworth's interesting account. We also disagree with his interpretation of parts of the route. He has Manly and Rogers going over the southern shoulder of Telescope Peak instead of the pass south of Porter Peak and says they crossed the Argus and Coso ranges instead of the Slate and Argus ranges (Southworth 1978:73).

Death Valley '49ers (1979) by Frank Latta is the culmination of a quarter century of work. The book's strong points are the excellent biographic material on the '49ers, particularly the Wade family, and the many pictures not previously published. Also, from interviews with descendants of the Wades, he learned they went by Saratoga Spring as they left Death Valley (p. 197). He collected most of his material by interviewing friends, relatives, and descendants of the '49ers. In 1974, he asked us to write the chapter on the Manly-Rogers routes, but we declined because we were not yet completely sure of our conclusions. To fill that gap in the '49er story Latta quoted extensively (128 consecutive pages) from Manly's *Death Valley in '49*. He used to advantage other quotes from '49ers, the Briers, and John Rogers. However, there are mistakes: Charles Wade was born in 1838, not 1883 (p. 75); John Brier's middle name was Wells, not Welsh (p. 79); Martha Bennett, born January 21, 1846, was 3 years old, not 1 (p. 81); and a page of a Brier letter is left out without noting the omission (p. 142). Latta provides no bibliography, and there are few citations in the text, possibly because he was not in good health when he completed the book. Latta (1979:xii) says he remembers when Manly interviewed his father, about 1902, but Manly was unable to travel at that time. L. Dow Stephens (JA 981) wrote on January 20, 1902, that Manly "met with an accident about six or eight months ago. He fell and broke his hip and has not been able to walk since."

George Koenig wrote an analysis of the Manly-Rogers and the Jayhawker routes in *Beyond This Place There Be Dragons* (1984). Of all the analyses it is the most likely to cause confusion. Koenig does not cite most of his references, nor does he include information that would contradict what he calls his "iconoclastic" conclusions. For instance, he concludes that Manly and Rogers crossed the San Gabriel Mountains by descending Bouquet Canyon (p. 195), but he ignores the volume of information that clearly documents they went down Soledad Canyon—the canyon later traversed by the Southern Pacific Railroad. Manly wrote T. S. Palmer in August 1894 (HM 50802), "We ware awful happy when we camped on the little brook in *Soledad* canion whare I killed some good fat meat." In addition, he said (1894:259), "The brushy cañon we have just described is now occupied by the Southern Pacific Railroad, and the steep and narrow ridge pierced by a tunnel, through which the trains pass." L. Dow Stephens (JA 898) wrote John Colton on March 16, 1884, that from where they buried Robinson they went "over a divide and struck on to the head waters of the Santa Clara River [and] followed it down to the San Francisco Ranch   the Southern Pacific R R now takes the same route." In addition, Tom Shannon (JA 881) said, "The Southern pacific rail road runs through the cannon that we came down . . . now known as Soledad" (see also note 56).

Maps are also an extremely important part of the literature. There are three extant maps that Manly drew "from memory after many years have passed by" (HM 50803). We designate them the Walker map (Death Valley National Monument Museum), the Jayhawker map (JA 1050), and the Palmer map (HM 50895). The Walker map has an exciting and romantic history behind its discovery, told by Ardis Manly Walker in *The Manly Map* (1954) and *Death Valley & Manly* (1962). Manly sent the Jayhawker map to Colton on February 17, 1890 (JA 616), "to show you according to my memory . . . the diferent trails we made." Manly included on his maps only the Bennett-Arcan exit route and the Jayhawker route as told him by various Jayhawkers, not the routes he and Rogers used to find and return with provisions. The Palmer map (map 2 in the present volume) was drawn about the same time as the Jayhawker map, although he sent it to Palmer on August 1, 1894, four years later. He said, "I sent you today my imaginary (no survey) map of the famous spot Death Valley." On December 24 of that year, Manly again wrote Palmer to elaborate: "I drew the map in 1890 while my Book was being printed   then my mind was much better tharn now   I have failed within the past 2 years in mind & body   my right hand is now too trembly to draw maps—so please *excuse my pencilship*." Manly may have drawn it to be included in his book. Several

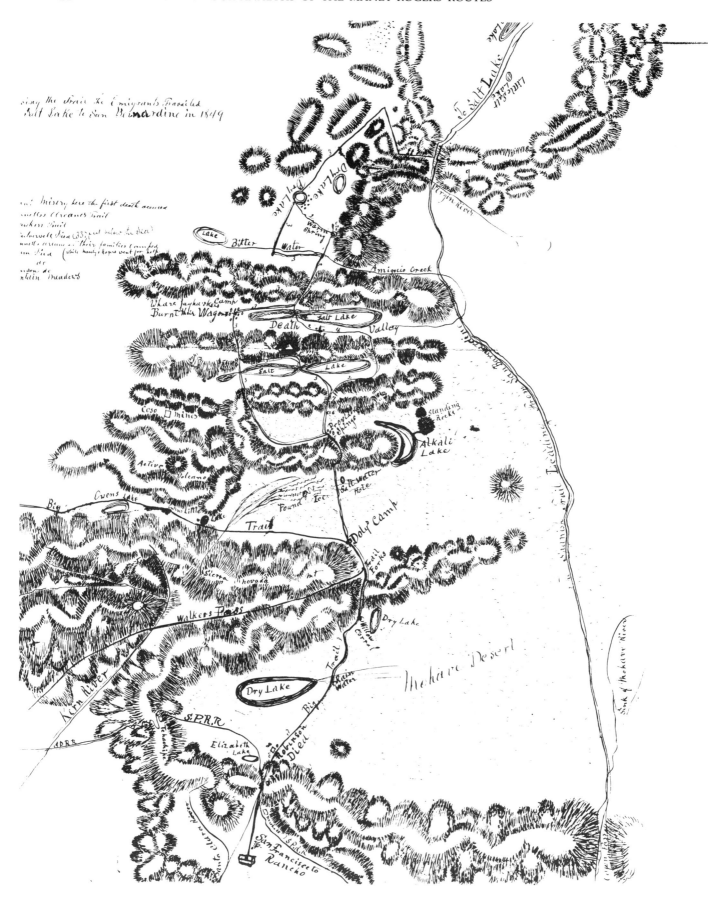

sketches were left out due to the extra cost, and the map may have met the same fate. However, Manly may have discarded it for some other reason. Palmer wrote Carl I. Wheat on December 31, 1938: "As to the *Manly Map:* It has always seemed to me that it would be unfair to Manly—due to the peculiar conditions under which his map came into my hands—to publish it unless accompanied by a modern map of the route and an explanation of the apparent discrepancies and a statement of why Manly discarded it." However, Wheat published it in *Mapping the Transmississippi West* (1959) without an explanation of the discrepancies or why Manly discarded it.

Manly's maps have cleared up one point of confusion—why his cardinal directions are wrong in portions of his narratives. The directions in his 1888 and 1894 accounts correlate well with his maps, but not with reality (also see note 54). It is probable that Manly and his writing assistant used one of his maps as a reference while writing his book (see also note 92).

Manly's maps have three major drawbacks to be kept in mind: (1) He drew part of the Jayhawker trail from hearsay. (2) The size, shape, and directions are not to scale. (For instance, they show the route going west when it really went south from Hobble Creek, and the Death Valley to Indian Wells Spring section is far out of proportion to the first and last parts of the trail.) (3) They are based on the memories of an event many years earlier. It is important to keep the value of these maps in perspective by balancing their advantages with their drawbacks.

The first published map that named Death Valley was Farley's mining district map of 1861, but there was an earlier unpublished map that Farley used as a basis for his map. It was drawn in 1861 by Aaron Van Dorn, assistant surveyor for the U.S. and California Boundary Commission, and is important in the search for the routes because the reconnaissance party traveled down Furnace Creek Wash and north along the Jayhawker trail to McLean Spring. We will publish the map and the story of how we discovered it in a forthcoming book (see also note 92).

A portion of Manly's map from the Palmer Collection (courtesy Huntington Library). Manly titled the map "Showing the Trail the Emigrants Travailed From Salt Lake to San Bernardino in 1849" and supplied this legend (spelling corrected):

1. Mount Misery here the first death occurred
2. On Bennett's and Arcan's Trail
3. On Jayhawker's Trail
4. Where Culverwell died (337 feet below the sea)
5. Where Bennett and Arcan and their families camped
6. Where Isham died (while Manly and Rogers went for help)
7. Where Fish died
8. Where Robinson died
9. Mountain Meadows

Helpful as maps have been, several published ones include mistakes that have led researchers astray. For instance, the view from Carl I. Wheat's "Manly Lookout" (1939b foldout map) in the Panamint Range south of Porter Peak does not fit his description in the text (see note 32). Another mistake is on the USGS Manly Peak, California, 15 minute, 1950, topographic map. The 180-foot fall labeled "Manly Fall" at the mouth of Redlands Canyon does not fit its official description. Dr. Wolff petitioned the U.S. Geographic Board to name a fall, a pass, and a mountain after William Lewis Manly. On April 6, 1932, the board (1932:6) accepted his recommendations, and the fall was officially described as: "Manly: fall. Inyo County, Calif., about 26 feet, the upper and highest of five falls within a mile of the mouth of Redlands Canyon, western slope of Panamint Range, near lat. 35° 56'.5N., 117° 11'.8W. Named for William Lewis Manly, a member of the Death Valley Party of 1849." We use "Ox-Jump Fall" to designate Wolff's Manly Fall (Ramsay 1979:166), the one that was such a formidable barrier to Manly, Rogers, and the Bennett-Arcan families in 1850. Ironically, Manly probably never saw the spectacular fall now bearing his name, because the Indian trails (still visible in places) circle to the north and south of it. The latitude and longitude given in the official description (possibly based on Wolff's petition) place the fall on the alluvial fan 0.5 mile northwest of the canyon mouth. The cartographer probably labeled the fall nearest to the given coordinates.

Another example of cartographic differences is the location of Towne Pass in relation to Pinto Peak. "Town's Pass" on the Wheeler map of 1877 is plotted the same place as it is on modern topographic maps, but the 7,267-foot peak bearing the name "Pinto Pk" on Wheeler's map is not the same peak with that name today (Wheeler 1877: atlas sheet 65D). The latitude, longitude, and elevation of Wheeler's "Pinto Pk" corresponds with that of an unnamed peak, elevation 7,284 feet, at the headwater of Panamint Canyon found on the USGS Panamint Butte, California, 15 minute, 1951, quadrangle map. This is 6.5 miles northeast of today's Pinto Peak. Peak 7613, east of "Town's Pass" on Wheeler's map, now bears the name "Pinto Peak." Another difference between Wheeler's map and current ones is the location of Needle Peak. Today, Wheeler's "Needle Peak" is officially named "Manly Peak," and Needle Peak is now located 4.3 miles southeast of Manly Peak (map 3).

Such cartographic mistakes have resulted in incorrect interpretations of the routes because the maps have provided incorrect data. Koenig (1964:6 & 1984:127) did not note that Pinto Peak was mislabeled and consequently assumed that Brier's mess did not exit Death Valley via Towne Pass as we know it today, but exited via a canyon south of today's Pinto Peak. Southworth (1978:49 & 106) was also led astray by the same mistake (see also note 153).

One result of our literature analysis and numerous on-the-ground observations was the decision to move the "Bennett's Long Camp" monument to Bennetts Well from Tule Spring, where it was placed in 1949. We concluded the emigrants started their "long camp" at Eagle Borax Spring but moved south to Bennetts Well in search of better water and forage. In January 1985, we wrote a proposal to Edwin L. Rothfuss, superintendent, Death Valley National Monument, recommending he petition the California State Historical Resources Commission for permission to move the "Bennett's Long Camp" State Historical Monument (Landmark 444) from Tule Spring 5.5 miles south to Bennetts Well (Johnson 1983). After the superintendent evaluated our request, he petitioned the commission using our proposal as justification. On May 18, Rothfuss was informed that "the Commission recommended the change of location of this monument," and it was moved shortly thereafter. The literature we cited in our proposal and the rationale behind our conclusion are in the notes (23, 81 & 84).

Placement of the monument was prophetically suggested in 1895 by "an old 49 Pioneer in Boston." Manly sent a copy of the old pioneer's letter to John B. Colton that said in part: "I have read your Book through & through. . . . You & Rogers should never die but live on & on forever   that was a brave & valerous act Manly & *the spot whare the reunion took place should bear a Monument* that would commemorate the act which to my mind is one of the most beautiful to modern history   it was a case of self sacrifice & self denial—I doubt whether another like case can be found upon the reckords of fame" (Manly JA 629; emphasis added). The "brave & valerous act" was Manly and Rogers's hike to the Rancho San Francisco for provisions and their return to save the Bennett and Arcan families stranded in Death Valley. The place where Asabel Bennett joyously cried, "The boys have come. The boys have come!" now has a monument to commemorate that reunion.

During our review we carefully evaluated all the literature to determine its value and its relevance to the research problem. Some evidence we rejected because we could not corroborate it or because it was so garbled that its credibility was questionable.

Choose a Method for Collecting Data

The third step in the scientific method was to choose a procedure to collect data and make observations. We decided on-the-ground research should be our primary one. We arrived at this conclusion early in our research on a very cold and windy afternoon when we found ourselves teetering on a small, obscure, meaningless nubbin in the Panamint Range after following a seemingly logical route we had plotted on the map. The evening before, in front of a cheerful fire, we had been armchair researchers and

decided this particular route looked logical on a modern topographic map. Fortunately, we had the sense to check our choice
(gather observations on our hypothesis), and what had seemed
reasonable on the map made no sense on the ground. From then on
we relied on our eyes, feet, and intuition first and used maps to
catalogue where we had hiked.

Our on-the-ground observations included simulated hikes to
cover the same distances in the same time spans as those indicated
in original documents of the '49ers. LeRoy accomplished one phase
of this when he and Dick Bush hiked the 270 miles from Travertine
Springs to the site of the Rancho San Francisco near Castaic Junction. Starting on January 14, 1973, the same time of year Manly and
Rogers hiked to the Rancho for provisions, LeRoy and Dick covered
the same territory in the same number of days.

Another time-distance problem became apparent when LeRoy
and Dick attempted to hike, in one day, from the floor of Death
Valley (starting 5.5 miles south of Bennetts Well) to Arrastre Spring
via Galena Canyon, a distance of 17 miles and a vertical rise of 5,800
feet. They didn't make it. So we were forced to doubt Manly's
implication that the Bennett-Arcan families, burdened with oxen
and children, had traveled from a camp about 4 miles south of
Bennetts Well to Arrastre Spring in one day. On another occasion
we again tested the hypothesis that the families had climbed that
distance and that elevation in one day. This time we did it with
women and children.

At the crack of dawn, LeRoy dropped Eric (12), Mark (10), and
Jean (?) on the west side road approximately where the families
would have camped after the oxen had their bucking spree. Since
none of us had climbed up the south fork of Six Spring Canyon, we
decided to test the hypothesis via this route. Unlike the men and
women who hiked up the Panamints in 1850, who were encumbered by oxen and sick babies, we had boots, comfortable pack-
sacks, and plenty of food and water. We also had a reservation at
Furnace Creek Ranch that night—a definite incentive to get to the
top of the canyon since that was where LeRoy parked the Jeep. As
we entered a narrow part of the canyon, a cold wind swept down
upon us. LeRoy, who had our jackets, was hiking down the same
canyon we were hiking up—we hoped. At one point the canyon
opened up a little and was cut by many ridges of alluvial material
about 12 feet high. Further on, above some rocky falls, we came to a
beautiful sandstone formation molded and layered in pastel shades
ranging from purple to orange. On the hill above the head of the
canyon we found a couple of lonesome petroglyphs. When we
finally arrived at the Jeep it was pitch dark: we had covered 12 miles
of rough alluvial fan and rocky canyon with an elevation gain of 1
mile, and we were still 5 miles from Arrastre Spring.

We hiked other possible canyons and each time fell short of our goal—Arrastre Spring. Therefore, we concluded that the families who were encumbered with sick children and who were driving a herd of oxen could not have made the trip in one day from the valley floor to Arrastre Spring (see also note 90).

Additional observations were made from an airplane to get an overall picture of the land and to gain a new perspective on possible trails. We also took thousands of photos in both color and black-and-white to use for reference or to prove a point in a lively discussion.

Formulate Hypotheses

After choosing a particular miniproblem to work on, we proceeded with the fourth step in the scientific method—to make a hypothesis to provide a framework for our data.

A hypothesis is a logical supposition, or an educated guess, that aids in solving a larger problem. For instance, we hypothesized that Manly and Rogers ascended the east side of the Panamints through the south fork of Six Spring Canyon. We then gathered data that would ultimately cause us either to accept or to reject this hypothesis. We also hypothesized that Manly and Rogers ascended the east side of the Panamints through either Galena, "Carbonate," Warm Spring, or Anvil Spring canyons. Each canyon had to be considered; the data had to be collected, analyzed, and interpreted; and finally a hypothesis had to be tentatively accepted or rejected. We also tested hypotheses of previous historians; some we accepted and some we rejected.

Collect Data

Our next step was to collect the data. We started collecting data in 1972, a year before LeRoy's long hike. After he was "hooked" on finding the Manly-Rogers routes, he infected the rest of the family with his obsession. Instead of calling our sojourns to the desert research trips or observation outings, we called them family vacations.

On the floor of Death Valley we wanted to locate the route the wagons took across the salt pan. Since "the whole valley [was] filled with water" as Nusbaumer said, it was logical to assume the '49ers followed a proven route across it. That would have been the Indian trail that we think became the same route used by the '49ers, prospectors, miners, and finally the first borax wagons. During part of Eric's hike down the full length of the Monument, Eric and LeRoy followed the Indian trail southward from the mouth of Furnace Creek Wash and found what appeared to be Indian food caches near the old wagon crossing 0.25 mile north of the present west side road crossing. Along the dim tracks of the old wagon road that crossed the valley, they found pieces of wood and metal signaling that people had passed that way long before. Now only coyotes pad along the thin, raised dikes that pointed in parallel streaks across the valley, barely discernible in the low winter sun.

Probably the prettiest areas for hiking are the upper elevations of the Panamint Range. When we were pinning down the exact location where Manly and Rogers stood as they looked out over hundreds of miles they had yet to cover, we made an interesting discovery—a pinyon nut gathering area. On "Manly Lookout," as we call hill 7478, we found a large Indian nut gathering camp composed of nut caches and over twelve habitation sites. One of the sites (often called sleeping circles) is 15 feet in diameter and paved with slate collected from a nearby outcrop. Dutcher (1893), a member of the Death Valley Expedition of 1891, observed Panamint Indians collecting and extracting pinyon nuts in a similar camp.

> In the shadow of a small group of piñon trees a number of small circles or "corrals" had been built. . . . In diameter they measured eight or ten feet, and their walls consisted merely of the broken piñon branches and of the small bushes that grew around, piled up into a loose row two or three feet thick and about as many high. The circle was broken . . . where entrance or exit was needed. . . . There uses seemed to be few—to secure a little privacy for the occupants; to serve as a slight wind-break during the night. . . . In the center of each circle was a small area where the fire was kindled. . . . The floor was smooth, clear of stones and weeds, and carpeted by a thick layer of fine, gray dust.

Near the Indian site is one of the most beautiful camping spots we have ever used. It is east of the road ascending the knob, overlooking Butte Valley in the foreground and Charleston Peak farther east across Death Valley. Many years ago prospectors cleared and flattened the area on which to pitch their tent. The spot is still flat, but a bent pinyon spreads its branches where men once spread their blankets.

A particularly difficult subproblem to research was: Which fall in the Panamint Range did Manly and Rogers have so much difficulty surmounting with the one-eyed mule (the same fall the families pushed the oxen and mule over on their way out of the desert)? We knew it could not be in the same canyon the boys used when they went for provisions because Manly said, "We had to try a new pass in the last range, for the way we came over could not be crossed by a dog, let alone our horses. We tried a canyon further south" (1888:July). Again we went to the literature to check old hypotheses. We suspected the fall could not be in South Park Canyon as Carl I. Wheat and Dick Freeman concluded because we had climbed the extremely rugged lower portion of that canyon. There is no way the oxen and mule could have descended the several high falls in the lower reaches of South Park Canyon. Also, we felt South Park Canyon or Middle Park Canyon might be the one used by the boys on their outbound search for provisions; if so, it could not be the one used by the families. However, we checked the fall anyway, guided by the pictures from a *Desert Magazine* article, "On Manly's Trail in the Panamints," by Dick Freeman (1941:5). There were elements of similarity between the fall and Manly's description; however, it was easily bypassed by a trail on the north side. So we rejected South Park Canyon as the one Manly and Rogers had difficulty ascending with the mule on their return trip to the stranded families.

We then checked Dr. Wolff's analysis. He felt the families came down Redlands Canyon. First we visited the fall at the mouth of Redlands Canyon labeled "Manly Fall" on the topographic maps. There it was, 180 feet tall; a far cry from Manly's 10-foot fall and certainly too tall to push oxen over and expect them to live. We went farther up the canyon after talking to Harry Briggs, then owner of the Homestake Mine, who built his residence and guest house at the mouth of the canyon. Harry asked us to take a look at his water pipe as we went up the canyon and to check the spring, if we got that far, because he was having problems with his water pressure.

The canyon had great chunks of rock washed into it. The walls were high and almost perpendicular in places. Small rock falls were smooth from years of gully washers. Clumps of yellow flowers and white Jimson-weed trumpets brightened our way. We measured each fall as we came to it, but kept in mind height changes from year to year as sand is deposited or removed during the notorious desert gully washers.

Since Manly had said the fall just below the spring was the one they had trouble getting the mule over, we went first to the spring to work down-canyon from there. At the spring we found that burros had pawed mud into the holes around Harry's water pipes; the screens around the openings were filled with willow roots. We cleaned the screens and carried big rocks to cover the spring so the burros could not muddy it. Finally we backtracked to the fall we now call "Ox-Jump Fall." We asked Mark to go down the canyon a short distance and find a way to climb the south wall so that he would be about 50 feet above the canyon, as Manly described, yet come out even with the top of the 10-foot fall. Mark was 12, a perfect age for such a quest, and he did find a way! Sometimes the ledge was only 4 inches wide, just as Manly described it. Sometimes it was wider, sometimes narrower, as it wound up and down, in and out. We all clambered around the wall to try the route. It certainly fit Manly's description and the sketch in his book.

After checking other likely falls in Goler Wash and all canyons north, including Pleasant Canyon, we were satisfied the uppermost fall in Redlands Canyon fit Manly's description best. We tentatively accepted the hypothesis that the families came down Redlands Canyon and we found additional support in the literature. The 1867 report of Lieutenant Bendire's scouting expedition and an 1893 mining claim also supported Redlands Canyon as the family exit route (see note 74).

This example illustrates the continuous problem we had with several locations fitting the same description. It required us to change the question from Which canyon fits Manly's description? to Which canyon *best* fits Manly's description? The question could only be answered by examining all possibilities and fitting what we saw on the ground with what was described in the literature.

While collecting data to pinpoint the boys' route down the west side of the Panamints, LeRoy climbed Middle Park Canyon—alone—a practice we do *not* recommend. The night before the climb he was a guest of Frenchie's, the current tenant on Harry Briggs's homestead at the mouth of Redlands Canyon. Frenchie, his wife and daughter, six cats, and five dogs had moved into the "Hilton," as Harry used to called his old guest house overlooking the canyon. In Harry's day, the one-room cabin was festooned with garlands of beer cans draped from the four corners. It even had a kitchen sink, but of course no water. Frenchie had made a singular improvement. The Hilton finally had an outhouse, and it was completely carpeted—floor, walls, stool, cover, everything! The large windows provided a spectacular view of Panamint Valley and Manly Pass in the Slate Range. Frenchie's wife and daughter were gone for the weekend, so LeRoy stayed in the guest house—Harry's old residence. While Frenchie prepared a plate of hors d'oeuvres fancy enough to have come from a fine restaurant, he regaled LeRoy with stories about the local rattlesnakes—how they lived under the guest house and how the big ones could bore right through a wood floor. Little did he know that, as a Boy Scout, LeRoy had killed many a rattler in the area—and what he killed, he ate, the bigger the better.

After a good night's sleep in the tidy cabin, LeRoy was awakened at 5 A.M. by a call from Frenchie to come over for coffee. Now, if you haven't tasted miner's coffee you haven't tried *real* coffee. It was boiled for several hours, and the "mud," as Frenchie called it, was left from the day before. After breakfast, Frenchie watched as LeRoy measured Manly Fall by standing at the top and dropping a rock attached to a long cord over the edge. Then he pulled the cord up and measured it with a tape; it measured 180 feet. All the while Frenchie never asked why a fellow would come all the way from Minnesota just to measure his fall.

LeRoy drove north along the Panamint Playa to the Middle Park Canyon turnoff and headed up the mining road as far as a two-wheel drive would go. The junkyard at the mill site would keep any tinkerer happy—trucks and cars and piles of assorted metal. He slipped into his backpack, which contained water, maps and books, thermometer, and a plastic air splint—just in case. From the mouth of Middle Park Canyon he could see miles up and down Panamint Valley. Across the way, Water Canyon cut into the upper reaches of the Argus Range, but the only logical route from here to cross the nearest range—the Slates—was Manly Pass. A year before, when he climbed South Park Canyon first with a friend and then with Eric, they found several falls in the lower part of the canyon, the highest being 22 feet. But Middle Park was more strenuous and dangerous. There are numerous falls ranging from 12 to 80 feet. After a difficult morning of climbing up the canyon, he had an even worse afternoon getting down. Don't believe anyone who categorically says down is easier than up. After finding that the falls could either be climbed or circumvented, although not without a struggle, he decided Middle Park might well be the canyon Manly and Rogers had descended. Of this trip we can say, as Manly did, that "the worst part is left out."

On another trip we climbed Manly Pass in the Slate Range via Fish Canyon on the east side. High on the canyon wall we investigated an Indian cave with a soot-blackened roof. For some reason LeRoy had left his watch in the cave on a trip two years before, but it ran just fine as soon as he wound it. As we climbed the long winding gash of Fish Canyon, the high perpendicular walls closed in and we imagined the Indians were watching us from the towering canyon rim much as did Reverend Brier (JA 76) and his three young boys. Soon Mark began to complain about what he considered dull trudging; however, his whole attitude changed when we found a tarantula. It was big and black and hairy; Mark thought it beautiful and wanted to take it home. We let him carry it around in his packsack, and his eyes were alert to every dark spot or shadow for the rest of the day.

On still another trip into the Slate Range, Eric and Mark found water "where there was none," according to Manly. This was a major discovery and extremely important in pinpointing the routes. Manly and Rogers dropped into a canyon where they found the tracks of some of the emigrants who had taken the northern route over the Panamints. Manly and Rogers dug where the others had dug, but found no water. The tracks belonged to Reverend Brier's mess according to one of his letters (JA 76). Brier found water in a canyon "with walls on either side overhanging or perpendicular—*A Silent Sepulcre . . .* scooping out a hole a little water arose."

In order to find where Manly and Rogers camped the night of January 16, we had to locate Reverend Brier's silent sepulchre (map 4). Before scouting the Slate Range for Brier's water hole, we interviewed Harry Briggs, who spent many years prospecting in the Slate and Panamint ranges. He assured us there was no water in the Manly Pass area. Geologists from the U.S. Geological Survey familiar with the area gave us the same answer. But we looked for water anyway—Reverend Brier said it was there, and we were determined to find it.

According to his letter, Brier left camp (at Post Office Spring, 0.5 mile south of Ballarat), crossed Panamint Valley, and scouted "some 12 or 15 miles" south along the eastern side of the Slate Range. He then went 2 or 3 miles up a canyon (Fish Canyon) that closed to 20 feet with perpendicular walls. We found an area fitting Brier's silent sepulchre 2 miles up Fish Canyon where the south fork makes a sharp dogleg turn to form a box canyon. We offered Eric and Mark a dollar reward if they could discover water here while we went up the canyon to look for Reverend Brier's windrows of sand. After digging with a 4-ounce juice can as far down as their arms could reach, they found potable water! This pinpointed the location of Brier's camp and also the place where Manly and Rogers dug for water but found none.

Brier's water source was in a stone basin, or *tinaja*, scoured out of the rock by thundering water cascading over the falls. Sand deposited in the *tinaja* or tank acts as a cover to keep the water from evaporating. When it was silted in, the only way to extract the water was to dig out the sand and scoop up the water as it filled the hole. After the Briers used all the water, there would be no more until another hard rain recharged the sand-filled basin.

As we stood at the mouth of a canyon or atop a mountain pass looking westward as Manly did so many years ago, we were guided by what he said when he was asked to retrace his trail ten years after his escape from the desert: "I followed in the most favorable and likely places that we would naturally have traveled" (in Woodward 1949b:69).

In addition to finding information on the ground and in the conventional literature, we also searched old courthouse records, dusty boxes at the National Archives, obscure library and historical society references, and even fog-shrouded graveyards.

It was in the latter—the Evergreen Cemetery in Santa Cruz—that we discovered information that, although it did not shed light on the location of the routes, gave us additional insight into the trials and difficulties the families suffered along the way. In the

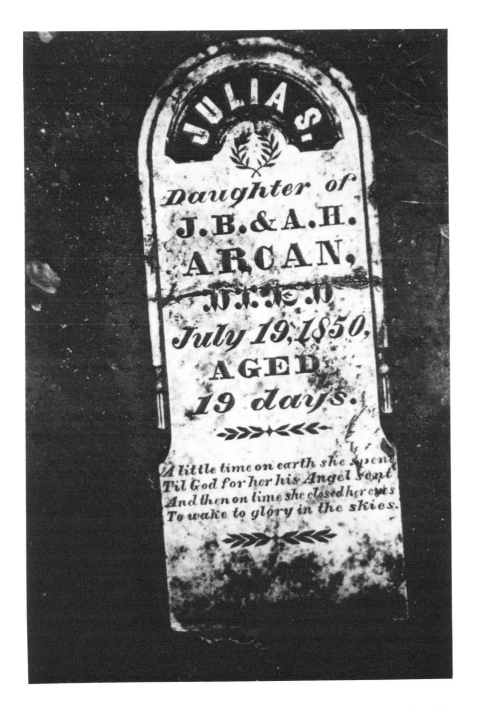

Julia S. Arcan's tombstone covers her final resting place. Hers is the oldest recorded burial in Evergreen Cemetery, Santa Cruz, California.

Arcan burial plot, a small, typed card said, "Julia is the oldest recorded death in Evergreen. She died at the age of 19 days in July 1850." Julia was born July 1, which meant Abigail was about five months pregnant when she struggled across five mountain ranges and four deserts on foot. It is difficult to imagine the strength, stamina, and determination demanded from Abigail, well advanced in pregnancy and caring for an ailing 2-year-old, to make the arduous passage through the rugged mountains and sand-filled valleys of the Great American Desert.

Little is known about Abigail. She apparently had some experience on horseback or she would not have tried to stay on her frightened ox when it joined the bucking spree as the families left Death Valley. Then again, it may have been sheer determination and tenacity—or paralyzing fear. She displayed a sense of humor when she wore her gayest Sunday best to ride out of the desert astride a bony ox. The funniest incident in Manly's accounts is his description of Abigail hanging on for dear life as Old Brigham tried to buck her off while her many "high colored ribbons" and things that hung loose flew round and round as in a circus. Her choice may have been a frugal one as well since Manly said they each took only one set of clothes, and her Sunday best was probably made of the most durable material. But Abigail wore something in addition to her clothes—she tied a prized possession around her waist, a tablecloth she had woven. It is the only article known to have survived to this day belonging to those who took the southern route through Death Valley. Etta Arcan, Abigail's daughter-in-law, said, "Abigail treasured it as a keepsake and used it only for very special occasions" (Johnson 1981:19). It was exhibited during the Centennial Gold Rush Celebration in Death Valley in 1949, and we hope it will someday be donated to the National Park Service or to the Death Valley '49ers so it can be displayed for all to appreciate.

After months of hiking the desert and collecting the pertinent literature in libraries and from helpful friends, we had to correlate, compare, discuss, evaluate, and put meaning to what we found. In short, we had to interpret the data.

Interpret Data

Data or observations are meaningless in themselves. Their significance depends upon how they are interpreted. Two historians might study the same events, both being equally competent, honest, and sincere in their analysis, and still arrive at different interpretations. Worthy interpretation of data is based on several factors: (1) knowledge of the literature, (2) clear understanding of the data, (3) experience in the field of study, (4) frank and candid discussion with colleagues and other experts, (5) ability to piece together meaningful parts to make a coherent whole, (6) health good enough to carry out the needed research, (7) ability to be objective and not intimidated by past hypotheses, (8) intuitive sense of being on the right track, and (9) desire to be historically correct.

Another important aspect of interpreting historical research is to try to understand why people acted as they did. Their frame of reference—how they perceived themselves in the context of the things around them—was tinted by their attitude, faith, health, and background. Their daily records and later memories varied according to their individual perspectives. For example, a carefree young man would view the adventure of a wagon trip across the western plains in the quest for gold and fortune quite differently from a young mother with children in her care leaving a secure home and cherished friends and family for the hardships and uncertainties of the same trip. The pressures and stresses from constant struggle, disappointment, and worry, as well as loss of health and loss of treasured property, etched in bold relief the personal qualities, both good and bad, of each individual.

To help us interpret the data, we tried to see things the way the emigrants did. We had to erase from our minds what we knew of the topography ahead to see the landscape fresh, as though for the first time, to experience the same impact it made on those who first saw it. We had to assume their frame of reference and feel what motivated them; to do this we had to look at the country around us with several points in mind.

First of all, the Jayhawkers and others in the northern contingent felt they had been driven far south of the route described on the Barney Ward map. Their goal was not only westward, but northward to regain their original route to Owens Lake and Walker Pass. Second, those who went south in Death Valley thought they were looking at the snowy Sierra Nevada and therefore that Walker Pass must be to the south. When Manly and Rogers reached the crest of the Panamint Range on their search for provisions, they could see the whole panorama around them. They probably had Frémont's map etched in their minds; for the first time in many weeks, they suddenly knew where they were.

Overlooking the expanse that lay before them, Manly (1888:April) outlined the way he and Rogers must proceed: "Two low barren ranges [Slate and Argus] and three desert valleys [Panamint, Searles, and Indian Wells] to cross before we could reach the foot of the big snow mountain, then we would be compelled to go westerly [southerly] across another wide level plain [Mojave Desert] for the big mountain [Sierra Nevada] was so covered with snow that we would not dare to cross it." Their goal was no longer due west into the high part of the Argus Range and snowy Sierra Nevada beyond. Their immediate goal was to reach the base of the Sierra Nevada, but from there they must turn southward. Any step north or northwest meant two steps wasted. Any step southwest was heading toward both Owens Peak in their Sierra Nevada goal and the Pueblo de Los Angeles southward from there.

We, too, had to stand on the small knoll near the pass above Pleasant Canyon (hill 7478, map 3) to see the lay of the land the way Manly and Rogers did: not knowing there was a spring in South Park, not realizing Pleasant Canyon was the best route off the mountain, not suspecting Middle Park was a shorter canyon but steeper and without springs. We had to force ourselves to rely on just what we saw with the only background being our knowledge of Frémont's map and knowing we had to get beyond the coast range to find provisions.

Because historical data require more subjective interpretation than mathematical data, there is greater opportunity for differences in interpretation. Therefore, we include in the notes the reasons *why* we came to our conclusions.

Make Tentative Conclusions

The seventh step in our scientific method was to make tentative conclusions and piece them together to see if the whole made sense. This became a continuous process. It could be compared to working on a jigsaw puzzle where several pieces are the same shape. You tentatively stick one in the hole to see if it fits with the surrounding pieces. Sometimes it looks okay and you leave it there only to find out later it was the wrong piece. Then you try another piece, but you also take a critical look at the pieces around it at the same time. Often we came full circle, rejecting an initial conclusion, embracing others, and finally returning to the first. During this process LeRoy's field notebooks were invaluable not only for recording immediate opinions and impressions, but to read again after months of desk work.

Reexamine Tentative Conclusions and Form Final Ones

Check and recheck, question again—the process is repeated over and over because the scientific method is circular. The researcher constantly goes back to the main problem and repeats the steps of reexamining conclusions, reformulating hypotheses, collecting more data, and again seeing how conclusions fit into the whole picture. This process also occurs after new literature is reviewed or new observations are made. Reexamining one's conclusions can be the most exciting but also the most distressing part of research. It is difficult to let go of strongly held convictions, to admit that you have been wrong in the light of new information, or to attempt visualizing information in a new way. But examining a new possibility and finding it better can also be exhilarating.

A case in point was our reexamination of the boys' route down the west side of the Panamints when they went for provisions. For years we had accepted South Park as the canyon the boys used, but after hiking the full length of Bighorn, Middle Park, and South Park canyons, we again discussed that part of the route. After looking at our slides and making special trips back to the Panamints, we struggled with what we saw and with the information left us by Manly and Rogers. What was the most logical route off the mountain based on what they saw, what they knew, and where they were heading? Middle Park Canyon, the nearest one in their line of travel with its smooth, open entrance, was the most logical route. It *looked* like the logical route from where the boys stood on the Panamint crest (map 3). In addition, Rogers said they found "water in some rocks," but neither he nor Manly mentioned a spring such as the one in South Park Canyon. So after reexamining the data we had to change our previously held conclusion. Although South Park Canyon fits most of the data, Middle Park fits it better. Koenig (1984:177–178) dismisses Middle Park Canyon by saying the "opening is not easily discerned" from Manly Lookout (hill 7478), but it is clearly visible in his photograph.

Once the data has been collected, organized, analyzed, and debated, final conclusions must be chosen. Some are easily arrived at because the data are sufficient and clear. Other conclusions, such as the location of the sulphur water hole, are decided upon only after complicated analysis and strenuous debate. Still others must be relegated to the category of preferred choices based on our experience and background. After years of research, on the ground and in the literature, we made our decisions and settled on our final conclusions; they are found in the final step and in our notes.

Present Findings

The last step in the scientific method is to present the conclusions so they may be questioned and tested by others. We have given talks to several organizations and published *Julia, Death Valley's Youngest Victim* as part of the task of presenting our findings. This book is the major effort toward our goal to share what we feel is the correct location of the routes Manly and Rogers used during early 1850 to hike from Death Valley to the Rancho San Francisco, return to Death Valley with provisions, then lead the families out of the desert to the Rancho.

Location of the Routes

Briefly and without benefit of explanation here, we conclude the routes are as follows: Manly, Rogers, the Bennett and Arcan families, and their drivers crossed the Amargosa Desert (49 miles southeast of Beatty, west of Highway 95) in the company of at least three other wagons and entered the east side of Ash Meadows near Devils Hole. After camping at Collins Spring, where they found firewood, grass, and water less than a mile south of Devils Hole, they headed almost due west through the brackish sloughs in Ash Meadows, crossed the Amargosa riverbed, and ascended the slope of the Funeral Mountains about where Highway 190 makes its way west from Death Valley Junction (notes 1–3; references are to notes that explain our conclusions). They descended the western flank of the Funeral Mountains through Furnace Creek Wash to Travertine Springs 3.5 miles east of where Furnace Creek Inn now stands. Manly scouted west into Death Valley then headed north following the Jayhawker, Brier, and Georgia-Mississippi boys' road. At McLean Spring north of Salt Creek he found the Jayhawkers burning their wagons and preparing to cross the mountains north of Telescope Peak (note 14). Manly returned to Travertine Springs while John Rogers and another man (not Manly) scouted south into Death Valley. Upon their return and on their advice, Bennett and Arcan decided to head south without waiting for Manly to scout that direction (note 19).

They crossed Death Valley about 0.25 mile north of the present valley crossing and threaded their way south on the smooth sand between the salt flat and the rough alluvial fans to Eagle Borax Spring, where the four Bennett-Arcan teamsters left the families and turned north to follow the Jayhawkers. About January 10, Manly, Rogers, and the two families headed south again, arriving at a small sulphury water hole that no longer exists. However, we think it was in the general area of Mesquite Well, 10 miles south of Eagle Borax Spring, a site later used by the borax freight wagons at the southernmost potable water on the western valley floor. From here Manly, Rogers, and at least one other man scouted for a route out of the valley. When Manly returned, he found the families preparing to head west up the mountain because Rogers felt they could cross via Warm Spring Canyon.

Manly hurried ahead to scout Anvil Spring Canyon hoping to find a better route than up Warm Spring Canyon. He decided they could not get the wagons across the mountains that way, so he returned and met the wagons high on the smooth Pleistocene alluvial fan where the Bennetts and Arcans were camped for the night. The oxen were unable to continue pulling the wagons up the steep grade, so the party returned to the sulphur water hole on January 14; on January 15, Manly and Rogers headed up the ancient uplifted alluvial fan to Warm Spring Canyon and arrived at Arrastre Spring high on the side of Butte Valley about dark. After preparing dinner at the spring, they continued up the Indian trail toward the pass and spent the night somewhere off the trail (note 31; camp A, map 3; see also appendix A).

The next morning they crossed the pass (southern headwater of Pleasant Canyon) and ascended a small knoll (hill 7478) to have a look around. The view was not only impressive, it was frightening. They were not atop the Sierra Nevada as they had hoped. From what they could see around them they determined where they were and where they would have to go for provisions (notes 32 & 33). They descended the Panamints on the west side through Middle Park Canyon, obtaining rainwater from small basins in the rocks. They helped each other down and around numerous rock falls and emerged from the canyon 1,000 feet above the floor of Panamint Valley (note 35; map 3). They had an extensive view up and down the valley, and directly west of them was the southern playa covered with mud and water. They headed for the lowest pass they could see—Manly Pass in the Slate Range—by circling the playa to the south and crossing the valley at its narrowest point, where they found a little stream of saltwater. The boys headed up the mountainside, but finally dropped into Fish Canyon hoping to find water. Here they came across tracks of the Brier contingent, which had crossed that way a few days before. They found where the others had dug for water, but Manly and Rogers found none (note 38; camp B, map 4).

The next day, January 17, they crossed the Slates and headed west across Searles Valley, but seeing Searles Lake to the south they changed directions and headed for the lake. They crossed the mud on Borax Flat before they reached the lake, where they were as disappointed as the Jayhawkers had been to find its water undrinkable (note 42). From the lake they headed directly west to cross the Argus Range via an unnamed canyon (west of Trona) that heads into Burro Canyon. They spent another night without water and descended the west side of the Argus Range through Burro Canyon (camp C, map 5). Far across Indian Wells Valley they could see the snow on top of Owens Peak and knew they would die from lack of water before reaching the base of the peak where they hoped to find water. Although they could see China Lake about a mile south of their route, they feared that it, too, would be salt, so they headed north toward a snow-capped volcanic cone at the north end of Indian Wells Valley. Soon Rogers found ice suspended above water-less rivulets. They gathered all they could—enough to drink, cook their meat, and fill their canteens (note 45). Then they struck due south down the valley, taking as their goal a bluff that sticks out from the toe of Black Mountain. When they realized they could not reach their goal for another twelve hours, they turned west toward the foot of Owens Peak. They saw smoke rising from the base of the mountain and headed for it (note 46). To their great delight, it was Doty's group of Jayhawkers camped at Indian Wells Spring. Here Manly and Rogers spent the night among friends who were in the same desperate plight (camp D).

On January 19, they followed the broad trail south along the foot of the southern Sierra Nevada, crossed southern Indian Wells Valley to the southeast, and descended the El Paso Mountains, where they found Asa Haynes's group camped at a tiny spring along the horse thief trail in Last Chance Canyon (camp E). The four teamsters who had abandoned the Bennett-Arcan families in Death Valley were also there—in desperate straits, being entirely without food (note 51).

In the morning Manly and Rogers descended Last Chance Canyon and followed the Indian trail to Desert Spring, a small oasis 1 mile southeast of Cantil (map 6). They drank as much as possible and filled their canteens, then headed south to a dry camp on the Mojave Desert (camp F). The route led them south all January 21 until they camped at some shallow rainwater holes just south of the Rosamond Hills (note 55; camp G). They spent some time looking for the trail in the Antelope Valley area, but finally headed for a low place in the San Gabriel Mountains. They were fortunate to find Barrel Springs 4 miles southeast of Palmdale, a site long used by Indian horse thieves and their pursuers (note 106; camp H). On January 23, they crossed Soledad Pass over snow, where they lost the trail. Because Manly became lame, the boys took two days to descend Soledad Canyon as they followed the intermittent stream through its brushy channel into the broad wash (note 56; camps I, J, & K). They climbed the spur of hill just east of Saugus and headed for the Rancho San Francisco hacienda, which overlooked the Santa Clara River 0.5 mile south of Castaic Junction. After a conversation in sign language with a Californio they continued west; due to Manly's lame leg, they traveled only a short distance and camped the night of January 26 under a live oak tree (camp L).

They returned to the ranch house the next morning, where they were loaned two horses to ride to Los Angeles. On the way they met Mr. French, who told them to return to the rancho because provisions were more plentiful there than in the pueblo. They spent the night at Mission San Fernando (camp M), returned to the rancho on January 28, and spent the next two days grinding corn and wheat and preparing their provisions to take back to Death Valley (note 78; camps N & O).

When they left the rancho with two pack horses on January 30, they headed north up San Francisquito Canyon, where they bought another horse and a one-eyed mule from some road builders. After spending the night with the laborers (camp P), Manly and Rogers traveled up South Portal Canyon and down Munz Canyon to Elizabeth Lake (note 68). From there they headed east to get back to their previous trail (camp Q). After a night at the rainwater holes near Rosamond Hills (camp R), they traveled to Desert Spring near Cantil in one day (camp S).

The next camp was at or east of Indian Wells Spring on February 3 (camp T), and the following camp was at or east of the saltwater hole at Paxton Ranch, about 2 miles north of China Lake (camp U). From the saltwater pond they followed the Jayhawker trail up Deadman Canyon, which is 2 miles north of Burro Canyon, the one the boys had used on their outbound trek (note 71; map 5). Rogers's white mare died in Deadman Canyon. On February 5, they descended the eastern side of the Argus Range via east Wilson Canyon and camped at Indian Joe Spring, 5 miles north of Trona. They had to bury some wheat there because the remaining two horses were now very weak from poor water and lack of grass (note 72; camp V, map 5).

On the eastern side of Searles Valley they made a slight detour to view Mr. Isham's grave, then ascended the Slate Range through the middle or south fork of Isham Canyon and crossed Manly Pass (note 73). They spent the night on the east side of the pass (camp W, map 4). From here they forged a new trail across the Panamints through Redlands Canyon, where they had to leave the last two horses to die and almost lost the little mule getting around Ox-Jump Fall (notes 74 & 75). They spent the night at Redlands Spring, 150 yards above the fall (camp X, map 3). The next day, February 8, the boys turned northeast in Butte Valley, passed Striped Butte, descended Warm Spring Canyon, and arrived at the little sulphur water hole at or near Mesquite Well that night (camp Y, the 25th night). The following day, February 9, they found Culverwell's body along the trail (note 79).

Later that day, the boys cautiously approached the Bennett-Arcan camp, which at first appeared to be abandoned. To their great joy, the families were safe, but were preparing to leave the long camp, which had been moved from Eagle Borax to the better grass and water at Bennetts Well.

About noon on February 11, the four men, two women, four

children, one dog, and eleven oxen headed south until the oxen
started a bucking spree 4 or 5 miles south of Bennetts Well. After
they established camp, Rogers and Bennett went south to bury
Culverwell's body while Arcan returned to Bennetts Well for water.
The rest repaired broken straps and other gear the oxen had dam-
aged (note 89; camp 1, map 7). The next day they took a nearer
route up the Panamints through the main branch of Galena Canyon,
and the families camped at one of the two springs in the canyon
(note 90; camp 2, maps 3 & 7). On February 13, they continued to
Arrastre Spring (camp 3, maps 3 & 7). While the cattle sought out
the sparse bunchgrass and the women rested, Manly, Bennett, and
Arcan climbed the trail to the little knoll (hill 7478) beyond the pass
so they might study the route of their journey to come (note 91). As
they descended, they gazed east over the deep, narrow valley below, and one of them intoned a final benediction over Captain
Culverwell—"*Good bye Death Valley!*"

The next day they turned south from Arrastre Spring into Butte
Valley and camped at Redlands Spring in Redlands Canyon (camp
4, maps 3 & 7). On February 15, they safely pushed the oxen and
mule over the fall below the spring, crossed the southern part of
Panamint Valley and had a dry camp in Fish Canyon on the east
side of Manly Pass in the Slate Range (camp 5, maps 4 & 7). The
next day was a short but difficult drive over the pass. They camped
in lower Isham Canyon almost in sight of Indian Joe Spring across
Searles Valley (note 97; camp 6, maps 4 & 7). The next night found
them at Indian Joe Spring at the base of Argus Peak, where they dug
up the wheat the boys had cached there a few days before (camp 7,
map 5).

They ascended the Argus Range through east Wilson Canyon
and spent the night on a plateau in the Argus Range along dry
Sweetwater Creek in view of the southern Sierra Nevada (camp 8,
maps 5 & 7). Descending the west side of the Argus Range they
worked their way through boulder-strewn Deadman Canyon and
camped at a saltwater pond, later the site of Paxton Ranch, on the
east side of Indian Wells Valley (camp 9, maps 5 & 7). The next
camp was a dry one about halfway across the valley, (camp 10; map
7), and the next good water was at Indian Wells Spring, their next
camp (note 101; camp 11, map 7).

On February 22, they headed south from Indian Wells Spring
and had a windy camp southeast of Freeman Junction within sight
of Robbers Roost (camp 12, map 7). The next camp was in the upper
part of Last Chance Canyon, where Manly and Rogers had caught
up with Asa Haynes's mess while on the way out for supplies (camp
13, maps 6 & 7). They had hoped to reach Desert Spring southeast
of Cantil the following day but had to camp at a small playa near
Gypsite about 2 miles from the mouth of Last Chance Canyon (note

105; camp 14, maps 6 & 7). This night brought a cold blanket of snow, and the next morning, February 25, they continued the 3 miles to Desert Spring, where they rested the remainder of the day (camp 15, maps 6 & 7).

They spent February 26 and 27 on the Mojave Desert (camp 16, map 7) before reaching the rainwater holes south of Rosamond Hills (camp 17, map 7). Because the footing was slippery from the rain and melted snow, it took two more days, February 28 (camp 18, map 7) and March 1, to reach Barrel Springs in the northern foothills of the San Gabriel Mountains 4 miles southeast of Palmdale (camp 19, map 7). Now that they were out of the desert, they slowed their pace; on the night of March 2, they camped at the edge of the snow on Soledad Pass (camp 20, map 7) and the next morning they started early to cross it while there was still crust enough to support their weight. The passage was difficult down brushy Soledad Canyon. It took four more days (camps 21–24, map 7), but they finally arrived at the Rancho San Francisco on March 7, 1850. It took the Bennett-Arcan party twenty-five days (map 7 & appendix B) to escape from "the cursed hole," as Manly called Death Valley (HM 50802).

Part II

William L. Manly's Account—
The California Desert Portion of
"From Vermont to California"

From Ash Meadows, Nevada,
to Los Angeles, California.
Written for the *Santa Clara Valley*, 1888

William Lewis Manly's portrait, taken February 1893 when he was 72 years old. (Courtesy of Huntington Library, San Marino, California.)

Introduction

The year was 1830; the season was summer, as an apprehensive 10-year-old boy mounted the driver's seat of his family's light wagon. The young adventurer received advice from his father and was "hugged and kissed and cried over by the best mother that ever lived" (quotes are from Manly's accounts). Young William Lewis Manly waved good-bye to his parents, sister, and younger brothers as he headed the Morgan mare down the narrow road near St. Albans, Vermont, to follow his aunt and uncle as they drove west to find new farming land on which to settle. Ohio was their goal, but after spending the winter south of Cleveland, where Manly went to school briefly, they received a message to meet the rest of the family in Michigan Territory. The Manlys homesteaded 240 acres in Jackson County west of Detroit, where "there were no stones to plow over and the land was otherwise easy to till." The family prospered except for the yearly bouts of "fever'n ager"—Michigan malaria.

As a child, Lewis had been brought up to be self-sufficient. "Everything consumed was produced upon the place. . . . Our summer clothes were of home-made linen, and our winter garments . . . made from the wool of our own sheep. . . . All we bought at the store was a little tea and once in a year or two some nice calico for mother [to make] a new Sunday gown."

Lewis's strict New England upbringing is evident throughout his accounts. He was taught that cruel treatment of people or animals was wrong and to swear was a sin. On the trip from Vermont with his aunt and uncle, he saw a canal boy throw stones at the barge-hauling team and "swear as loud and as bad as the oldest sinner." He considered such people "vulgar and wicked." A few years later he saw a father curse a small child who fell while learning to walk; the father's insensitivity remained a lifelong memory. The first time Manly saw a slave sold at auction he said, "With my New England notions about the sin of slavery it made a very deep impression on me to see a fellow creature, black though he might be, sold at auction as I would sell a steer." On the way to California, his New England ideas of honesty were shocked when Mr. Dallas, his employer, hid some army horses among his own and did not return them when the soldiers asked if Dallas had seen them.

As a young man he exemplified that special breed of pioneer whose mettle had been tested in the uncompromising wilderness. In the north woods he developed confidence and pride in his ability to be self-sufficient. He followed his trap line through the harsh Wisconsin winters wearing buckskins and moccasins he had sewn, eating what he could shoot, hook, or trap, living in shelters he constructed himself, and keeping his scalp attached to his head by steering clear of the local Indians.

Manly was also respected and admired by the men around him. When the drivers from Dallas's wagon train decided to float down the Green River in an attempt to reach California, they "organized into a company, and much against my wishes, I was elected captain, and assumed command." His reticence to push himself forward was also described many years later by Professor Hunt, who taught Pacific Slope History at the University of the Pacific, College Park, in San Jose. He met Manly shortly after *Death Valley in '49* was published in 1894, when Lewis and his wife lived near the college. Hunt invited Manly to speak to his class, and "with some reluctance and timidity" he consented. After a brief introduction Professor Hunt turned to Manly but was "dumfounded when [he] noticed that the old man's hands were shaking violently, and his whole body was agitated. Even worse, he could not speak a word, seemed to be completely tongue-tied and stage-struck." Manly gradually relaxed with Hunt's gentle coaxing and was soon telling his story: "What a contrast . . . did this dear trembling pioneer present when compared with others I have known, who seemed to thrive on their own loquacity, and the larger the crowd the better it pleased them. Yet not one of them had a greater story of personal courage displayed, or more intense suffering endured, than William Lewis Manly. In that quality there is something that stirs my admiration. A man's life speaks out more loudly than his words" (Hunt 1962).

But Lewis was a mortal man and had prejudices as do others. Upon meeting six heavily armed Mormons while on the way to California, he said, "I had heard so much about the Mormons and their doings in Nauvoo and other places that I looked upon them with suspicion, and thought I would not like to meet them if I had a desirable mule which they wanted, or any money, or even a good looking wife." He also had been brought up to believe that "Spaniards were a race of pirates and robbers, and to be in a land where they lived was very dangerous," but he changed his mind after he had personal contact with them. When he received help from the Spanish woman at Rancho San Francisco, he said, "The woman was quite intelligent and as interesting as one could expect. She put me in mind of my mother, only she was of dark complexion." When he again received aid from the Californios he said, "We bade our kind friends good bye . . . and with 'adios, adios,' many times repeated we parted as good friends."

To those of us who have read Manly's words and traced his footsteps for so many years, he has become larger than life. In reality, though, Manly was shorter than average, and during his desert trek, he wasted away to little more than skin and bones. John B. Colton, a young Jayhawker, said that when Manly "found our trail, and came into our camp, trying to get out [of the desert], and get succour for the women and little children, he was a skeleton, but did not look older than 25 years, but he had the nerve of a cata-mount" (in Powell 1971:40). The census records reveal Manly was 5 feet 7 or 8 inches tall. A neighbor who knew Manly as an old man said he was "a small man, about 5 feet 4 inches in height, bent over and walking with a manzanita cane held in a palsied hand, palm outward. His eye was clear and keen with a snow-white beard and his mind was like a basket, filled only with the events of his trip through Death Valley. He had the reputation of having been the keenest rifle shot in the entire party" (in Powell 1971:42). About this last subject, a companion once replied, "Manly, if I could shoot as well as you I would never follow any other occupation," and Manly once said of himself, "I really considered myself a good shot, and had no fear of any four footed beast I ever saw."

When Lewis was 20 he decided he should try to make his own way in the world. His father gave him all the cash he had—$3.00—which made a grand total of $8.00 with which to make a trip from Michigan to Wisconsin. Louis started his life away from home by taking a lonesome float down the Grand River with a friend also in search of himself. When they finally arrived at Lake Michigan they took a schooner to Wisconsin.

Work was difficult to find among the widely scattered settlers in Wisconsin during 1840; few had money to buy the services of some-one else. Not until Manly walked 130 miles west to Mineral Point did he find employment. By then he was down to his last 35 cents. He split ten cords of wood into 1-inch pieces to mix with charcoal for smelting iron ore, and for this he was paid $12.50. He found odd jobs on neighboring farms and cut wood for a collier who made charcoal. While on this trip Manly had his first cup of coffee, which he thought tasted "much like a mild dose of quinine." He was much taken by this new land; it seemed healthier than Michigan.

After a trip back home in the spring, where he had an attack of "bilious fever" (Michigan malaria) he returned to Wisconsin to trap for marten and otter. But before the trapping season arrived, he used his hunting prowess to provide fresh venison to the Cornish miners of Mineral Point for 25 cents a hindquarter.

In the fall, Manly and a companion headed north to trap. When their provisions ran out, they "tried to eat the marten but it was pretty musky and it was only by putting on plenty of salt and pepper that we managed to eat them." After spending all winter trapping and dodging Indians in the wilderness, they arrived at Prairie du Chien, where Mr. Brisbois, a fur trader, was surprised to see them, having heard they were killed or lost. He paid them $100.00 each for their pelts, saying they were the best fur handlers he had ever seen. Manly invested his $100.00 in 80 acres of government land near Mineral Point, but instead of farming he spent the next eight years hunting and trapping north of the Wisconsin River and mining unsuccessfully in Mineral Point.

In 1845, there was much talk about the Oregon Territory—rich soil, plenty of timber, mild winters, and "some Indians, just to give a little spice of adventure to the whole thing." But Manly could not yet go because it would take two years to put together enough money for an outfit. By 1847, the fur market was poor, so Manly tried unsuccessfully to join the army for the war with Mexico.

In the winter of 1848–49, while Manly was staying with his friends the Bennetts near Mineral Point, convincing news of gold discovered in Alta California coincided with the poor fur market. On February 2, 1849, the *Wisconsin Tribune* carried the following titillating information: "Letters have been received at the State Department, dated Monterey, November 16th [1848], confirming all the previous accounts of the inexhaustible supply of gold in California. . . . Lieut. Larkin saw lumps of gold weighing one and two pounds, and heard of lumps weighing sixteen and twenty-five pounds." The adventure of going west and the possibility of making a fortune at the same time were inducement enough for Manly and Bennett to pull up stakes.

Asabel Bennett, a hunter who had a farm a few miles northeast of Mineral Point, decided to sell out and take his family to the California gold fields. In 1840, Asabel had married Sarah Dilly (Dille, Dilley); by 1848, they had three children: George, Melissa, and little Martha. They may have read and heeded the advice given by Wm. P. Parkinson in a *Wisconsin Tribune* article (February 2, 1849) about "the proper outfit, time of starting, difficulties and hardships of the trip, &c. &c." It included the following information:

> Wagons should be light and strong, made of thoroughly seasoned wood and well ironed . . . covered with a double sheet of cotton drilling, as this is most comfortable, durable, and best, for protection from the rains. Painted covers draw the heat, and are more liable to crack or split than those that are free from oil or paint. . . . A wagon for the conveyance of a family should be entirely closed up at each end, with a side door, as it is much more convenient for the family to get in and out . . . these

wagons should be drawn by three or four yoke of good sub-
stantial fast-traveling young oxen, not exceeding seven years
old. Much depends upon the proper kind of oxen. . . . The
cooking utensils should consist of a tea-kettle, coffee-pot,
frying-pan, a few tin cups and small pans, tin-plates, &c. &c. No
heavy article in this line should be taken, with the exception of a
brass or other light kettle for washing. . . . they can have water
for cooking purposes by carrying water kegs with them, which
every one should not fail to do. . . . Every family should be
supplied with a good roomy tent, either painted or dipped in
oil, so as to exclude the rain which is sure to fall . . . the first
three or four weeks.

Manly was to go west with the Bennetts, but first he went to
Prairie La Crosse to buy a Winnebago pony because no suitable
horse was available in Mineral Point. He altered his gun to a pill lock
and packed enough ammunition for two years. A new outfit of
tanned deerskins provided his comfortable and durable traveling
clothes.

Unfortunately, the Bennetts started west before Manly returned from Prairie La Crosse. But, expecting to meet Manly at the
Missouri River crossing, they took his gear with them. When Manly
arrived at Council Bluffs, the primary river crossing for wagon trains
heading west, he searched in vain for the Bennetts. Unbeknownst
to him, the Bennetts had crossed at Kanesville north of Council
Bluffs. With only his gun, his pony, and the clothes on his back,
Manly decided to continue west anyway. Many months and hundreds of miles later, Manly finally—and quite by accident—crossed
the Bennetts' path near Hobble Creek south of Salt Lake City.

Between the Missouri River and South Pass in the Rocky Mountains, Manly's trek across the continent was similar to that of
thousands of emigrants. He was hired—for board only—by Charles
Dallas of Lynn, Iowa, to drive one of five wagons to California.
Another driver in this small train was John Rogers, a large, quiet
man from Tennessee.

Manly and Rogers intended to go all the way to California with
Mr. Dallas. But just before they crossed South Pass, they learned the
train would overwinter in Salt Lake City because the season was too
advanced to attempt a Sierra Nevada or Cascade Range crossing
into California.

Rogers, Manly, four other ox drivers, and the cook left the
wagon train when it reached the Green River, north of what is now
Green River, Wyoming. Manly and others had studied a government map, possibly Frémont's 1848 map, and reasoned they could
float down the river to California. They conferred with an army
captain, who told them the only obstacles he knew of were some

bad cataracts downriver. These adventurous souls had no concept of the treacherous waters of western rivers. They assumed, incorrectly, that they could navigate the Green River as they had the calm rivers east of the Mississippi. With bad advice, a sketchy map, a salvaged boat, and excess enthusiasm they headed down the Green River toward the Pacific Ocean and the gold fields.

On their harrowing trip down the river the seven men lost their boat and most of their guns and heavy supplies. They were forced to carve three dugout canoes from pine trees to continue their bold adventure. They navigated over 300 miles of twisting river before they chanced upon the great Ute chief Walkara (Wakara) and his band camped where the Old Spanish Trail crossed the river 3 or 4 miles north of Green River, Utah. This spot was a favorite camping place for the chief and his tribe. B. Chateau (in Hafen and Hafen 1954a:369) had encountered Walkara there in 1848. Possibly Walkara (whom Manly called Walker) chose this location in order to secure tribute from pack trains during peak travel periods, a policy he practiced on wagon trains that passed through his territory during the gold rush.

When Manly's party said they were *Mormonee*, Chief Walkara befriended them and by sign language convinced five of the river runners to abandon their foolhardy venture and travel cross-country to Salt Lake City. After a ten-day march, the men chanced upon the Asabel Bennett family at Hobble Creek, 45 miles south of Salt Lake City. At last Manly found the friends with whom he had intended to start his trip six months before. The Bennetts owned two of the over one hundred wagons about to embark on the southern route to California. He joined the Bennetts and invited John Rogers to travel with them to the gold fields.

There had been considerable controversy among the emigrants arriving in Salt Lake City late in the season about how best to proceed to California. A letter from James Wasley written October 21, 1849, after arriving in California via the northern route, explained the dilemma:

> It was very late in the season when we arrived there [Salt Lake City], and the Mormons told frightful stories about the dangers to be encountered on the Northern route so late in the season. There is a new route further South, which they advised emigrants to take. A Mormon named Capt. Hunt offered his services as guide by the southern route; he had been through there with a train of pack mules, and said that the route was practicable for wagons by working the roads. There never has been more than one wagon through that route, and that in one instance it had to be taken to pieces and let down by ropes. . . . They recalled to our recollection the fate of the "Donner party," and also of Frémont and his men last winter. All this, you know,

was enough to appall the stoutest heart, but we suspected that it
was nothing but a trick of theirs, to induce us to go the Southern
route, and break a road for them. . . . So we concluded to run
the risk of the Northern route, but knowing that we ran a great
risk of being caught in the snow in the mountains.

Those who successfully negotiated the northern route arrived
in California more than four months before those who took the
southern route and the disastrous western "cutoff."

The large caravan moved slowly south paralleling the mountains along the natural course now traversed by Interstate Highway
15. As they neared what is now Cedar City, Utah, the slow progress
and fear of losing many animals in the desert led to dissension in the
caravan. When copies of Barney Ward's map circulated among the
wagons showing a cutoff of 300 to 500 miles to the gold fields along
a route with grass and water, most of the emigrants defected from
Hunt's leadership and headed due west from Enterprise, Utah.
They were also led astray by Frémont's 1848 map showing, incorrectly, a mountain range extending west that appeared to create
a southern border to the Great Basin.

As the Bennett party headed west into unknown territory in
hopes of finding a shortcut to the gold fields, they spent precious
time and provisions breaking a road around the many dry mountain
ranges in the uncharted Great Basin. Manly realized they had been
driven far from the route drawn on the Barney Ward map and must
find their own way out of the deserts. Since he did not have any
specific responsibilities, he took it upon himself to scout the country
ahead to find the best way through. His pace was strong and fast,
and other men had a difficult time keeping up with him. Many a
night he stayed alone in the wilderness on his treks to distant peaks
from which he could see more of the territory. As water and grass
became scarce, he covered incredible distances as he dipped into
canyons and skirted ridges looking for small seeps and patches of
grass.

By the time the small train of seven wagons, including the two
Bennett wagons, reached the Amargosa Desert east of Death Valley,
they were already on short rations; the oxen were so weak they
could hardly pull the heavy oak wagons.

Ten years before, when Manly left home to seek adventure, if
not fortune, his mother bade him good-bye with the admonition to
"remember our advice, and honor us for we have striven to make
you a good and honest man, and you must follow our teaching, and
your conscience will be clear" (1894:31). Little did he know that in
the winter of 1849, in the heart of Death Valley, he would wrestle
with his conscience and choose what he thought was certain death
with honor rather than life with disgrace. He said, "If I were alone,

with no one to expect me to help them, I would be out before any other man, but with women and children in the party, to go and leave them would be to pile everlasting infamy on my head. The thought almost made me crazy but I thought it would be better to stay and die with them, bravely struggling to escape than to forsake them in their weakness" (1894:142). Only a few days after Manly's temptation in the wilderness, four men from his party, the Bennett and Arcan teamsters, faced the same monumental decision and chose to save their own skins—to hell with the women and children.

It is not just because Manly performed a great and memorable feat by saving the families left in Death Valley that we admire and respect him, but because he did it with compassion, bravery, and honor. John Rogers deserves an equal share of our admiration for choosing, as Manly did, to do all within his power to help his friends, even if it meant death.

Manly and Rogers's heroic exploits are well known through the popularity of Manly's book *Death Valley in '49*. In the past only a few historians and scholars had access to his earlier account, "From Vermont to California," upon which his book was based, but now all Death Valley buffs can read the Death Valley and California desert portion of Manly's serialized account, which Burr Belden said was "more Manly."

Fortunately, the eleven issues covering the California desert portion are intact. However, the first five paragraphs of February deal with the emigrants' travel in eastern Nevada. This area is now in the atomic weapons testing range, and we have not yet followed the route through that area. Therefore, we excluded these paragraphs and join the families as they enter the Amargosa Desert through a narrow gap near Point of Rocks now threaded by Highway 95 between Beatty and Las Vegas, Nevada. They skirt the southern edge of the playa in the Amargosa Desert and enter Ash Meadows.

Into Death Valley

[February 1888; Volume IV, Number XII, page 187]

We now started on again. On the second or third night we camped near a hole of clear water [Devils Hole, Ash Meadows, Nevada] which was quite deep and had some little minus [minnows] in. Grass was good and plenty for our cattle.[1] The next day we crossed a shallow stream of peculiar tasting water [in Carson Slough].[2] It seemed to be medicated in some way by the

1. The Bennett-Arcan wagon train entered Ash Meadows from the east through a low pass in the hills and followed an Indian trail southwesterly to Devils Hole and Indian occupation sites nearby. The trail, paralleling the current dirt road, leads to Devils Hole, a small pool hidden 50 feet down in a fault fissure at the base of a limestone hill (not "volcanic cliffs" as Koenig says [1984:94]).

Devils Hole is on the right-hand side of the trail at the entrance to Ash Meadows just as Nusbaumer described it (sheet 9). It harbors "little minus"—the endangered Devils Hole pupfish (Cyprinodon diabolis), one of the rarest fish on earth (Soltz and Naiman 1978:17 & 24). These fish are not blind, as Koenig says (1984:94).

Fairbanks Spring and Big Spring have been suggested as the campsite (Long 1941:213), but they fit neither Manly's nor Nusbaumer's description. We conclude the emigrants stopped at Devils Hole since it was the first water they had encountered in many miles, but that they camped 0.75 mile south at Collins Spring. There are numerous ash, screw-bean mesquite, cottonwood trees, wild grapes, and "good and plenty grass" here. It was logical to continue on to Collins Spring because it had firewood and grass and is in a direct line to the pass in the mountains ahead. Collins Spring is not shown on the Ash Meadows USGS quadrangle map, but is in Dudley and Larson (1976:13).

Nusbaumer said he and Hadapp bathed in the pool (Devils Hole), but surely they would not have bathed in the camp's water supply—the only interpretation possible had they camped at Devils Hole. Also, the soil around Devils Hole cannot support a stand of "good and plenty" grass. Nusbaumer goes

on to say (sheet 9), "The temperature of the water is about 24–26° [75–79° F] and the saline cavity itself presents a magical appearance." The word "saline" is left out of Koenig's Valley of Salt, Memories of Wine (1967:42), but "saline cavity" accurately describes the ring of white saltlike deposits encircling the pool in what Dudley and Larson (1976:10) call "horizontal depositional rings of calcite or dolomite." The current temperature of Devils Hole is 92–93° F, well above Nusbaumer's estimate. Other water sources in Ash Meadows such as King Pool near Point of Rocks Springs more closely approximate Nusbaumer's estimate, but these do not fit his description as well as does Devils Hole.

In 1866, Nevada's Governor Blasdel (1867:144) traversed Ash Meadows and visited Devils Hole. He described the meadows: "Six miles across . . . with some small white ash timber and grape vines . . . [they entered] a range of low coralline limestone hills, with a fine spring [Devils Hole] on the summit, in a cave thirty feet long and ten feet wide."

2. This was the brackish water in Carson Slough that flowed into the Amargosa River. The water now flowing from the many springs in Ash Meadows is impounded for domestic or agricultural use and rarely reaches the river. Previously water from the slough entered the riverbed south of Death Valley Junction. The Brier accounts (Juliet Brier 1913; John Wells Brier 1903 & 1911) indicate the Amargosa was dry except for muddy pools north of Death Valley Junction.

The riverbed meanders south to the tip of the Black Mountains, where, just north of Salt Spring, it curves northwest and terminates in Death Valley. Had the pioneers followed the riverbed south for 36 way in which it acted on those who drank much of it. I think it came from a mine of salts.

Here we came in the road of those who had gone and left us.[3] The path led up hill and it looked like a very long pull [near highway from Death Valley Junction westward]. I went ahead until I could see that the road was a very long one with no prospects for water. I then turned back to see if our party had filled their kegs with water. I found they had not. I told them they might have to go forty miles without the way the country looked. They then unloaded the lightest wagon and went back for water.[4]

I then pushed on and near the summit I found a dead ox. Someone had cut a big gash square across the ham and it had dried. I cut a big slice from it and ate as I went along. I was hungry and it tasted very good.[5] I turned the summit and pushed on down the canyon [Furnace Creek Wash] and found a little water on the face of a clay bluff in a hole that held about a quart.[6] I got a good drink and passed on. The canyon, as well as the whole range was barren, dry and very volcanic. It was now a heavy down grade, but not rocky. No more water was found till near the mouth of the canyon. I walked on down the lonesome dry bottom and about an hour after dark came to Mr. Brier's camp, where there were numerous weak springs and a little grass [Travertine Springs].[7]

---

miles, they would have struck the Old Spanish Trail near Tecopa, California. Captain Hunt's wagon train, from which the Bennett-Arcan party split near Enterprise, Utah, camped on "Salaratus Creek" (the Amargosa River) November 30 and reached Salt Spring on December 1, 1849, according to Addison Pratt, a member of that train (in Hafen and Hafen 1954b:94).

3. These were tracks of the Brier mess, the Georgia-Mississippi boys, and the Jayhawkers, who had parted from the Bennett-Arcan group in Emigrant Valley, Nevada. This day, the day before Christmas, the Jayhawkers were 30 miles west attempting to cross Death Valley with their wagons. The Briers and others were picking their way down Furnace Creek Wash.

4. Their return for water, probably from the outflow of Big Spring, is confirmed by Nusbaumer (sheet 9). They had not filled the water kegs so the weakened oxen could more easily pull the lighter wagons through Carson Slough, which Nusbaumer called "horrible alkali marshes." The Ash Meadows area has numerous fresh water springs, so the parties may have assumed they could obtain water along the trail ahead of them.

5. In this account, Manly neglects to say he bivouacked between Ash Meadows and Travertine Springs somewhere "pretty near the summit" (Manly

1894:136). We conclude he slept near the pass through the Funeral Mountains, 11 or so miles west of Death Valley Junction.

6. This unmapped seep, which we call "Clay Bowl Spring," is 0.25 mile west of Navel Spring and 8.5 miles east of Travertine Springs. Manly (1894:137) described it: "In one of the perpendicular portions it seemed to be a variegated clay formation, and a little water seeped down its face. Here the Indians had made a clay bowl and fastened it to the wall so that it would collect and retain about a quart of water." Because the Jayhawkers had pioneered the wagon road down Furnace Creek Wash, Manly was free to follow the Indian trail, which he suspected would lead to water. The Indian trail to the spring is still traceable, and even today potable water seeps down the clay formation. Navel Spring is not a contender for Manly's "clay bowl" spring because it is not located at the base of a "variegated clay formation."

7. The Briers were camped at the most easterly of several springs collectively called Travertine Springs, but named Hadley Spring on old maps (Palmer 1980). Owen (1861), leader of the U.S. and California Boundary Commission reconnaissance, said that in March 1861, Furnace Creek flowed "about three miles or less from its lower outlet into Death Valley. . . . we found an abundance of grass of var-

He and his family, consisting of his wife and two [three] boys, were the only ones in camp.[8] The others had out traveled him and as he did not belong to their organization they would not pay much attention to him nor accept his advice. He was not very well liked among the boys and up to this time had received little favor from them. He was a great talker. When I came to his camp he was delivering a lecture to his boys on education. I thought this a queer place under the circumstances to teach school, but perhaps they have remembered the lecture and profited by it. I slept by their fire without any blanket, for I never carried any bedding and always slept very near the fire.

Mr. Brier started on in the morning, but as I was in no hurry I staid after he had gone and looked the camp over to see if anything had been left. I found only some bacon rinds which I gathered up and devoured. They seemed the best I had ever eaten. I now turned back to meet the teams, which I found seven or eight miles up the canyon. The cattle were nearly worn out, and we found it necessary to lay over and let them rest. The night was foggy and showed signs of rain but none fell. We could hear geese quacking over our heads and we thought that we must be near civilization. The little springs came all together and ran down the canyon some distance and sunk in the sand. I went along the little stream and saw and shot a wild goose, which I suppose had been drawn here in the night, by seeing our camp fire. Near the end of the canyon and under a high precipice [Furnace Creek Inn stands near here] was quite a cave which had the appearance of once being occupied by Indians.[9] I observed a curious crooked track going down towards the valley. I followed it out into the sand hills, which were but a few feet high and here in the top of one was a hole dug deep enough for a small man to crawl in out of sight. The hole was occupied by an old white headed Indian who was a cripple and blind and had crawled from the cave

ious kinds, all green and luxuriant . . . [but] when chewed, it had a sharp sour taste, so decided, as to be unpleasant to the taste." Van Dorn, assistant surveyor for the 1861 boundary commission, described the creek as a "bold torrent, which dashes noisily down the rapid descent, and is lined by a fringe of grass and willows" (in Woodward 1961:50). On April 20, 1866, Nevada's Governor Blasdel (1867:144) said the creek flowed a "little more than four miles." The springs discharge about 2,000 gallons of water per minute (Hunt et al. 1966:B36), but most of the water is now diverted for irrigation and domestic use at Furnace Creek Ranch and Inn.

8. The Briers had their three sons with them: Christopher, 8; John, 6; and Kirke, 4 (Wheat 1939d:108). According to Juliet Brier (in Belden 1954:23), there were others in camp who "asked Mr. Brier to speak to them. . . . So he made them a speech." When Manly arrived at Travertine Springs about dusk, the Briers were alone in camp. The others had followed the Jayhawkers north.

9. Manly (1894:139) said the camp had "the appearance of being continuously occupied by Indians." Van Dorn said, "a rancheria of over a hundred of them [Indians] existed at the mouth of this creek" (in Woodward 1961:49). The Indians called the village Tumbica from *tumbi* meaning "rock" (Steward 1938:92). A vestige of this ancient camp still remains. A 17-foot-long boulder with several mortars ground into it rests in the gravel parking lot of Furnace Creek Inn.

this far for fear of his enemies. It appeared that he had dug the hole himself, as no other tracks could be seen in the sand. The old man laid very still as if hiding, but he was alive for I could see him breathe. But I journeyed on and left him alone in his glory.[10]

We were now close up to our big snow mountain [Telescope Peak] that we had been steering towards for the past month.[11] The valley [Death Valley] was not very wide and seemed to rise gradually to the north. The road now turned north and led up the valley.[12] I followed it and reached camp [McLean Spring] at about nine o'clock at night and stopping at Doty's camp, I inquired if they had explored Martin's pass now near by.[13] They said they had and that there was no possible way of getting over with wagons. They were burning their wagons and killing some of their cattle and intended to pack the oxen with the provisions and bedding. This was indeed bad news to take back to my camp. The water here was very poor and brackish and the grass very scarce.[14] They would have to hurry along and find a better camp. I started back for our camp [at Travertine Springs] before daylight and on my way met Mr. Fish

10. Manly (1894:139) said the old man's "skin looked very much like the surface of a well dried venison ham. I should think by his looks he must be 200 or 300 years old." The Briers also saw the old Indian (in Belden 1954:23).

11. Telescope Peak, 11,049 feet, is the highest point in the Panamint Range. Its base, at Eagle Borax Spring, is 251 feet below sea level. The continuous vertical rise of 11,300 feet in 13 air miles is one of the greatest ascents found on earth. No wonder the emigrants thought they were looking at the eastern escarpment of the mighty Sierra Nevada.

12. Manly followed the Jayhawker wagon tracks along Furnace Creek and west into the valley. At the salt flats he found where they returned to higher ground and headed north. The Jayhawkers were following an Indian trail, parts of which are still traceable from Furnace Creek to McLean Spring. The road they forged eventually became the early wagon and auto road to McLean Spring. It lies west of and generally parallel to the present highway.

13. Martin's Pass was named for Jim Martin, a leader of the Georgia-Mississippi contingent. Manly (1894:123) first referred to Martin's Pass near Papoose Lake, Nevada. "In a due west course from me was the high peak [Telescope] we had been looking at for a month, and the lowest place was on the north side, which we had named Martin's Pass and had been trying so long to reach."

14. This wagon burning site is near McLean Spring, the headwater of Salt Creek. It was called

Lost Wagon or McCormick Spring on some old maps (e.g., Holt 1869 & 1875).

The Jayhawkers abandoned their wagons at two different locations in Death Valley. The first site was recorded by Van Dorn, assistant surveyor of the 1861 U.S. and California Boundary Commission (in Woodward 1961:52 & 53), who wrote, "Riding along the border of the plain, we observed the faint tracks of the emigrant wagons of '49 running along its margin, and this morning we came to a spot where they had camped [near Cow Creek], and which was evidently one of the scenes of their sad disaster. It was strewn with the relics of their wagons—the spokes, tires and hubs of the wheels, and the iron of the running gear, chain, broken pots and other remains of camp equipage marking the abandonment and destruction of part of the train." At McLean Spring he noted, "Here again we find the traces of the emigrant encampment, bones of cattle in plenty, and the less perishable parts of their abandoned wagons, trace chains, broken pots, etc." Koenig (1984:246) claims that the members of the commission found wagon remains "at McLean Spring *and* to the north of it." However, Van Dorn clearly states the first site was *south* of McLean Spring. Blasdel (in Stretch 1867:143) observed in 1866 that "many remains of the wagons belonging to emigrants who perished here in the attempt to reach California, lie scattered round these springs. . . . Water at Lost Wagons [McLean Spring] strongly alkaline." No emigrants died here in winter 1849–50.

of Indiana and another man with their packs on their backs.[15] They were both of our party and were nearly out of grub and their cattle being poor and weak they had given them to their traveling companion, Capt. Culverwell, and were going to try to make the balance of the journey on foot.[16] They were both past middle age, Mr. Fish being fifty or more years old. We had half an hour's talk over our prospects. I encouraged them by saying it might not be so far out as I had predicted.

An ounce of food that could be left and could not be eaten had better be thrown away, but Mr. Fish had wound around him a beautiful long whiplash which he would not throw away. He said he might meet a chance to trade it for something to eat. We then shook hands and parted. As I went back towards our camp, I thought of the poor prospects of these two old men ever seeing a settlement.

[March 1888; Volume V, Number I, page 10.]

On reading over my last month's article, many little incidents came up, which I saw I had forgotten to put down. As they might give a clearer light on our travels, I give a few little additional notes as I now recall them. [Manly's reflections relate to incidents in southeast Nevada that, although not covered in this book, do poignantly show the desperate situation some of the emigrants were in.]

When I returned [to Cane Spring, Nevada?] from my trip of exploration on the high mountain, with a sad and discouraged heart, my companions told me that after I had left, they had found a small pile of squashes covered over with sage brush. They had divided them in camp and all were eaten with a relish as they were very good. I told them this was a bad thing to do, to rob the poor

---

15. The other man was Mr. Gould (Manly 1894:142). Reverend Brier (JA 76) referred to "M. Gould" as being in their party as well as Fish and Isham when they crossed the Slate Range, and Mrs. Brier (in Belden 1954:26) said Gould "would pick up everything the rest threw away, until he had so much that Mr. Brier gave him an ox to carry his load." Isham and Smith, from Nusbaumer's mess, were also on the trail north from Travertine Springs, although Manly does not mention them. Nusbaumer said, "here on the 28th our other fellow travelers left us, all but Culverwell who is too ill to go further with the others." That is, Fish, Isham, and Smith left Travertine Springs on December 28 and went north to join the Jayhawkers at McLean Spring. Nusbaumer and Hadapp remained at Travertine Spring until January 7, when they went south following the Bennett-Arcan mess.

16. Richard Culverwell, 48, and son Stephen, 22, started to the gold fields with Goldsborough Bruff as members of the Washington City and California Mining Association. Richard fell ill at Fort Kearny; Bruff (in Read and Gaines 1949:xlvi) said of him, "One, I find, I must leave, a too elderly man is in such feeble health that he cannot proceed, with us . . . and we shall leave him here. . . . I advised him to remain till he recovered, and then to accompany the first train in to Missouri, and so get home.—His son, a hearty and intelligent man, (a good carpenter,) continues with us." Stephen later told Bruff (in Read and Gaines 1949:484) that his father recovered and traveled on to Salt Lake with a Mormon family. Here Culverwell teamed up with Nusbaumer, Hadapp, Fish, Isham, and Smith. They left Salt Lake City on October 7 and caught up with the Hunt wagon train ten days later.

Indians in this desert country, and as they are generally revengeful, they would sometime get even with us.

Two nights after this at about three o'clock in the morning Mr. Bennett got up to renew the fire and fix his kettle of meat, so as to have it ready cooked for breakfast. But when he looked in his kettle he found the meat nearly all gone. He woke me and said in a low voice, "did you see any one up during the night?" I said "no." "My meat has been stolen," he said, "and I would like to know who the thief is." I did not know who was starving and forced to steal. This was bad news among our little party and we wondered what we were all coming to. Was some one to be killed to save others? We thought we could put our fingers on the starving man, but were not sure. We talked this over in a low voice for some time and finally concluded it was best to keep it all to ourselves, for the present at least, and wait and see what might be done if anything of a similar character should happen again.

I slept no more that night. I was quite certain that some were getting short of grub but I had not for once thought that any one would try to get any dishonestly at such a risk of discovery, as there were four or five camp fires in our small circle and one would be very liable to be seen. At daylight all our party were up. I surveyed them all carefully as did also Mr. Bennett, to see if we could detect any signs of guilt, but we could not so we said nothing to any one and agreed to wait further developments. But we never were troubled again in all our journey by having meat stolen, and the hungry thief never turned up again.

The night that I spent at Doty's camp [McLean Spring, Death Valley], we talked nearly all night over our prospects as well as of the troubles and trials we had endured. The camp was composed of men of all kinds of dispositions, some were well educated others illiterate; no one could be judged by his looks. Some of the men could talk on any subject and at this particular time were free to talk and give their opinions having no fear of offense for language was free and there was not respect of persons. Some seemed to believe this section was made of what dregs were left after the world was made and all the salt that the ocean could not dissolve and Lot's wife included.

The desolation as far as animal life was concerned was almost complete. The coyotes were too smart to come out here and starve and the buzzards could not fly over here and live. There was no game larger than a jack rabbit, and not more than one a week could be seen of them; then they did not allow one to get nearer to them than half a mile.

Before I went to sleep I asked about Mr. Brier, how they liked him and how they got along. As I have remarked before he was not generally liked. They told me that his wife was the best man of the two and they were followers and poor councilors. He was all talk and little work, and as now he had got where preaching was poor pay and was not in God's own country, his prayers did not get far above his head. He is willing for us to do all the work and does not seem to realize that we now have to all trust to muscle, poor meat and lots of ambition to ever get to a better country. He follows in our broken road, takes the easiest place and only works with his tongue, following his old habits of life in a settled country where grub was cheap and plenty.[17]

I left this camp before daylight and started back to my party; on my own way, I met Mr. Fish and a companion, whom I mentioned in my last article.

When I arrived at our camp I found that three of the oxen had been shot with arrows by the Indians. One was shot fatally and we killed the poor beast and ate his flesh. The other two got well. I told the men they were now getting their pay for stealing their squashes and might possibly fare worse. I think the object of the Indians was to cripple our cattle so that we would leave them, they would then use it for food.[18]

Our party now concluded to go down towards the south end of the valley and to try and find some pass where we could get over the mountains.[19] The valley here was quite narrow. The snow capped mountains now before us seemed high enough to hold snow all the year and its east side was so steep and rocky that a man on foot could hardly climb it. The snow could be seen drifting over the summit of the mountain, but in the valley it was as warm as a July day. We concluded that rain must be scarce in this region for the gravel in ravines seemed to be so little washed. About fifty miles south the mountain gradually sloped down forming low black barren buttes without snow or any sign of timber. It looked as if the barren buttes might continue on forever in that direction.

There was no way possible to get through with our wagons but by going south, so we all started on together, without waiting for

17. As a vocal proponent of the cutoff route, Reverend Brier was a logical scapegoat when troubles arose. He was quite ill in the latter part of the journey. Lummis (1911:41) said he began the trek weighing 175 pounds and wasted away to 75.

18. The oxen were shot the night of December 27. The Indians often suffered from acute hunger in winter and early spring after their stores of mesquite beans, pinyon nuts, and grass seeds were eaten (Steward 1938). This attack was simply an attempt to get food.

19. The decision to head south immediately was based on information from a scouting trip made by Rogers and another man. Rogers (1894) said, "We traveled [south] about ten miles and struck a bunch of willows and a spring of fresh water. In prospecting ten miles farther we struck a lake. . . ." This was Tule Spring, 15 miles south of Furnace Creek Inn. Willows do not tolerate alkaline or saline soils; thus, the bushes were probably arrow weed (*Tessaria sericea*), which now grows here. It resembles willow when it is leafless in winter. The lake was the standing water at Eagle Borax Spring. Rogers does not say the lake was 10 miles beyond the spring but that he scouted 10 miles and during that time found a lake (see also notes 118 & 119).

me to go before as I had been doing.[20] We thought it impossible to get the women and children through and leave the wagons so we took this pass [path?]. When we had all got fairly started I went ahead and out into the valley and part way across it. Here it seemed to me were large blocks of salt with dirt on their tops, and I thought for sure here must be the place where Lot's wife was left.

We went a short way down the valley and crossed an arm of the lake that was in view farther south. The water was very clear and not very deep. Before the wagons drove in, I went and cut a *mesquite* about the size of my arm and four feet long; this I used as a feeler to tell the depth of the water. The bottom of the lake I found quite uneven, it having many holes two feet deep. As I jabbed my stick down, I noticed it made a white spot, so to see what the bottom was made of, I broke off a piece and found it to be pure salt.[21]

When we got to the west side of the valley, we found a good spring of fresh water that came from the snow mountain above, also quite good grass.[22] The next day we got nearly as far down as the

20. Nusbaumer stayed eleven days at Travertine Springs, December 28 to January 7. We conclude the Bennett-Arcan party left Travertine Springs December 31 or shortly thereafter. The palatable grass around the springs had been eaten by the Jayhawkers' cattle; thus, Bennett wanted to leave even though Manly had not scouted a southern route. The fear of further Indian attacks also figured heavily in Bennett's decision to move camp to the spring John Rogers discovered—Eagle Borax Spring (see also note 119).

21. The wagons crossed the valley through Devils Golf Course about 0.25 mile north of the present road. This old wagon crossing was found by the noted geologist Charles B. Hunt (Hunt et al. 1966:B-63; Hunt 1975:177). It was first reported by Army Lieutenant R. Birnie, Jr. (1876:352), who reconnoitered Death Valley for Lt. George M. Wheeler, U.S. Army Corps of Engineers. Birnie recorded, "From Bennett's Wells we moved northwardly along the western border, and crossed to the northeast, over the old emigrant road to Furnace Creek . . . [past] Salt Springs." On Wheeler's map (Wheeler 1877:atlas sheet 65D) "Salt Sprs" (now extinct) is drawn 7 miles south of Furnace Creek—precisely where the eastern remnant of the road can still be seen. Explorers and miners used this crossing before the current roadbed was built to accommodate heavy borax wagons. We traced this old roadbed across Death Valley and found bits of old wagons and salt-encrusted iron along the route. In the middle of the valley, the clear waters of Salt Creek must be crossed. West of the white salt flat is a muddy area where fill just wide enough for a wagon is still discernible. Most of this raised portion has been washed away by flash floods from Trail Canyon.

After crossing the valley, the wagons headed south. They kept to the narrow belt of firm ground between the soft, moist silt of the valley floor and the rough, boulder-strewn alluvial fans.

22. Actually, they found two springs, Tule and Eagle Borax. The latter is named "Emigrant Spr." on the Wheeler map (Wheeler 1877:atlas sheet 65D). The "quite good grass" is alkali sacaton grass (*Sporobolus airoides*), which forms large stands around Eagle Borax Spring and Bennetts Well (Hunt 1966:36). Sacaton grass is not very nutritious, but livestock eat it when preferred forage is not available. Eagle Borax Spring—with its potable water, abundant forage, and firewood—was a good spot to camp so the oxen could recuperate. One of the Bennett-Arcan wagons was probably burned here. Nusbaumer said he "reached a place [Eagle Borax Spring] where the company that had gone before us had burned a wagon and slaughtered oxen and dried meat. They with their families also are in a sorry condition" (sheet 13). The families remained here until January 11 or 12 and then continued south.

To this point there were eight men and four wagons in the Bennett-Arcan party. But Silas Helmer and C. C. (or S. S.) Abbott, Bennett's two teamsters, along with Arcan's two teamsters (unnamed), "concluded their chances of life were better if they could take some provisions and strike out on foot" (Manly 1894:146). They left Eagle Borax Spring about January 7 and backtracked to the Jayhawkers' trail. On January 14, the four drivers plus two other men caught up with Sheldon Young at Providence Spring, now known as Indian Joe Spring (in Long 1950:277). Manly and Rogers overtook them January 19 in Last Chance Canyon in the El Paso Mountains (Manly 1894:162).

snow mountain and camped at a small sulphury water hole.[23] They now thought it best to try and cross the mountain and not to wait for me to go ahead and view the way.

We were now at the mouth of a wash coming down from the west, and it was decided that they would go up it and take their chances.[24] I took my gun and went on ahead. I got within a short

23. The exact site of the sulphur water hole will probably never be determined because it is extinct and the available information describing its location is contradictory. After considering all the evidence, we conclude it is somewhere between 6 and 13 miles south of Bennetts Well, the most probable location being at or near Mesquite Well, 7.5 miles south of Bennetts Well (USGS Furnace Creek, Calif.–Nev., 60 min., 1910; reprinted 1920).

Manly (1894:148) described the water hole: "Out in the valley near its mouth was a mound about four feet high and in the top of this a little well that held about a pailful of water that was quite strong of sulphur. . . . About the mouth of the well was a wire grass that seemed to prevent it caving in. It seems the drifting sand had slowly built this little mound about the little well of water in a curious way."

Our biggest problem was to reconcile the contradictory mileages between the sulphur water hole and the long camp given in Manly's two accounts. First we had to decide where the long camp was. We concluded it was at two locations: first at Eagle Borax Spring, then at Bennetts Well. The wagons first went back "to the good spring we have just left [Eagle Borax Spring]" (Manly 1894:151), and later they moved south 2.25 miles to fresh grass and better water. The water quality is much better at Bennetts Well than at Eagle Borax Spring. Bennett and Arcan either improved the Indian wells or dug a new one, thus giving Bennetts Well its current name. Burr Belden (1954:12) says Charles Bennett dug the wells during the borax mining days; however, "Bennett's Wells" are named on the 1877 Wheeler map and "Bennetts Spr" appears on Holt's maps of 1869 and 1875, many years before Charles Bennett arrived on the scene. The California Historical Landmark (#444) commemorating the long camp has been moved from Tule Spring to Bennetts Well based on our analysis (Johnson 1983).

We next considered Manly's contradictory mileages. He said (1894:197) that on their return from getting provisions they came upon Captain Culverwell's body 7 or 8 miles north of the sulphur water hole. This account says they had "gone about a mile or two" north from the hole before finding Culverwell's body—a discrepancy of 5 to 7 miles. Both accounts agree on the other mileages. Thus, bracketing Manly's contradictory mileages, the sulphur water hole was between 6 and 13 miles south of Bennetts Well—or, put another way, somewhere be-

tween 1.5 miles north of Mesquite Well and 2.5 miles south of Salt Well.

We found the site of Mesquite Well in 1975 while Eric was on his 130-mile pan-Monument hike. It is 230 feet south of benchmark −246 (map 3). Contrary to Koenig's statement (1984:108) that "there is no longer any obvious sign" of it, we found tin cans, baling wire, and other camp debris remaining from the 20-mule–team borax days when it was the only potable water between Bennetts Well and Lone Willow Spring at the southern tip of the Slate Range. John Spears (1892:145) camped at the well and commented that "it was a pleasing desert camp . . . sheltered by the mesquite grove . . . [and] the water of the well is counted excellent." But before they could drink the water they had to dredge several drowned rats from the well.

Koenig (1984:256) contends "Mesquite Well slipped into Salt Well," implying the two are synonymous. But Salt Well is 2.5 miles south of Mesquite Well. Dr. Coville (1891:Jan. 20) recorded both wells when the Death Valley Expedition entered the valley. They "passed an old watering place called Salt Wells. A hole about twenty-five feet deep . . . and we drew up some water which was found to be a nearly saturated brine." The next day "after a few miles . . . we came upon a shallow well containing amber-colored water of disagreeable taste, and known as Mesquite Well." T. S. Palmer (1891:Jan. 20), also with the expedition, said, "Salt Wells are two holes about 25 ft deep with a little water in the bottom. Water is a saturated solution of salt." Fred W. Koch (1893:49), who joined the expedition in April, said, "we reached Mesquite Wells, a large, rectangular hole filled with salty and sulphury water, far from good, but nevertheless eagerly swallowed by the thirsty horses. After a hasty lunch . . . [we traveled] six miles, which fortunately brought us to Bennett's Wells, where the water was much better than at the last stopping place."

The salty water at Salt Well suggests Manly's small well was not that far south. The Mesquite Well area (1) is the southernmost known potable water source; (2) has been described as sulphury; (3) has mesquite growing on 4-foot-high mounds of earth; and (4) fits the mileages given in this account.

24. Regardless of the exact location of the little hole, the canyons the men considered to make their ascent into the Panamints were the same—Six Spring, Galena, Carbonate, and Warm Spring. From

distance of the top of the canyon, which all along had been very narrow; it suddenly spread out and seemed walled in on all sides by steep cliffs and there seemed no possible way out with wagons. They would have to go back.[25]

It was now near night and I had seen no water or grass all day. I turned and started back to join our party. After dark I slipped and fell on the rocks breaking the breech off my gun, which was quite a misfortune to me. It was near midnight when I reached camp. I told them what I had found and that they could not get over by the way of this canyon. So we were on the morn all obliged to retrace our steps.

This venture proved to be a bad one, for Mr. Bennett lost one of his best oxen, which laid down and could not be pursuaded to go any further, and Mr. Arcane had to leave one also. They dressed Mr. Bennett's ox and put it on a wagon, and as the road was a heavy down grade, it was not hard for the cattle to haul it. When we got back to camp [at the sulphur water hole] Mr. Arcane took a bucket

Mesquite Well, Six Spring Canyon was due west; above it loomed Porter Peak covered with snow. Galena Gap, the headwater of Galena Canyon, was clearly visible and offered a possible low pass over the range. Carbonate Canyon obviously terminated a short way into the range, and Warm Spring Canyon could hardly be seen behind the shoulder of the ridge that separates it from Carbonate Canyon.

Some historians have assumed Six Spring Canyon, 8 miles south of Eagle Borax Spring, was ascended, since Manly (1894:148) said that after leaving Eagle Borax Spring they "went over a road for perhaps 8 miles and came to the mouth of a rocky cañon leading up west to the summit of the range. This cañon was too rough for wagons to pass over. Out in the valley near its mouth was . . . a little well. . . . [two paragraphs later] The men with wagons decided they would take this cañon and follow it up to try to get over the range." Why would they attempt a canyon Manly had just said was "too rough for wagons," one leading to the snowy summit of the range? They did not go up Six Spring Canyon, which clearly heads into the base of snow-covered Porter Peak with a very rough alluvial fan leading to it. Manly's writing assistant has exacerbated the problem by implying the "too rough" canyon and the one they decided to ascend were one and the same.

While the families rested at Eagle Borax Spring, Rogers and another man scouted Warm Spring Canyon and Manly scouted the southern reaches of the valley.

25. Based on Rogers's assessment, the wagons headed up the smooth Pleistocene alluvial fan that extends from the valley floor to Warm Spring Can-

yon. There were two compelling reasons why they chose this unlikely and uninviting canyon when Anvil Spring Canyon, the next one south, was a more logical and feasible route. First, there was the clear Indian trail leading into it. At Travertine Springs, Nusbaumer (sheet 12) said they "intend to follow an Indian trail about 4 miles west and then south . . . and intend, if our supposition in reference to Walker's Pass does not deceive us again, to arrive in a short time at the diggings." Second, they were looking for Walker Pass. The emigrants were using Frémont's map (Manly 1894:120 & 145), which showed his 1845 route paralleling the eastern toe of the Sierra Nevada, and some of party thought the Panamint Range was the Sierra Nevada. Walker Pass, although not labeled on Frémont's map, was well known and appeared on other maps of the era (e.g., Mitchell's 1846 map in Woodward 1949b:xi & facing 168). The prominent Indian trail along the toe of the Panamint Range turned sharply into the mountains, as did the trail on their maps.

Manly met the wagons at the little sulphur water hole and learned "the men with wagons decided they would take this cañon [Warm Spring] and follow it up to try to get over the range, and not wait for me to go ahead and explore" (Manly 1894:148). Because he had seen the seemingly more logical route up Anvil Spring Canyon on his scouting trip southward, he rushed ahead to scout it. Manly's description (1894:149) of finding no water and entering "a kind of basin" fits Anvil Spring Canyon best. Snow-clad Manly Peak appeared to block further progress for the wagons, so Manly turned back before reaching the springs at the headwater of the canyon.

of water back to his ox and succeeded in reviving it and bringing it back to camp.

This place was without grass and there was poor water as well as sage brush. Our situation was now becoming very critical and was talked over with long faces without any jokes. We could not live here and we would be compelled to return to the good spring we had left and stay there until a way out was found. After a long council and much argument, it was decided to send Rogers and myself to find the way and return as soon as possible, for bread now was only given to the children and the cattle must be saved as they were the only means of livelihood. They, or most of them, believed that they were at the foot of our last range; for we had been told that only a narrow range lay between the desert and Los Angeles. They thought we would be able to make the trip in a week or ten days, so we consented to go.[26]

26. The "week or ten days" was changed to fifteen days in his book and in a newspaper article (Manly 1894:154). His 1877 report (in Woodward 1949b:10) said they were allotted eighteen days, and Rogers said three weeks.

Manly and Rogers Go for Provisions

[April 1888; Volume V, Number II, page 26]

After we had consented to go and hunt for a settlement, all hands turned in and helped us to get ready. We all went to work and cut the meat from the bones of an ox and a half. We killed Arcane's ox and cut it up small and dried it over a brisk fire all night. The women made us each a knapsack and put all the meat we had dried from the two oxen in them. You can believe me, when I tell you that the oxen had not a speck of fat on them, and when their bones were broken the marrow ran out like corruption, and a camp kettle cooked full of meat would not show an eye of grease. They gave us a little tea and a few teaspoonfuls of rice to take along in case we were sick. I had a pair of buckskin leggins that I brought from Wisconsin which I wore, I also took one half of a small blanket. Rogers wore his coat and went without any blanket.[27] We had new rawhide moccasins on our feet. Rogers took Bennett's double barrel shot gun, and I took his seven shooter repeating rifle. We had each a canteen made of two one pound powder cans put together and covered with cloth.[28]

They gave us all the money they had in camp, about $60 in all, with the instructions to bring them something to eat and some animals if we could find any. They said they would wait for us eighteen days and if we did not get back in that time, they would conclude we had perished in the snow or the Indians had killed us.

We were about ready to start, when Capt. Culverwell, who was a sea-faring man, said he would tell us how to find our way back, if we should get lost.

Before he could say more Bennett spoke up and said, Lewis don't need any such instructions for I have known him a long time and he never went to a place in the day time, but he could go back in the night.

27. The boys had to cross the Panamint Range. The paucity of sleeping gear and warm clothing indicates they did not anticipate spending a night in the snow. Since Telescope Peak was covered with snow and Manly Peak to the south was also blanketed, and since neither Manly nor Rogers mentioned snow during the crossing, we conclude the low portion of the range south of Porter Peak was snow-free. We have seen the Panamints exhibit similar conditions.

28. A one-pound powder can holds four cups of water; thus, they carried one gallon of water. Rogers said they had a quart canteen.

Before I go further with my narrative, I would like to speak of Mr. Wade and wife and three children, as being among our party and camping with the rest who were going to await our return. I had forgot to mention them before, because they never seemed to seek our acquaintance, and always camped a little ways behind us and seemed independent and able to take care of themselves. I never saw them after I left this camp.[29]

Resuming my narrative from where I left off a moment ago. They fixed on our knapsacks and we got ready for our search for a better country.

The whole camp gathered around us to say good bye and to wish us a safe and speedy return to them. Such language as, "God bless you," "God save you," "Hope for your speedy return," "Good luck to you," seemed sad. Some could not say anything, but the water could be seen in their eyes. The women with grief were silent, they wept, shook our hands tightly and turned away. Mrs. Bennett seemed more effected than any one else. Our whole party stood and watched us till we disappeared up the canyon [Warm Spring] out of sight.[30]

29. Although Manly said he "never saw" the Wades again, Glasscock (1940:33) says Manly visited them while preparing his book. The Wades arrived at Los Angeles a good month before Manly did. Their success in driving a wagon out of Death Valley may have been a difficult feat for Manly to accept. Had the Bennett-Arcan group followed the Wades, they possibly could have taken their wagons out of the desert. Weeks of agony would have been avoided; tools, equipment, and treasured household goods would have been saved.

Both Manly and Charles E. Wade, one of the children who traveled through Death Valley on Manly's heels, were members of the California Pioneers of Santa Clara County Corporation (Mars 1901:268 & 275). We think Manly must have known the Wades made it out of Death Valley with their wagon.

Why the Wades traveled behind the main wagon train was never made clear by Manly. According to Latta (1979:77 & 199) the Wades carried 50 gallons of water in numerous milk cans. Apparently they lingered a day behind the others so small springs had time to refill (Burrell in Woodward 1949b:161). Also, it was easier for their oxen to follow a trail broken by those ahead. The Wades had four (not three) children (Foote 1988:536; Burrel 1894).

30. Manly (1894:153) said there were "eleven grown people in all, besides a Mr. Wade, his wife and three [four] children" at the sulphur water hole that night. He mentioned eight of the party—Mr. and Mrs. Bennett, Mr. and Mrs. Arcan, two Earhart brothers and a grown son, and Captain Culverwell.

The three others were apparently a Mr. Schaub and two unnamed companions; these three later joined forces with the Earharts, making a company of six. We agree with Reed and Gaines (1944:1230) that Nusbaumer, Hadapp, and Schlögel had continued south and were not present at the sulphur water hole when Manly and Rogers left (see also note 144).

From the sulphur water hole, the boys followed the Indian trail into Warm Spring Canyon. They ascended the smooth desert pavement of the ancient Pleistocene fan, which provides the easiest walking in the southern part of the valley. These fans extend down from the canyon mouths almost to the salt pan in the area south of Salt Well. An old road up the fan shown on some maps may trace the Indian trail (USGS Avawatz Mt., Calif., 60 min., 1933; USGS Wingate Wash, Calif., 15 min., 1950). Warm Spring Canyon appears to be an illogical choice when compared to Anvil Spring Canyon, the next one south. However, Manly had already investigated Anvil Spring Canyon and found no water as far as he had explored. The well-traveled Indian trail to the spring in Warm Spring Canyon was a strong inducement to go that way. Some historians reject Warm Spring Canyon because Manly did not mention the spring (Wheat 1939b:103). Since he did not record other water sources, we attach no importance to this omission. Southworth (1978[1980]:125) suggests Warm Spring suddenly appeared as a result of the 1872 Owens Valley earthquake. However, the waterworn rocks and nearby Indian habitation sites indicate it is an ancient water source.

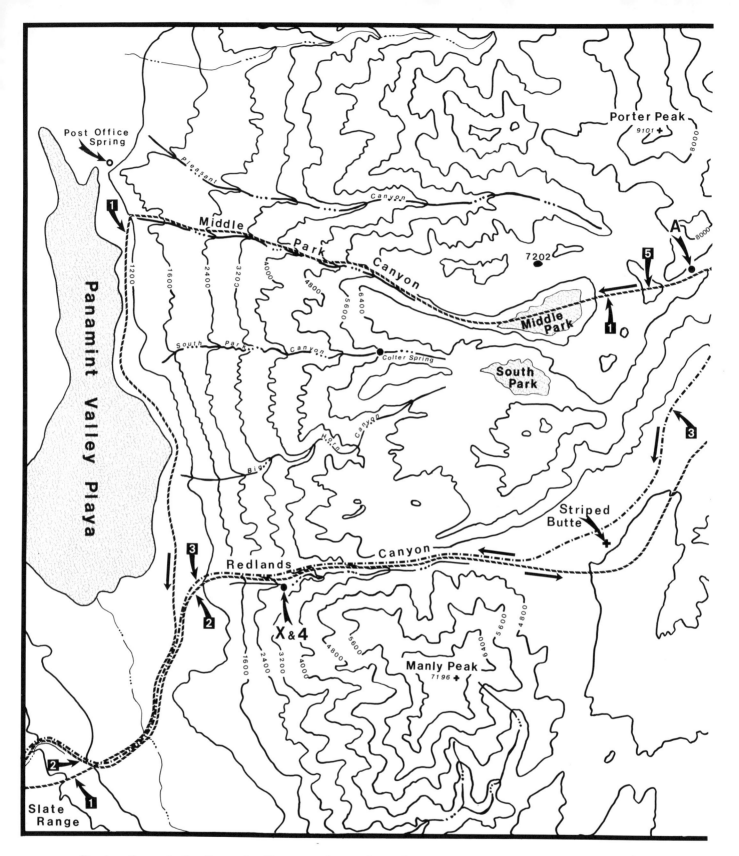

Routes through the Panamint Range, redrawn from the Bennetts Well, Wingate Wash, Telescope Peak, and Manly Peak, California, USGS 15 minute quadrangle maps, contour interval 800 feet.

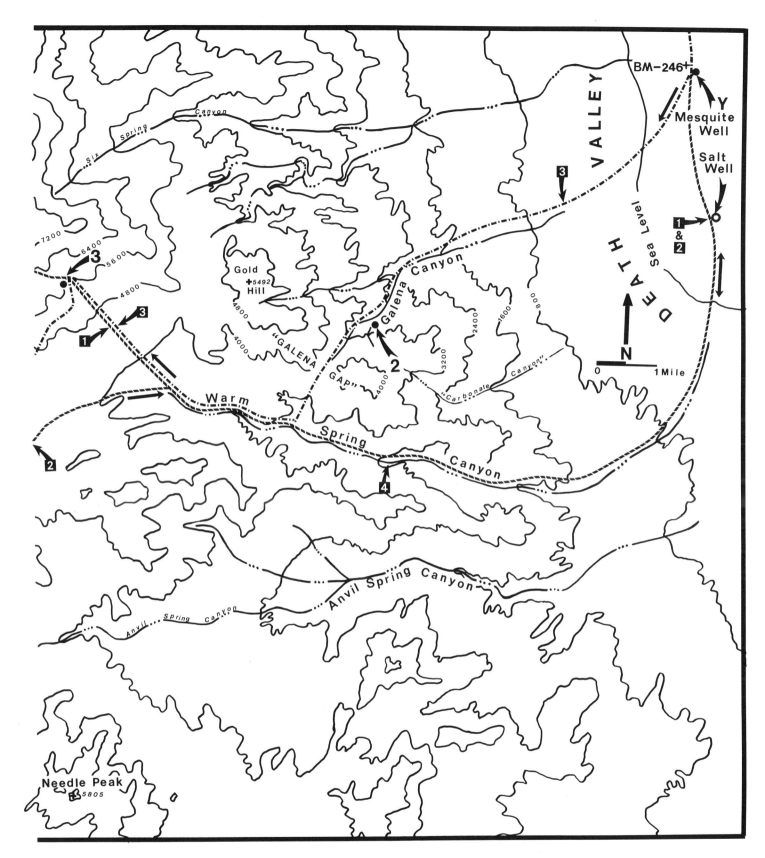

- **1** Manly and Rogers's route out for provisions
- **2** Manly and Rogers's route back to Death Valley
- **3** Bennett-Arcan families' route out
- **4** Warm Spring
- **5** Manly Lookout (7,478 feet)
- **A** Manly and Rogers's 1st camp, above Arrastre Spring (approximate)

- **X** Manly and Rogers's 24th camp, Redlands Spring
- **Y** Manly and Rogers's 25th camp, at or near Mesquite Well
- **2** Families' 2nd camp at or near Talc Mine Spring, Galena Canyon
- **3** Families' 3rd camp, Arrastre Spring
- **4** Families' 4th camp, Redlands Spring

When we got near the summit [of the Panamint Range], night came on. We built a fire and ate our supper of dried meat. When it got dark we traveled on some ways further and found a small washed revine. Here we lay down out of the wind in spoon fashion and put the one-half blanket over us. I had slept many times in this way without a fire to avoid being found by the Indians and had escaped being filled with their arrows.[31]

As we were at quite an elevation [about 6,000 feet] the night was cold and we had rather an uncomfortable night of it with our scant cover and hard bed.

We started in the morning as early as we could see to travel safely in such a rough country. We soon reached the summit and saw what was west of the mountains we had seen so long and had been wondering how the country looked beyond. We were in a rather low pass but at a great elevation and could see a great distance east and west. We could see more than 150 miles to the west and north and but 60 or 70 miles before us was the highest, broadest, biggest mountain we had ever seen, covered deep with snow, and beyond were white peaks beyond peaks as far as the eye could see [the Sierra Nevada].[32]

We now stood and looked some time at the grand picture before us, and wondered if such a mountain would hold its snow all the year. The high mountain glittering and gleaming in the morning sunlight and the lesser peaks clothed in dazzling crystal was the grandest and sublimest sight we had ever seen. In strange contrast to this in the west and south were dark low barren mountains

Rogers may have known Warm Spring existed, because he said he and another man "went up the mountain to spy out a route that would lead us to the other side. Finding we could cross it we went back to camp."

The Indian trail divides into three branches where it enters Butte Valley. The boys took the middle fork up the mountainside to Arrastre Spring (map 3).

31. We conclude the boys slept uphill from Arrastre Spring near the Indian trail to the pass above (camp A, map 3). Manly (1894:153) mentioned a spring in his book and said they stayed there all night; Rogers said they camped "near a spring." Dr. Wolff (1931:26) thinks they camped at Arrastre Spring; Wheat (1939b:84) places this camp near one of the springs in Six Spring Canyon, 2 air miles north. The spring is named after the old gold mining *arrastre* hidden in the brush nearby.

32. The boys hiked up the Indian trail that crests at a saddle (7,160 feet), the southern headwater of Pleasant Canyon. We have named it "Rogers Pass" after John Rogers. The trail from Arrastre Spring to

Rogers Pass is traceable most of the way.

Manly implied they could see a great distance west from the pass, but this is not possible. The view west is totally blocked by the ridge that separates Pleasant and Middle Park canyons. From the pass the boys ascended a prominence (7,478 feet) 0.25 mile to the southwest. We have named this prominence "Manly Lookout." It is not the same hill labeled on Carl I. Wheat's map (Wheat 1939b & Wheat's 1949 edition of Manly's *Death Valley in '49*). Wheat's "Manly's Lookout" corresponds to the location of hill 7202 (USGS Telescope Peak, Calif., 15 min., 1952), 2.5 air miles west of the Death Valley National Monument boundary and 1.2 miles southeast of Stone Corral in Pleasant Canyon. Wheat's description of the view from his "Manly's Lookout" closely fits the view from our Manly Lookout, hill 7478, with one exception. Telescope Peak cannot be seen from hill 7478, but Sentinel Peak can. We feel Wheat mistook it for Telescope Peak. We conclude the two lookouts are the same point, but Wheat's cartographer incorrectly mapped his "Manly's Lookout."

devoid of snow and without any signs of timber, grass, or water. They had the appearance of a barren, desolate region; but in the very far south and west we could see a range that seemed to have some snow on its highest peaks, but it was very dim [San Gabriel Mountains]. A long way off the snow mountain [Sierra Nevada] seemed to drop off suddenly into an almost level plain and the mountains in the distance seemed to start out on its most western spur.

We now knew we would have to steer for the big snow mountain, and it would probably take us three days to reach it, as the country looked barren and dry and we had two ranges to cross.

After looking our proposed route west carefully over, we turned and looked east over the country we had just come over. We could see over a hundred miles over the poorest country in all America. The valley we left, the morning before, was so deep in the ground that it could not be seen through the distance. Across to the mountains east looked but a little ways.[33]

After this survey of the surrounding country, we were satisfied that we could not reach a settlement and return in one week nor in twenty days either. We sat on a rock and looked at our prospect ahead; two low barren ranges [Slate and Argus] and three desert valleys [Panamint, Searles, and Indian Wells] to cross before we could reach the foot of the big snow mountain [Sierra Nevada], then we would be compelled to go westerly [southerly] across another wide level plain [Mojave Desert] for the big mountain was so covered with snow that we would not dare to cross it; no, we would not be able to return in eighteen days.[34] We, as well as those we left in camp, would be disappointed for we might never return.

Our task now before us looked very hard for two lone men to

33. The view from Manly Lookout is spectacular. Immediately east loom the Black Mountains—Manly's (1894:216) "Coffin's Mountains." Clearly visible 125 miles to the south stand the San Gabriel Mountains, which Frémont called the Coast Mountains. Prominent on the western skyline is Owens Peak—"the big snow mountain" the boys would steer for. The two dry, barren ranges in the foreground are the Slate and Argus ranges. Now the boys knew they were not atop the Coast Mountains with the Pueblo de Los Angeles at their feet as some at the sulphur water hole had hoped. Nor were they traversing the southern tip of the Sierra Nevada as others thought. From their familiarity with Frémont's map (in Jackson and Spence 1970:map portfolio, map 6), they knew Walker Pass was to the southwest.

Here they faced the stark reality of their situation. They had to travel three days just to reach the Sierra Nevada, continue 120 miles south, and cross the snow-clad San Gabriel Mountains to find provisions. They could not possibly return in the allotted time.

34. A difficulty in deciphering Manly's accounts arises from incorrect cardinal directions in this part of his narrative. The three extant maps Manly drew—Jayhawker (JA 1050), Palmer (HM 50895), and Walker (in Walker 1954 & 1962)—show the general routes taken by the Jayhawker and Bennett-Arcan parties. The Palmer and Walker maps incorrectly trace the route from Death Valley to the Rancho as bearing westerly (as indicated by the north-south arrow on the Walker map). The Jayhawker map shows generally correct directions as far as the San Gabriel range, but shows the trail down Soledad Canyon as going south instead of west. In reality, the route from Death Valley is west to the Sierra Nevada, south to the San Gabriel Mountains, and west to the Rancho San Francisco.

accomplish. Language is inadequate to express any one's feelings without realizing our situation or without some realistic comparison. Those behind us anticipating more than they could realize. Maybe we were all lost, who could tell? Maybe we all might starve, who could tell from the situation as we now saw it? These were very sad reflections, and we weighed the matter to the best of our ability and came to the conclusion that there was no other course for us to pursue than to go ahead live or die.

Go ahead we did, and pushed our way on down the mountain [in Middle Park Canyon]. Some places we found it so steep that we had to help each other down over the steep places. We took good care to keep our little canteens filled with water wherever it could be found, as well as drink ourselves.[35]

When we got near the foot of the mountain, we could see a large lake to the north, but the valley where we were to cross it was very narrow and had a small clear stream of slowly moving water going towards the lake. As this water had floating dust on its surface, we thought it was not good to drink, but we could not pass

---

35. Of the several possible descent routes—Pleasant Canyon, a ridge, Middle Park Canyon, or South Park Canyon—we opt for Middle Park Canyon for the following reasons: (1) It is the most logical route down the west side of the Panamints as seen from Manly Lookout (hill 7478). (2) The flow of the land and its smooth, broad entrance invite the hiker to take it (map 3). Koenig (1984:177) incorrectly says Middle Park "is not easily discerned" from the lookout, but his photograph (p. 178) clearly shows it. (3) It fits Manly's description of ruggedness, fits Rogers's description of finding water in holes, and fits the view Manly describes upon their exodus from the canyon. Although Middle Park Canyon veers to the north and is very rugged, neither of these drawbacks is apparent until you are committed to the canyon (map 3).

Southworth (1978 [1980]:120) accepts what he says is Wheat's conclusion that Manly and Rogers went down Middle Park Canyon. But Wheat did not make that conclusion: he (1939b:87) says, "It seems likely . . . [they] kept to some ridge . . . [but the] exact identification of the route . . . down to the floor of Panamint Valley is not possible." Neither Southworth nor Wheat traversed Middle Park Canyon.

We reject Pleasant Canyon because of its easy descent, its abundant water, and its direction toward the highest part of the Argus Range, all of which does not fit Manly's descriptions. We reject a ridge descent since Manly and Rogers were too experienced to have attempted such a rugged route just to "survey the terrain" as Wheat (1939b:87) suggests. And we reject South Park Canyon because it is not as logical a route as Middle Park when viewed from the lookout and

even less logical from the lower elevation of the South Park Playa. In addition, South Park has a spring, and neither Manly or Rogers mentions getting water from a spring.

Additional support for our decision comes from Manly's description of the view from the lower exit of Middle Park, where you can see a great distance up and down the valley, whereas at the mouth of South Park you must climb north out of the wash onto the ancient Pleistocene fan to see northward. In addition, Rogers said they "passed a hole of water in some rocks" rather than a spring. We found several holes or tanks in Middle Park Canyon; the largest held about 3 gallons.

A disturbing piece of information is that Manly said he went without water for 60 hours (in Woodward 1949b:10 & JA 632) during this part of their trek. We think Manly's statement was figurative, since they found "water in some rocks," and that he was referring to 60 hours from a spring (Arrastre) to the ice in Indian Wells Valley.

A question that must be asked is: Did the boys follow an Indian trail on their descent? A hunting trail probably went down South Park Canyon, but it would have left the Panamint crest from the Indian encampment on the east side of the lookout. Since the route the boys chose was obvious from the lookout, they did not backtrack to seek a trail, but instead made a beeline for the smooth entrance of the nearest route down the mountain within their line of travel— Middle Park Canyon. A distinct foot trail goes down the canyon, but it is not clear whether it is of Indian origin.

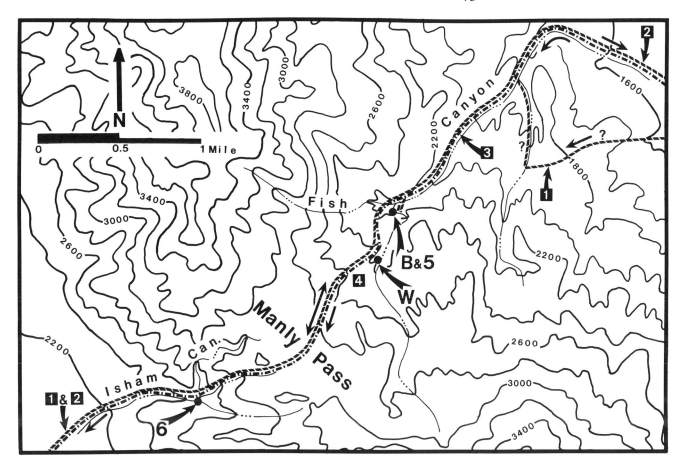

Routes through Manly Pass, Slate Range, redrawn from the Manly Peak and Trona, California, USGS 15 minute quadrangle maps, contour interval 200 feet.

1	Manly and Rogers's route out for provisions	**B**	Manly and Rogers's 2nd camp, "Silent Sepulcre"
2	Manly and Rogers's route back to Death Valley	**W**	Manly and Rogers's 23rd camp (approximate)
3	Bennett-Arcan families' route out	**5**	Families' 5th camp, "Silent Sepulcre"
4	Where Fish died (approximate)	**6**	Families' 6th camp, lower Isham Canyon

without trying a taste, but it proved to be as salt as any brine. The banks on each side of the stream, were perhaps fifty or a hundred yards wide and of mud dried hard as bricks and without any vegetation of any kind.

The day was clear and warm in the valley [Panamint Valley], and as we had heavy packs and sweat freely we wanted a good deal of water. Our canteens held but little more than a good drink, and we soon found water scarce and the tasting of the salt water increasing our thirst, consequently we suffered much, but we pushed on up the mountain [Slate Range] due west and before we reached the summit night was near.[36]

We went down into a canyon [Fish Canyon] to camp and look for water. When we reached the bed of the canyon we found a trail made by oxen from the camp of those before us that I had visited fifteen days before and left them burning their wagons.[37] We followed this trail until near dark, and coming to a damp place where there was considerable sand, we stopped for the night, thinking we could dig and get water, but we were disappointed.[38]

In searching up the ravine we found the body of Mr. Fish with some sage brush thrown over him. This was the old gentleman I met when returning from the camp where the wagons were burned;

36. From the outwash of Middle Park Canyon, a low gap in the Slate Range—Manly Pass—is clearly visible. The boys did not attempt to cross Panamint Valley directly, but instead skirted the east shore of the muddy or wet playa and went south to the narrow part of the valley. Here, near the toe of Manly Peak, they headed "due west" up the Slate Range toward Manly Pass. Two of Manly's comments support this conclusion: (1) "There were two low, black rocky ranges directly ahead of us which we must cross [the Slate and Argus ranges]" (1894:155); and (2) "the valley where we were to cross it was very narrow and had a small clear stream." Had the boys gone directly across Panamint Valley from Middle Park Canyon and up Water Canyon or some canyon still farther north, as Koenig suggests (1984:181–188), they would have crossed only one range, the Argus. This northern part of the range cannot be described as "low"; the valley is not narrow here; nor is there a stream in this wide section of the valley.

37. Manly assumed these tracks were made by the Jayhawkers, whom he saw at McLean Spring in Death Valley on December 28. Actually, they were tracks of the Brier contingent, with the additional oxen given them by the Georgia-Mississippi boys, and several independent men who chose to travel with the Briers. Twenty days had passed (counting January 28) since he left McLean Spring.

38. As the boys gained elevation, it became

apparent no water would be found on the high ground, so they dropped into Fish Canyon. There they found tracks of the Brier mess that led to a box canyon in the south fork of Fish Canyon, where Manly and Rogers spent the night (camp B, map 4). Here too the Brier mess "had camped . . . and had dug holes in the sand in search of water, but had found none" (Manly 1894:155). Manly was wrong in his conclusion. Reverend Brier (JA 76) described the spot this way: "I reached the mouth of the canyon [Fish Canyon] about 2 pm went up 2 or 3 miles untill it closed up to 20 feet in width, with walls on either side overhanging or perpendicular—A Silent Sepulcre. Here I found a little damp sand & scooping out a hole a little water arose." Juliet Brier (in Belden 1954:25) said, "Seeping up from the sand Mr. Brier found a little water, and by digging the company managed to scoop up about a pint an hour." Manly and Rogers also dug in the same area about five days later but found no water—enough time for even a weak spring to replenish itself.

Reverend Brier found water in a silt-filled tinaja or tank. The only way to extract the water from it is to dig a hole and scoop the water out as it fills the excavation; once the trapped water is depleted, it can only be recharged by another hard rain. Between the time the Brier mess left and the boys arrived a few days later, there had been no rainstorm.

Aerial view of Trona Pinnacles south of Searles Lake, Searles Valley. Manly and Rogers crossed Searles Valley north of the lake, and Manly wrote: "We saw a lake to our left only a mile or two off, and on its opposite side, perhaps two or three miles further, we believed we could see trees." On the Palmer map (map 2) he labeled the pinnacles "standing rocks."

so my predictions that he would not be able to reach a settlement proved correct.[39]

We now followed the trail [down middle fork of Isham Canyon] and found that those who had gone before had consumed all the water clear out to the foot of the canyon. We found no living water and we concluded it would not do to follow the trail of so many cattle, for if no spring was found we would never get another drink.[40]

39. Mr. Fish managed to climb out of Fish Canyon by holding onto the tail of an ox. When he surmounted the ridge above Brier's "Silent Sepulcre," "he reeled & fell to rise no more" (Brier JA 76). In the winter of 1860–61, while searching for Charles Alvord, Manly saw "Mr. Fish's bones scattered around among the rocks" (in Woodward 1949b:69).

40. The boys descended the unnamed middle fork of Isham Canyon that joins the main canyon at the dogleg bend (map 4). We came to this conclusion after hiking several times all the canyons along the western flank of the Slate Range between Isham and Goff canyons. We correlated our observations with the only known description of the descent—a letter written by Reverend Brier (JA 76): "After going down the western slope in another canyon about 300 yards

When we got clear out of the canyon, we came to a valley [Searles] several miles wide to cross before we could reach the next range and chose a canyon that we could see looked the most favorable for water and easiest of ascent.

When we got fairly out into the valley, we saw a lake to our left only a mile or two off, and on its opposite side, perhaps two or three miles further, we believed we could see trees; and, if so, the lake must be fresh.[41]

We then turned due south and went for the lake, for we were now very much in want of water, for the weather was warm and our road sandy. Our canteens were empty and we were very dry. Before we reached the lake, we came to soft mud where the water had receded. We had half a mile yet to go before we reached the water we so much desired. We waded on as fast as we could through the mud, but alas, when we got to the water to our disappointment it was a strong alkali, red as wine and slippery to the touch.[42]

we suddenly came to a jumping off place of about 6 feet. Groscup & I built a stone Bridge down to the level over which all passed in safety. Groscup then took the lead with his one ox, & mine followed. He soon found other jumpoffs but the madcap did not wait for a Bridge but forced his Ox to jump & mine followed suit. So on we went until about 3 PM We found ourselves faceing what is now known as Borax Lake [Searles Lake]."

Upper Isham Canyon has a 20-foot fall that would be very difficult to get oxen around. The only branch obvious from the pass is the middle fork.

41. These were not trees, but the Trona Pinnacles south of Searles Lake. They could easily be mistaken for conifers when viewed through the shimmering heat waves rising from the lake. Manly discovered they were rocks rather than trees on his return trip ten years later, because he called them "Standing Rocks" on his Palmer map (HM 50895).

The pinnacles are various shapes and sizes, some rising to 140 feet (Scholl 1960). According to Dr. G. I. Smith (1980), "the Trona Pinnacles were formed in two stages during the Pleistocene Ice Ages when large lakes occupied Searles Valley. The first, which accounts for about 95 percent of the pinnacles' volume and height, took place between 40,000 and 130,000 years ago. . . . These accumulations . . . tended to form in a ring around where the spring water was entering into the lake, and as successive layers of limestone crystallized, they eventually grew to form towers. . . . algae . . . contributed to the continuing buildup."

42. This alkali lake is now named after John Searles, but it was called Borax Lake in the late 1800s; the mud flat north of the lake is now called Borax Flat.

The wine color is from halophilic bacteria found in salty or brackish lakes throughout the world. These bacteria are so numerous in northern Great Salt Lake that the red color is visible from outer space (Post 1977:150). Searles laid claim to Borax Lake in 1862 and shortly thereafter built a plant along its northwestern edge. According to Koenig (1984:136–140), none of the '49ers entered Searles Valley; instead he believes they went to Carricut Lake in Etcheron Valley high in the Argus Range. Koenig overlooks firsthand accounts that support Searles Lake as the lake they approached with hope of finding fresh water; however, they were bitterly disappointed.

In spring 1873, Reverend Brier retraced part of his 1850 trail when he guided a group of miners into the Panamint Range. This refreshed his mind as to the route he and the Jayhawkers took; in 1876, he wrote Charles Mecum (JA 70) that "the Lake was not salt but Borax It is now famous for that Mineral." In 1879, he wrote Luther A. Richards (JA 71), "Well that lake is not salt as we supposed, but is Borax. Here are the great Borax Mines or washings." Again in 1896 (JA 76), he wrote his "Old Comrades" that the lake they went to "is now known as Borax Lake." Carricut Lake was never called Borax Lake, nor were there borax mines or washings on its shores—it has no borax deposits.

On the Palmer map (HM 50895) Manly drew the "Alkali Lake" at the end of the mountain range with "Standing Rocks," the Trona Pinnacles, on the far side of it; this is certainly not descriptive of the Etcheron Valley, as Koenig suggests. When Manly and Rogers went to the lake on their journey out, they walked through a half-mile of mud before reaching the water. Since Carricut Lake is only a half-mile

We had now to return to our course, and as we did so, we found that cattle had been driven here for water and had had to go back as thirsty as they came.

We got back to the line of our route very tired and thirsty. As we ascended the canyon [due west of Trona], we watched to gather every green spear of grass that might grow on the north side of a rock, to eat and quench our thirst.[43] We had carried bullets and small stones in our mouth all day, and had kept from talking as much as possible. We traveled with our mouths closed to keep from wanting water. We were now unable to eat, though very hungry. We got near the summit of the mountain and had seen no signs yet of water; a few spears of grass was all we had found. We had often before found pools of water in holes in rocks in the canyons left after rains, but we found none in this one.

We turned the summit of the mountain before night, and could see a level plain [Indian Wells Valley] at least thirty miles before us, before we could expect to find any good water.

[May 1888; Volume V, Number III, page 46]

There were now no more mountains between us and the big snowy one [Sierra Nevada]. When we got about half way to the foot of the mountain [in Burro Canyon, west side of Argus Range], we came to an old Indian camp, and, as it was after sundown, we concluded to camp there for the night and search for water, for we believed it could not be very far off. We put our packs in the little brush hut and commenced hunting for water, but we found none. We tried to eat, but could not swallow. We built a fire, and as it was

wide even when completely full of water, the boys would have walked all the way across it had they been there.

Ironically, these gold seekers were standing on several billion dollars worth of minerals (Smith 1979:4) at Searles Lake, but they did not know it—or, more accurately, did not care. Potable water was the only treasure they sought.

There are numerous springs in the Argus Range north of Wilson Canyon. Had Manly, Rogers, and the Brier mess followed the Indian trail west from the mouth of Isham Canyon to those springs, much suffering could have been averted. Some of the Jayhawkers may have found water coming from a "pile of tremendous rocks" (Manly 1894:340), possibly in Great Falls Basin, while those with oxen went directly to the lake, where the Brier mess found them. The Jayhawkers had separated from the Briers in Panamint Valley and crossed into Searles Valley over what we call "Jayhawker Pass" 1.25 miles northwest of where the Trona–Wildrose Road now crosses the north end of the Slate Range. Reverend Brier (JA 76)

and Captain Town discovered "an Indian Trail over a very steep pass which I [Brier] condemned as impassible. . . . [and the] next morning the Jayhawks packed up & started for the condemned pass." The Briers took a route south down the east side of the Slates and crossed over Manly Pass.

43. From the mouth of Isham Canyon, the logical route across the Argus Range is up Wilson Canyon. However, their detour to Searles Lake put Wilson Canyon north of their westward route to the Sierra Nevada. The boys traversed the canyon due west of the lake in "the line of our route." It is the nameless canyon directly west of Trona and heads into Burro Canyon on the western flank of the Argus Range (camp C, map 5). The Brier mess and the Jayhawkers ascended the Argus Range in east Wilson Canyon and dropped into Indian Wells Valley through boulder-strewn Deadman Canyon. These canyons are in the Naval Weapons Center, China Lake; no one may enter this area without permission from the base commander.

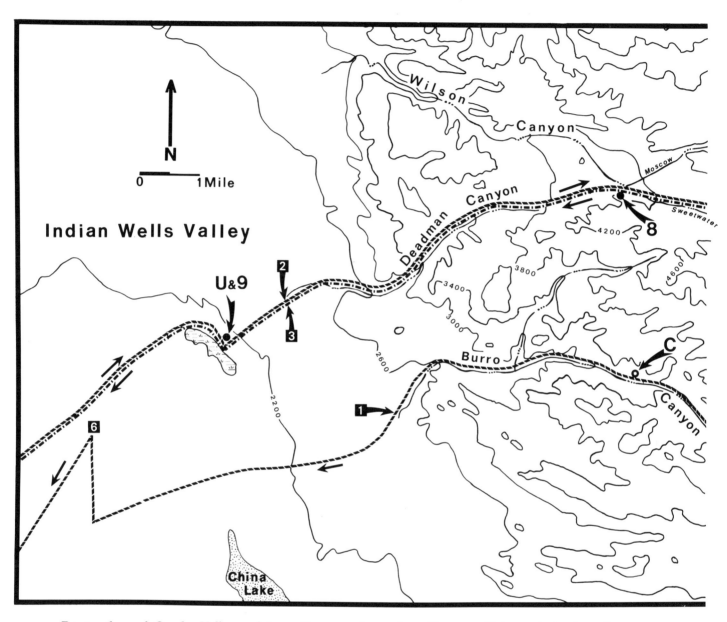

Routes through Searles Valley and Argus Range, redrawn from Trona and Mountain Springs Canyon, California, USGS 15 minute quadrangle maps, contour interval 400 feet.

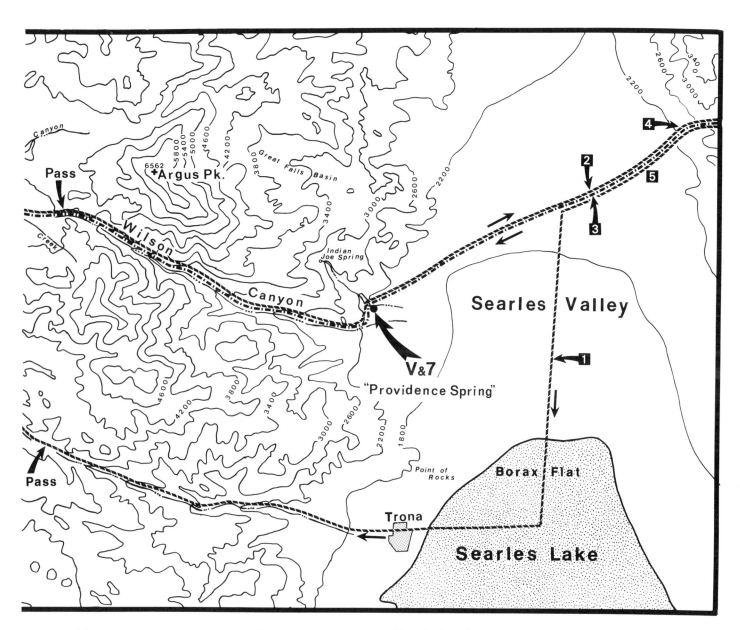

1 Manly and Rogers's route out for provisions	**C** Manly and Rogers's 3rd camp (approximate)
2 Manly and Rogers's route back to Death Valley	**U** Manly and Rogers's 21st camp, Paxton Ranch
3 Bennett-Arcan families' route out	**V** Manly and Rogers's 22nd camp, Providence Spring
4 To Isham Canyon	**7** Families' 7th camp, Providence Spring
5 Where Isham died (approximate)	**8** Families' 8th camp, Sweetwater Creek
6 Where Manly and Rogers found ice (approximate)	**9** Families' 9th camp, saltwater hole, Paxton Ranch

moonlight, one continued to search for water while the other kept up the fire. When out of sight of camp we could call to one another and so find our way back. We worked in this way all night long, never sleeping a wink nor eating a mouthful.

We now began to feel that our chances to get to water were poor, for it would take us all day and perhaps longer to get across to the snow mountain. We felt very much discouraged but had to push on with all our strength and all the courage we could master.

As soon as we could see the morning star in the west, we started and worked our way along over the rough, rocky road. We made slow progress, but we could make some little advance in this way, while it was cool, and every step brought us that much nearer to water. We got to the foot of the mountain about sunrise and could see a lake to our left, perhaps a mile away [China Lake], but for fear we would be as badly disappointed as before we kept on our course.[44]

We had had but two chances to get water since we left the wagons and it was now the fourth day.

As the sun came up, it soon became hot and scorching, and we thought we could not hold out through the day. Our thoughts now went back to the women and children we had left behind. What chance was there for them to get over such a desert, dry country! We thought of them every day and compared their case with ours.

As we came out into the valley [Indian Wells], we soon came to what to us seemed to be very small water courses, which wound around little islands of small salt or alkali weeds or brush, hardly more than six or eight inches high. These little dry water ways came from the north and spread over a belt or strip about one fourth of a mile wide.

We now concluded to separate and follow up these channels and see if we could find some hole that would still have a little water left in it. We were now going out of our course, but water we must have or die. We had gone perhaps a mile, when Rogers fired his gun and I went to him to see what was the matter. To our united joy he had found a little ice that the sun had not melted. It was about as thick as window glass. We gathered it all, there was no water under it, and put it in our little two quart camp kettle and melted it and had a good drink.[45] We made a fire of the sticks that grew on the

44. China Lake contains potable water during the winter. A hill on the north side of Burro Canyon wash (not evident on the USGS Mountain Springs Canyon, Calif., 15 min., 1953 quadrangle map) blocked their view of the saltwater pond at Paxton Ranch where Sheldon Young camped the night before on January 17. Thus, they missed the water there.

45. On January 21, 1973, we found similar sheets of ice in almost the same place Rogers did (map 5). LeRoy's diary (Johnson 1973:27) says, "As we crossed [the valley], we went over 3 N/S rivulets that had ice on the banks. There was alkali so I assumed the water to be salt. After going 20 yards, I returned, broke the ice and tasted it. FRESH. I ate a large chunk and it was quite good."

little islands and ate a big breakfast of meat and water, but before we had finished our meal our water was gone to the last drop. We now felt much better and thought this might be some of the manna from heaven. We now believed we were safe and would be able to reach the foot of the big snow mountain. As the country was now a gradual ascent the entire way and level, we would have to get there without another drink. The day was clear, warm and no wind. The walking now was hard. We had no trail and the brush got taller as we pushed along.

We steered west [southwest], taking a little bluff as a guide [the toe of Black Mountain], and leaving the big mountain a little to our right, believing we could reach the bluff, which we had made our objective point, by night. The distance was a deal longer than we had thought and by the time we had gone as far as the point of the mountain, the sun had gone behind it and left its shadow on our side. Our little bluff we were steering for, could not be reached in less than another twelve hours walk.[46]

We soon saw rising at the foot of the mountain [Owens Peak] on our right a sage brush smoke like that we had seen on our road before and thought they were Indian signals, for what purpose we did not know; perhaps they were warning their friends that enemies were in their country.

We stopped and consulted a while and talked over what was best to do. The bluff ahead was too far off, and if the smoke we saw was an Indian fire, we might have to fight for water and be over-powered. We thought the party with oxen a great deal farther along

---

Rain from the winter storms percolates immediately into the sandy soil, but on playas such as China Lake, fine clay sediment clogs the pores in the sandy soil and retards percolation. The rivulets where John Rogers and LeRoy found ice are minute playas. The surface of these shallow puddles freezes during the cold winter nights. Daytime temperatures near the ground remain cold enough to keep the sheets of ice from melting while the water underneath slowly percolates into the soil. It may take several days for these thin sheets of ice to melt or sublimate.

Manly (1894:159) said they found the ice early in the day. The statement that "an hour after the sun had risen that little sheet of ice would have melted and the water sank into the sand" is an editorial embellishment interjected by his writing assistant. Manly clearly stated in this account that Rogers found ice *after* the sun became "hot and scorching." We know from our own experience these thin sheets of ice with no water under them persist all day, so we feel this account correctly describes what happened.

46. After melting the ice, the boys headed again for the Sierra Nevada but quickly changed their direction from west to southwest toward Pueblo de Los Angeles, their goal for provisions. Manly did not specifically say they changed direction, but they did. First, they headed for the "foot of the big snow mountain," Owens Peak, the most prominent mountain in the southern Sierra Nevada. In the next paragraph he said they were "steering west," the correct direction for Owens Peak, but he added they had taken "a little bluff as a guide." The only bluff visible from the middle of Indian Wells Valley is the one jutting from the toe of Black Mountain 22 miles to the southwest. Manly was right when he said the bluff "could not be reached in less than another twelve hours walk." Thus, after first heading west toward the Sierra Nevada, they turned southwest toward the bluff at Black Mountain in line with their ultimate destination. This put "the big mountain a little to our right." Still in need of water and realizing the bluff was another day off, they again changed direction and headed due west toward the snowy Sierra Nevada, where they hoped to find water.

LeRoy Johnson holds a sheet of ice found on January 20, 1973, near Paxton Ranch site in Indian Wells Valley. Rogers also found ice here, on January 18, 1850. Manly said: "Water we must have or die. . . . To our united joy he had found a little ice . . . about as thick as window glass."

and it must be an Indian camp; perhaps they had killed the white folks and were now eating their oxen.

The situation now looked bad for us, for water we must have, and prospects of it before us were not very promising.

We now screwed up our courage and turned due north [west], starting straight for the smoke, for we must have water or die in the battle for it. As it was now getting dusk and cool, we pushed on as fast as we could go. The moon soon came up and before we got near it was light and clear. When we got within a mile of the camp, we stepped into a trail, knowing it by the earth under foot being much harder than on either side. The greasewood was two or more feet high and the branches grew quite near together.

We wanted to know who made the trail, so we got down and felt in it with our hands, and we could make out what were oxen tracks.

We now left the trail and went a fourth of a mile west and found the camp [at Indian Wells Spring] was on a bench some higher. We now expected every minute to see an Indian dog, but none came. It was now considerably up hill to the camp and nobody could be seen about it, no noise was heard. We now crawled along keeping as low down as we could, expecting at any time to be met by a shower of arrows, but water must be had or we must die for want of it. We now thought the chances were much against us. We stopped frequently and listened, putting our heads close to the ground; sometimes we could hear sounds, but could not tell who made them. We kept on advancing toward the camp and when we were within shotgun distance we could hear sounds that we thought were not Indians and after some very low talks we concluded to make ourselves known; so we raised up with our guns in full cock and said in a shrill voice, "Hello" and were answered. We said, "Don't shoot;" the answer came, "We won't."

We now approached camp and found, not Indians to our great joy, but E. Doty, Tom Shannon, L. D. Stevens and others.[47]

We now had many questions to ask, and the first was, "What were the prospects?" "Well," they answered, "right here we came into a large trail coming down from the north and seeming to follow around the foot of the mountain in a westerly [southerly] direction, and we have all determined to follow it let it go where it may, even if it go to Mexico, it certainly goes to some settlement, and we don't care where it leads to, we must soon have more oxen to eat or something else, for there are now several that have nothing of their own to eat and we have to divide with them, we cannot see them starve."[48]

I asked if Bennett's and Arcane's teamsters had been seen, and they said, "Yes, they were ahead with others, but had to depend on the liberality of those around them for something to satisfy their

47. Indian Wells Spring is on a bench, the water impounded in a cave dug into the hillside (camp D, appendix A). When Reverend Brier (JA 70 & JA 71) returned to Death Valley in 1873, he found a hotel here. Today the spring supplies water to the restaurant and residences at Homestead on Highway 395. State Historical Monument #457 commemorates the site where the "Manly-Jayhawker parties of 1849 found their first water after five days' travel from Argus Range." Actually, the Jayhawkers traveled from the Argus Range across Indian Wells Valley in two days or less; Manly and Rogers crossed it in one day. (The Jayhawkers were without water for five days in Nevada.)

48. A trail to Mexico would not lead west. This is another example of Manly's confused directions. The trail continued southward over the plain to the El Paso Mountains, across the Mojave Desert to the San Gabriel Mountains, and into the fertile coastal re-

gions. The trail was a branch of a great network of Indian trails that led from the California-Nevada deserts into the richer coastal areas, where the Indians found plenty of Spanish horses to steal. The Spanish told Zenas Leonard (1839:62 & 1959:116), who traveled with Walker in 1833 and 1834, that the Indians "prefer eating domesticated horses because the act of stealing them gives their flesh a superior flavor—and it would be less trouble for them to catch wild horses, if they could thus gratify their stealing propensities."

Joseph Reddeford Walker, for whom Walker Pass was named, traversed this trail north from Walker Pass in 1834 with 52 men, 315 horses, 47 beef cattle, and 30 dogs (Leonard 1839:64 & 1959:119–123). This was part of the Bonneville-Walker expedition (Cleland 1963:282). In 1843, Walker led members of the Joseph B. Chiles party over the same trail (Stewart 1953:21; Read 1923:72; Stewart 1962:41).

hunger. We had to stop to dry the meat of an ox that gave out, and we will go on tomorrow."

"Where is Brier?"

"He is behind perhaps a day or two. His wife has all the camp work to do, as well as pack the oxen, for he claims he is unwell." (Tom Shannon said he was lazy.) They did not seem to have much sympathy for him.

We inquired about water on the trail they came. They told us all the water places as well as their particular locations. We now told them that our party would remain in camp for us to return, if we returned in fifteen or eighteen days and if we lived long enough we would come back and help them out. We may follow your trail, and knowing the water places may help us.

They now offered us some of their meat to roast which we found better than ours. As some were sitting up tending the drying of meat and keeping up a fire, we sat up quite late talking with them, although we had not slept a wink the night before. They told us of the death of Mr. Fish and Isham, and the hardships and suffering they had had, and many other interesting incidents that have been forgotten.[49] They saw our one half blanket and all the cover we had and gave us a place in their bed which was thankfully received. They said that some of their train had gone on without any cattle. They carried as much killed and dried meat as they could and believed it would last them till they got to a settlement. None of them had ever been seen since. They then spoke of the big snow mountain beside us and said if their big trail led into it they would have to leave it. We thus spent a very pleasant night with real friends instead of Indians, and much real pleasure, as well as valuable information, was enjoyed and received.

In the morning we shouldered our napsacks and took the trail which followed along the foot of the mountain for seven or eight miles; here a small branch turned north [northwest to Walker Pass] and seemed to go into the snow, but the broad one bore south [southeast] and away from the mountain and across a level plain to a quite low range.[50] Our trail would lead us right to the summit of

49. Mr. Fish died on the eastern flank of the Slate Range, and Mr. Isham died in Searles Valley (Palmer map:HM 50895; James Brier JA 73; John Wells Brier 1903:335). Juliet Brier (in Belden 1954:34) said Isham could not keep up with his companions and stopped to recuperate, after which he crawled on his hands and knees for several miles. After the Jayhawkers and Briers reached "Providence Spring" (Indian Joe Spring), a rescue party took water back to Isham, but he could not drink and soon died. He was buried in a shallow, hand-dug grave (Manly 1894:340)

somewhere in the sandy valley a few miles north or northeast of Searles Lake (maps 2, 4 & 5).

50. The Los Angeles aqueduct west of Highway 395 closely parallels the old trail. The boys followed the trail from Indian Wells Spring to Coyote Holes, later known as Freeman's stage stop (Edwards 1964), located 1.5 miles southeast of the current junction of highways 14 and 178 (map 7). All that remains of Freeman's stage stop are some concrete fragments and rusting pipes. The "small branch . . . into the snow" was the trail heading to Walker Pass.

this range [El Paso Mountains]. All the ravines run out south and on to another big plain fifty or seventy-five miles wide [Mojave Desert]. We followed down a very steep canyon and when we came to its bottom, we found a weak little stream of water and here the party we were following were camped [in Last Chance Canyon]. No grass and sage brush scarce, a sorry place for a camping ground.[51] Here we found Bennett's and Arcane's four teamsters, with nothing to eat of their own. They were very glad to see us and told us of their troubles. They said an ox had been killed that night and they were not offered a mouthful. They talked pitifully and seemed to feel bad, so we gave them some meat out of our store, and we ate together. They said they had to depend on those who had oxen for every mouthful they got. We were a little better off for we had five or six

When the boys arrived at Coyote Holes, the ashes were probably still warm from the fires of the Asa Haynes contingent, which had spent the night here. By correlating Haynes's mileages to Sheldon Young's log and to Manly's accounts, it appears Haynes and company spent the night at Coyote Holes while Manly was with Doty's group at Indian Wells. From Coyote Holes, the boys followed the well-worn Indian trail and the tracks of the Asa Haynes party just ahead.

51. Passage through the El Paso Mountains was via Last Chance Canyon (map 6). Historic evidence points to Last Chance as the canyon traversed by the Indian horse thief trail (California Department of Parks and Recreation 1971:78). Frank Latta told us that in the 1940s the horse thief trail going into and out of Last Chance Canyon was visible from the air. Dune buggies and trail bikes have since obliterated most signs of this trail, but we found it (and an arrowhead chipping site) north of the mountain's crest. Many people have assumed the emigrants traversed Redrock Canyon because Manly (1894:235) said, "This cañon is now called Red Cañon." Since he was not in the area after the stage route was put through Redrock Canyon, he may have assumed the stage route followed the heavily used horse thief trail that the emigrants followed. Possibly his writing assistant added "Red Cañon" as a point of clarification assuming, incorrectly, that the stage route was in the same canyon as the horse thief trail. The red and pink cliffs bordering Last Chance Canyon are called Red Buttes (USGS Saltdale, Calif., 15 min., 1943; Saltdale NW, Calif., 7.5 min., 1967). In the western ones are located the Cudahy Pumicite Mines, where the abrasive for Old Dutch Cleanser was mined (Troxel and Morton 1962:264).

Freshwater springs in Last Chance Canyon are the main reason why the horse thief trail traversed it rather than Redrock Canyon. We have hiked all the canyons in this area and have found several un-

mapped potable springs in Last Chance Canyon. Some were developed by miners who worked the placer gold deposits.

A spring in the lower reaches of Redrock Canyon is unofficially called "Mother-in-Law Spring" because of its arsenic content. Another, called Tufa or Sullivan Spring, is 1 air mile due east of Recardo. However, it does not fit Manly's description of being at the bottom of a "very steep canyon."

Other support for Last Chance Canyon comes from Sheldon Young's log (in Long 1950:278). "(JAN.) 22ND. Went eight miles through a deep cañon and came into a valley—alkali bottom. [and on Jan. 23] Went five miles South-West. Found grass, water and plenty of willows." Had he exited Redrock Canyon, he would have gone 3 miles southeast not 5 miles southwest to arrive at the willow corral now known as Desert Spring.

Later in this account, Manly's mileages give additional support for Last Chance Canyon. He said they went 8 to 10 miles down the canyon and 4 miles further to the spring. If you backtrack 12 to 14 miles from Desert Spring up Redrock Canyon, you end up in southern Indian Wells Valley 3 to 5 miles north of the canyon rim. However, if you backtrack from Desert Spring 12 to 14 miles up Last Chance Canyon you find a spring that fits Manly's description. We call it "Forlorn Hope Spring," where Manly and Rogers caught up with the Asa Haynes contingent (camp E, map 6). It is located in a small side canyon that heads into the main ridge. An old stone house stands at the head of the canyon. Below the spring is a narrow spot, but today it is not as narrow as Manly (1894:164) described: "As we went down the cañon we came to one place where it was so narrow, that a man or a poor ox could barely squeeze through between the rocks." Large blocks of the soft white rock are strewn below the narrow portion. It is easy to visualize them in their original positions, thus narrowing the gap to more nearly the size Manly describes.

days meat on our backs. Here we got a history of their trip since they left the wagons. It was like the stories told by others, hard, hard indeed. We told them what we were trying to do for those we left behind, as well as their bad luck and how much farther from civilization they were than they supposed. We had a long serious talk; some had almost given up ever getting out.

There was a long level road before us and no water or grass could be expected on it. Some of the party were not physically able to endure the fatiguing walk across such a wide desert. Some, who had no cattle, said if they had a little meat they would go with us, but it could not be got, for there was no grub to be bought or begged. These poor hungry fellows were to be pitied.

When we got ready to start in the morning, many gathered around us and wished us good luck, for they almost knew we would get through. Some gave us their addresses in Illinois; among them, the oldest man in the camp, Capt. Asa Haynes, requested us when we got to San Francisco to go to the fort and have the news sent to their families, telling them how they suffered, starved, and choked to death on the desert. "None of us may get through," they said, "and if you do not, our folks will never know the dreadful fate of their relatives and friends."

After a great deal of mournful talk, that my poor gift of language cannot express, we commenced hand-shaking, and bidding each other goodbye, which brought tears to their eyes as they turned and walked away. This was a sad parting. Many thought they were doomed to perish and die alone and go without burial, like some of those who had fallen by the wayside, days before. Mr. Fish and Isham both died for the want of food and water and who could tell but that their turn would come next; their prospects were no better.

Rogers and I could not help feeling bad with them, for we thought some of them would not live long. Their cattle were very poor and when killed were soon devoured, and those who had none, what would they do? They knew no end to the road, as it now led across a wide level plain which in this country was never fertile but always dry and barren. The prospects did indeed look gloomy.

We finally bid them one and all goodbye and went sadly and silently down the canyon. In eight or ten miles we reached the open plain and our trail seemed to point across it. About four miles further, we came to a bunch of willows growing thick and perhaps ten feet high. They were growing on level ground and the grove was perhaps fifty feet or more in diameter. In it we found a good spring of water, but it did not run but a few feet beyond the willows [Desert Spring, 1 mile southeast of Cantil]. The willows in the center of the grove had been cut out and woven into those left so as [to] make a small corral; this was on our trail and seemed to us a little strange. We now filled ourselves with water as well as our canteens, and hurried on west [south] in the trail.[52]

[June 1888; Volume V, Number IV, page 62]

It now seemed up hill for at least twenty miles, and the country perfectly barren. We soon found bones along the trail. Some seemed to be very old, while other showed no sign of decay. There were often the bones of two, three or four animals in a place; this, we thought, proved that before us must be a long dry road, as horses did not seem able to stand it.

Our trail followed the highest ground on the plain and the traveling was good. As we turned south to follow a slight rise in the ground, we found that a little off of our high trail, the ground was very soft and light as snuff. An animal that might try to walk in it, would sink six inches at every step.[53]

Before night we got on the highest ground and could see off to the north [west] a large dry lake, and the plain extending northwest [southwest] about a hundred miles.[54] Near night we came to a tree about six inches through and perhaps ten feet high. The leaves were a foot long and all dead except some at the very top. This kind of a tree [Joshua] we had never seen before. When night came, we had reached the wash from the big dry lake with its numerous little channels, but no water was in them. Our strange trees now became more plentiful. After sundown we found a little pond of rain water and camped by it for the night.[55] We named the fine, strange trees,

52. The willow corral—at Desert Spring—had been woven by Indians to hold their stolen horses (map 6). State Historical Monument #476 stands 1 mile southeast of Cantil in a clump of tamarisk trees that have replaced the willows. The inscription reads, "This spring was [on] an old Indian horse thief trail and later (1834) Joe Walker Trail. The famished Manly-Jayhawk Death Valley parties (1849–50) were revived here after coming from Indian Wells through Last Chance Canyon. This was also a station on the Nadeau Borax Freight Road."

53. Manly (1894:165) later described this dirt as "finer than the finest flour"—a feminine touch that supports our hypothesis that Manly's writing assistant was a female. This area is now called Fremont Valley, and the "snuff"-textured soil supports lush fields of alfalfa.

54. Again we find confusion in Manly's directions. The Palmer map (HM 50895) shows a "Dry Lake" (Rosamond Lake) to the north of their westerly route, assuming north is to the left of the page as the directions are marked on Manly's Walker map (Walker 1954). However, they were not going west; they were heading south. Rosamond Lake was actually west of their route. If this portion of the map is rotated so their trail is oriented north and south—the actual direction of the trail—the map fits the route as hiked. Koenig (1984:116) mistakenly shows their trail west of, rather than east of, Rosamond Lake. They probably crossed the Rosamond Hills through the low gap 5 miles north of the eastern edge of Rosamond Lake.

55. Water in a shallow playa again saved their lives. These rainwater ponds are in the lowest part of the valley between the dry beds of Rosamond and Buckhorn dry lakes on Edwards Air Force Base (camp G, appendix A). We camped here January 24, 1973, and found less than 1 inch of rainwater on the same playas. In order to scoop the water we had to dig a hole; this made the water extremely muddy but still potable.

A literal reading of the text indicates Manly and

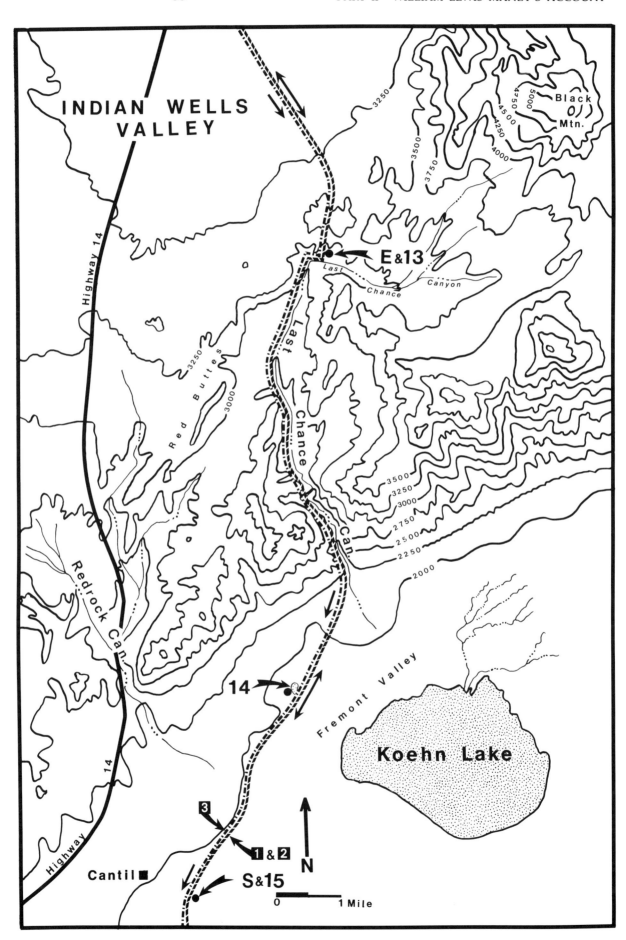

INDIAN WELLS
VALLEY

Black
Mtn.

Highway 14

E&13

Last
Chance
Canyon

Red Buttes

Last Chance Can.

Redrock Can.

Fremont Valley

Koehn Lake

14

3

1&2

Cantil

N

S&15

14

Highway

0   1 Mile

cabbage trees, as their bodies looked much like old cabbage stalks. The dead trees made a good fire, as they were like a honey comb. A man could easily carry a large dry tree on his back, but while green they were quite heavy indeed.

The next morning our trail seemed to end or disappear. The mountain before us was covered with snow and it would be almost necessary for us to cross it in a trail. We separated and traveled one northerly [westerly] and the other in a southerly [easterly] direction in search of a trail. We passed through considerable of this strange timber, our so-called cabbage trees.

We came together after noon and concluded to steer for what seemed to be as low a pass [Soledad Pass] as any within twenty miles, and try and cross. As we traveled into the hills we saw slight signs of a trail and the further on we went, the plainer it got. We followed on in this new trail and as we advanced the hills became more grassy and some trees could be seen on the higher hills.

We felt sure now we were coming to a better country. About sundown we came to some water holes [Barrel Springs, 4 miles southeast of Palmdale] and what had been a large camp at one time. Cattle skulls were laying around and there were many small places where fires had been built, perhaps years before. This looked to us like a rendezvous of thieves, and that horses had been drove over the trail we had come and stolen from some settlement. No man would follow the robbers across the desert.

The next morning, before we had gone far on our journey, we reached snow which was hard enough so we could walk on the top, and we got over without trouble. We soon killed a crow, the first

Routes through the El Paso Mountains, redrawn from Saltdale, California, USGS 15 minute quadrangle map, contour interval 250 feet.

1 Manly and Rogers's route out for provisions
2 Manly and Rogers's route back to Death Valley
3 Bennett-Arcan families' route out
E Manly and Rogers's 5th camp, Forlorn Hope Spring

S Manly and Rogers's 19th camp, Desert Spring
13 Families' 13th camp, Forlorn Hope Spring
14 Families' 14th camp, small playa where it snowed
15 Families' 15th camp, Desert Spring

Rogers hiked 46 miles in one day from Forlorn Hope Spring in the El Paso Mountains to this rainwater pond. It took them two days. Manly (1894:166) supported this conclusion when he said seven days had passed since they left the sulphur water hole. By listing the camps we can account for seven days of travel: (A) above Arrastre Spring, Panamint Range; (B) Fish Canyon ("Silent Sepulcre"), Slate Range; (C) Burro Canyon, Argus Range; (D) Indian Wells Spring at Homestead; (E) Forlorn Hope Spring, Last Chance Canyon, El Paso Mountains; (F) near California City, Mojave Desert; (G) rainwater holes between Buckhorn and Rosamond lakes, Edwards Air Force Base (appendix A).

thing we had seen to shoot since we had left the wagons. A little farther on Rogers killed a hawk. This kind of game, we knew, always lived in a better country than that we had come through and we were much encouraged.

The canyon [Soledad Canyon] we were now following led nearly west; the brush got larger and the trees at a distance looked good to us for they were a great change.[56] About sundown we came to another canyon that joined ours and in it we found a beautiful little babbling brook. Here we made our camp and had some good wood and water.[57] Rogers killed a quail; we knew that this kind of a bird knew better than to try and live on a desert. We felt sure we were coming to a fertile place.

We put our birds on to cook and found them all good, except the crow. He was as black and tough inside as he was out. Now we only wished that those we left were here, as these mountains must have game in [them] and we could live with our guns. We now talked some of going back for them, but our meat was so near gone that we could not go so far and live on so little; so in the morning we pushed down the creek and a mile off, on a grassy hill, we saw three horses. They looked wild and on seeing us, they ran away through the brush.

The creek bottom got very brushy and we passed some swampy meadows and had to follow a bear trail to get along. We could see

56. The boys descended Soledad Canyon, not Bouquet Canyon as Koenig (1984:194 & 226) says. The evidence supporting Soledad Canyon as the one used by Manly and Rogers, the Brier mess, the Jayhawkers, and others is overwhelming. L. Dow Stephens (1916:23) said, "we ascended a long hill, or divide, [coast range] and after crossing saw a brook with running water, the first we had seen for months. It looked good to us, and we concluded it must empty into the Pacific Ocean, which was correct, for this proved to be the headwaters of the Santa Clara River." The Santa Clara River flows down Soledad Canyon. Manly wrote T. S. Palmer in August 1894 (HM 50802), "We ware awful happy when we camped on the little brook in *Soledad* canion whare I killed some good fat meat." Manly's Palmer map (HM 50895) shows the "S.P.R.R." railroad going down the same canyon as their trail. In addition, Manly said (1894:259), "The brushy cañon we have just described is now occupied by the Southern Pacific Railroad, and the steep and narrow ridge pierced by a tunnel, through which the trains pass." Additional evidence that Soledad Canyon is the one they descended is found in letters in the Jayhawker Collection. L. Dow Stephens (JA 898) wrote John Colton on March 16,

1894, that they "struck on to the head waters of the Santa Clara River [and] followed it down to the San Francisco Ranch   the Southern Pacific RR now takes this route." On January 11, 1900, Tom Shannon (JA 881) wrote to the Jayhawkers that "the Southern pacific rail road runs through the canyon that we came down." The railroad is in Soledad Canyon, not Bouquet Canyon.

57. Manly's (1894:169) later description is considerably embellished, and again we detect the feminine touch of his writing assistant: "a beautiful little running brook of clear pure water, singing as it danced over the stones, a happy song and telling us to drink and drink again, and you may be sure we did drink, for it had been months and months since we had had such water, pure, sweet, free from the terrible alkali and stagnant taste that had been in almost every drop we had seen." This little brook springs from the ground at Thousand Trails recreation park, 2 miles down the canyon from the town of Acton, and flows for some distance before disappearing underground. The water in Soledad Canyon periodically comes to the surface, but soon disappears in the sandy creek bed (camp I).

their tracks, but no bear. It was a lucky thing for us that we did not meet any, for we did not know the danger in meeting a grizzly bear, and were ready to fight anything.

Before noon I got very lame in my knee and had to stop and rest quite often. After a while I told Rogers he had better go on and I would follow just as I could. He refused to go, saying, "We will either die or go together." By the next morning I was some better and was able to hobble along. Our road was very thick and brushy and we had to go slow.

The first sign of man we saw was what seemed to be ancient excavations, with trees growing on what had been thrown out.[58] We soon came to a stump that had been cut years before. It was about six inches through. Finding these things helped our spirits, and after awhile we suddenly came out of the brush.

The whole canyon was without brush, but sage brush was plenty. Our creek had sunk into the ground. The mountain on the north was covered thick with brush, and the south side had some grassy spots and a few oak trees. We could see the tracks of some animals in the sands, but we could not tell whether they were cattle or elk.

On the hillside about half a mile away, we saw some twenty coyotes feeding around some old bones.[59] This was a civilized sign, for where they can live, man can also.

We followed down the barren wash, but a point of land [east of Saugus] on our south side shut off our view, so we climbed up this point to get a glimpse of the country ahead.[60] It was a glorious sight that greeted us, one that filled our hearts with surprise and joy, for before us was a large level tract of more than a thousand acres, all covered with green grass.

In this pleasant field hundreds of Jacob's cattle, ringed, streaked and speckled, were happily grazing. We sat down to feast our eyes on the scene before us, and our conversation went back to our poor starved oxen, and we compared them with these.

After a good rest we walked on down the valley. A little way

58. The Spanish prospected for gold in this area (Bunje and Kean 1938:vol. II:36; Newhall 1958:39; Perkins 1957:107; Woodward 1949a:2), and this excavation was probably an early Spanish gold prospecting hole. On March 9, 1842, Francisco Lopez and two friends found gold in Placerita Canyon on the eastern boundary of Rancho San Francisco. This started California's first gold rush, but it was short lived. Gold valued over $60,000 was extracted from this area in 1842 and 1843, some being shipped to the Philadelphia mint. Interestingly, a map purportedly dated 1841 (Preston 1974:10–11) has the word "Gold" written in the general location of this "ancient excavation." Preston does not cite the origin of his maps, so they are of little value to scholars.

59. Manly (1894:172) said, "A pack of prairie wolves were snarling around the carcass of some dead animal," another editorial embellishment by Manly's writing assistant.

60. This point of land extends north from Saugus. Since there is a spring on the hill, there was surely a trail to it that the boys followed.

down, the stream broke out and made a deep gulch. As we got a little farther down the stream, we found a yearling calf near the bank. I crawled up slyly and gave him a shot, which killed him. We made our camp [about 4 miles east of the Rancho San Francisco house] by our game for the night and had a supper of good meat; but we had a little fear of the consequences, for we had killed an animal belonging to someone else and might be caught. We knew it was wrong to kill the calf, but we were hungry for something good to eat. There was plenty of wood scattered around and we worked all night drying the meat. One of us sat up and worked while the other slept. The coyotes came around and serenaded us with frequent open air concerts. They, no doubt, wanted some of our stolen meat. Some of them came within twenty feet of our fire. The moon was shining very brightly and we could see many more in the distance, and when they would all go to howling, Rogers would wake up and say, "Shoot the cursed things." But we let them alone and none of them were hurt. In the morning we emptied out our poor meat, and put in the meat we had just dried.

The soles of our moccasins had been worn out for several days, but we had kept them on to protect the top of our feet coming down the brushy canyon. We now made us some new moccasins out of our calf's hide and were ready to start on our journey early in the morning. Before daylight we heard the faint bark of a dog, which sounded as if down in the valley, so we started in the direction of the noise. I was still lame and we got along slow. About ten o'clock we saw in the trail before us, a man with a broad brimmed hat on and a woman by his side, dressed in regular Spanish fashion. As we were a little afraid to meet any one with fresh raw-hide on our feet, we turned to one side and let them go by. They did not seem to take much notice of us. We had always heard the Spaniards were a race of pirates and robbers, and to be in a land where they lived was very dangerous. We felt that any moment we might be set upon and killed. We went along slow; by and by at three o'clock, we came in sight of a low house on an elevation overlooking the whole valley.[61]

61. The seriousness of Manly's lameness can be imagined when you consider it took them all day to travel only 4 miles from their camp to the adobe house on the 48,612-acre Rancho San Francisco. Previously, their daily average was 22 miles.

The ranch house sat on a bench above the Santa Clara River 0.5 mile south of Castaic Junction. According to Perkins (1957:102), who excavated the site between 1935 and 1937, the five-room house was about 105 feet long and 17 feet wide. The floor was baked tile, the walls were adobe, and the roof was mission tile. Downhill and east of the house were several springs. Arthur Perkins told us the site was badly vandalized by treasure hunters seeking hidden gold and mission treasures before he could complete the excavation. The vandals shattered all the floor tiles and razed the remaining walls. After the site was vandalized, the rubble was bulldozed over the hill by the property owners. We collected and gave specimens of the floor and leg-molded roof tiles to the

We now stopped awhile and considered what was best to do. After we had talked matters over, we concluded to go to the house and stand the results.

The house was one story, had a flat roof and was made of big sun-dried bricks. There was a big corral near by and near the door of the house was a mule tied to a post. A middle aged man came out and said something we could not understand. We spoke to him but he only seemed to understand two words, Los Angeles and San Francisco. To Los Angeles he pointed west and San Francisco north, and seemed to want us to go to San Francisco. I showed him by signs that I was lame and wanted something to ride. I showed him some money and pointed to the mule, giving him to understand that I wanted to buy, but he shook his head and declined my offer. I had to make up my mind to walk.

Rogers wore a patent leather belt and on it a small box for matches. The man wanted this and we traded it for corn meal. I took the meat that was in both our napsacks and Rogers put the meal in his. The man looked inquisitively at our feet and we thought that he must know that we had killed something of his. We felt guilty but we could not talk and explain. He then pointed north and went away and there was nothing left for us to do but go on.

We soon came to where two small streams came together and we followed up the north branch along its north side. I got very lame and walked with great pain, and finally we sat down on a sandy place near the creek. We mixed a little meal in our camp pail and baked it on the lid. As we ate our meal we talked of our prospects. I told Rogers that this course wouldn't do. The country north where the man told us to go gets higher and rougher the further you go and no one lives there. This course will never do

Death Valley National Monument Museum. Rancho San Francisco is commemorated by California Historical Landmark #556 at Castaic Junction.

The ranch house was originally an *asistencia* (boardinghouse) of Mission San Fernando. In 1839, after the missions were secularized, Don Antonio del Valle was granted ownership of the Rancho San Francisco, and the *asistencia* became the del Valle home (Newhall 1958:35–48). Don Antonio died in 1841, and his widow married Don José Salizar. Manly consistently called the Rancho "San Francisquito Ranch"—possibly after San Francisquito Canyon which is nearby. The correct name is well documented as Rancho San Francisco (Cowan 1956:76; Perkins 1957; Newhall 1958:35; USGS Santa Susana, Calif., 15 min., 1903, reprinted 1924; USGS Southern Calif., Sheet 3, 1/250,000, 1910, reprinted 1931; Donley et al.

1979:13).

Cowan (1956:77) lists one Rancho San Francisco, but five called Rancho San Francisquito: one in Los Angeles County, one in Monterey County, and three in Santa Clara County. The 8,894-acre Rancho San Francisquito in Los Angeles County was adjacent to and west of the San Gabriel River, and originally encompassed parts of the land now occupied by Arcadia, El Monte, and Temple City. It was granted to Henry Dalton in 1845; the title book with a map and legal description is in the Huntington Library ([Dalton] HM 29329). Dalton paid $400 for this land and named it "San Francisquito" (Jackson 1977:77). It is shown on Stevenson's 1880 "Map of the County of Los Angeles" (in Preston 1974:25) and on the USGS Southern California map No. 1 (1/250,000, 1901; reprinted 1921; Donley et al. 1979:13).

according to geography, for the ocean is not north, and we will not be able to find help in that direction before all those we have left behind are starved to death. I have formed a bad opinion of Spaniards and as they have seen our money, they have sent us off here to get it and perhaps our lives too. I had hardly finished speaking, when looking up the creek, we saw the dust rise and come towards us, and soon we saw men coming on horseback at a furious gait. We said, "There comes some of those Spanish robbers."

We took our money and hurriedly buried it in the sand. We made our guns ready for action and waited with bated breath for their coming, for we felt that we were doomed to death. They came down the creek on a good strong gallop. When they were opposite us, they stopped and had a short consultation and one rode over to see us. We were ready for the worst and were sitting on the ground with our guns at full cock. We almost held our breath in those few moments of waiting. When the rider got near to us he proved to be a white man, one that could give us a good deal of information. We were happily disappointed and awful glad to find a man that we could understand.

We now told where we were from and what we wanted to take to those we left in the desert. "Now," he said, "I can talk Spanish and will try and help you." He pointed across the valley to a large live oak and said, "There is an American camped under that tree; go and stay with him till morning and then come to the ranch building where I will stay to-night."

Then with his companion he road away. We were now wonderfully relieved in mind, as we had found somebody to talk to and could learn where we were. After all, the Spaniard had meant us no harm; by pointing north he had tried to make us understand that an American was camped out this way who would be able to talk to us. All might look honest when properly explained.

We went over to our man, who was camped under the oak tree. He had come south by Santa Fe and Arizona and had lost all but his horse and a little grub.[62]

The night was quite cold and in order to sleep without any blankets we had to gather stuff enough to build a fire on the place chosen to sleep, so as to warm the ground or we would not have been able to get any sleep at all. After we had warmed the ground, we cuddled down like two dogs close together and were soon asleep, but we were forced out before morning from the disagreeable effects of the corn cakes. We had been so long living without

62. Bieber (1937:51) estimates about twenty-five hundred emigrants came to California via the Santa Fe Trail between April and September 1849.

vegetable food that it acted as a purgative, accompanied by severe pains. At times we thought we might have the cholera.

We started for the mud house early in the morning, without any breakfast, but we were so often attacked with pains in the stomach that we did not get along very fast. We thought such food was too strong for us and we had better touch it lightly for our good.

Manly and Rogers Return to Death Valley

[July 1888; Volume V, Number V, Page 78]

When we reached the house, the two men had their own horses saddled up and an unsaddled horse for each of us. This, then, was the way we were to go to Los Angeles, where they would help us all they could. We at once mounted the horses and started on to Los Angeles, which was about 30 miles away. We soon got very tired riding and got off our horses and walked. When the others would get about half a mile ahead, we would get on our horses and gallop up to them, and then get off and walk again. It was easier on us walking than riding.

After we passed the San Fernando Mission we met a Mr. French on his way to his ranch Tejon.[63] We all stopped and talked awhile. Our wants were made known and the object of our mission fairly told. He said, "If you will go home with me, I will give you a pair of fat, gentle work oxen, besides all the beans you can carry. That is all I have to give, but such as it is you are welcome." We thanked him for his offer, but told him that oxen could not be driven so far out on the desert and, besides, we were not certain we could get them over the mountain. The way we came it would be impossible. He then told us that we could not get any in Los Angeles if we went there, and he thought we had better go back to the place we came from in the morning. He was well acquainted with the folks at

63. Dr. E. Darwin French prospected in the Death Valley area for the fabulous Gunsight Mine in 1850 and 1860. However, he apparently did not enter Death Valley on the first trip. In a paper presented to the California Academy of Sciences, Henry G. Hanks (1869) said, "I am indebted to Dr. E. D. French . . . for the particulars which follow: In 1850, a party of 14 men came to his ranch, near Fort Tejon, and camped for the night. They told him that they were going over the mountains to look for a silver mine which had been discovered some time before by a party of emigrants." The party, now including Dr. French, got as far as Panamint Valley, and the surrounding mountains. "After making the most strenuous efforts, they did not discover the mine, but were compelled to return to the settlements" (Hanks 1869). Both Wheat (1939c:197) and Long (1950:312) credit Dr. French with the 1850 and 1860 expeditions. However, Palmer (1952) does not mention the 1850 trip in his definitive *Chronology of the Death Valley Region in California, 1849–1949*, nor does Hanks (1883:29–37) in his *Third Annual Report of the State Mineralogist*. The general route of Dr. French's first trip is shown on Gibbes's 1852 "New Map of California." The map shows the "Route of the Silver Mountain Expedition in the fall of 1850" as crossing Walker Pass and going north through the Coso-Darwin area.

the house, could talk their language and would tell them of our wants and try and persuade them to do all they could to help us. We concluded it would be best to turn back, for we must get back to the wagons as soon as possible. If we should go to Tejon we could not get the outfit wanted, still we had found a real friend with a willing hand.

He now went on and we turned and followed him, leading our horses. He was soon out of sight and we were left alone. As we traveled along we talked and studied over our prospects. I was feeling much better than a while back, for the horseback ride had driven the pain out of my leg and walking was quite easy.

We got back to the house the next day at about ten o'clock.[64] The folks seemed pleased to see us. The woman acted the most friendly; she took us into a part of the house used as a store house and showed us some wheat and a large coffee mill with two handles fast to a post. She then motioned for us to grind wheat for ourselves. We had to talk by the sign language, but the woman was a good talker in that way, and we got along well.

After we had worked awhile on the mill, she came in with a small child by her side and pointed to it and to us and then held up her hand and shut it one finger at a time. I now understood that she had been told we had children back in the mountains. To answer her, I put my hand on my breast and then held it up, keeping my thumb down. By this she understood that there were four children. In the same way she asked how many women, and I showed her two fingers.[65] Then she wanted to know how far away they were and I showed her how many sleeps or camps we had made while traveling the distance. She shook her head as if to say, "no good."

She now commenced to tell me the names in Spanish of many common things, and as I was anxious to learn, I took the pains to write down all the words I could understand in both languages. She gave me many words and I wrote them down in this way: Man, hombre; woman, moharee; horse, cavio; cow, vaca; wheat, trigo; beans, frijolese; corn, mice; squashes, calavases; oxen, mays; wagon, carisa; mare, yawa; Indian, Injiana; milk, lache; meat, carnay. In this way I gathered quite a list and committed them to memory, so as to be able to use them on our return.

64. Manly (1894:183) later recalled they spent the night at Mission San Fernando, where they were kindly treated (camp M, appendix A).

65. Manly was referring only to the women and children in the Bennett-Arcan party, not Mrs. Wade and her four children. Although the Wades were in camp when the boys left, Mr. Wade must have stated he would not wait for Manly and Rogers to return; so Manly did not count them. However, three women are mentioned in his book (1894:184). We think this is another addition by Manly's writing assistant, who knew Mrs. Wade was at the sulphur water hole when the boys left but may not have known the Wades did not plan to wait for their return. Manly and Rogers spent two nights here; during the day they ground corn and wheat (camps N & O, appendix A).

The woman was quite intelligent and as interesting as one could expect. She put me in mind of my mother, only she was of dark complexion. I could not help looking at her. As we worked, she brought us large pieces of roasted squash, which tasted especially good. We chewed dried wheat during our work, and in all we lived quite well.

When we got ready to start away they brought us two or three small sacks, and filled one with beans, one with wheat and the third with the coarse flour we had been grinding. They brought to the door two small gentle mares, with the addition of an old saddle tree and strips of dry rawhide. The woman came out with four oranges in her hand and pointed to her child and by signs gave us to understand we must take the fruit to the children and not eat it ourselves.

They then fixed the pack saddles on the horses. This was new work for us and we were glad of a chance to learn how the work was done. After they had finished fixing the packs, we laid our money down for them to take their pay. After a little talk among themselves, they took about $30. We thought they were cheating themselves and we were pleased with our bargain; we afterwards learned that they were not, for mares in those days were almost valueless.

Our horses were good enough for us, but there were not enough of them, for all the women and children could not ride on the two. We bade them good-bye and led our animals, that had cost us half of our little store of money, off up the valley to take our way back to the wagons.

A few miles walk brought us to the wagon road of a train, that had gone before. We followed in it [north in San Francisquito Canyon] till it led us to their camp.[66] Here we bought a beautiful little white fat mare. She was rather wild, but Rogers said he would tame her. He got on bare-backed and worried her around a little while and then tied her up.

As we were standing there, a man came up with a little black mule which he had found away out in the desert where it had probably been left to die. It had only one eye, its back had no hair on it for a space the size of the saddle, and it was still quite poor, but he believed it would stand the trip. After a good deal of horse jockey talk we bought the mare and the mule. They gave us saddletrees, straps and ropes enough to rig out with. They gave us a little more flour and helped us fix our packs all on two of the animals; thus leaving the other two for us to ride.[67]

66. Soledad Canyon was so full of brush that they had to find another route over the mountains, so they followed a wagon road that was being built up San Francisquito Canyon.

67. Manly (1894:187) said they were given "25 pounds of unbolted wheat flour." Rogers said they also procured coffee, sugar, and tea here (camp P, appendix A).

We now took the trail to the summit which was north [northwest] of the brushy one we came on. We could see, when we reached the summit, the desolate country we had to go back over. The road looked hard, but we struck out. Immediately on our right and near the top of the mountain was a small beautiful lake, which is now called Elizabeth lake.[68] It was full of good fresh water. We watered our horses and filled our canteens and then started southeast to get on our trail. We got out quite a little ways among the cabbage trees; night came on and we had to camp. We tied our animals to the trees and after a night's rest, started out again.[69]

We soon came to the ox trail of those we left behind us. We had missed them by coming over the mountain in a different canyon, further north. We got to our little rain water hole before sundown; here we camped. Our horses got water as well as ourselves.

At the break of day we were off again. We now walked part of the time to favor our stock, for they began to feel weak from their small supply of water and grass. We crowded them along over the trail as fast as we could walk and reached the willow corral near sundown. The horses here got water and some grass. We felt a little afraid of Indians in this camping ground, so, to make all safe, we concluded to stand on guard and do without a fire, and thus we might save our horses from the Indians.

The next night we camped at the place where we had before crawled up to and found to be E. Doty's camp [Indian Wells Spring]. There was good water here, and the horses, when they came to drink, put their heads up to their eyes in water. From here we had a two days' travel with only a little salt water hole, that no animal would drink, and hardly any grass.[70]

Our mule proved to be the smartest of them all. We gave her the heaviest load and let her go loose. She would go out of the trail for every bit of grass in sight and stood the work the best of anyone.

The next morning we had a canyon to go up [Deadman Canyon, Argus Range], and a part of it was well filled with boulders and

68. They ascended the mountain via San Francisquito Canyon and South Portal Canyon (Bear Canyon on old maps), crossed the western shoulder of Grass Mountain, and descended Munz Canyon to enter the San Andreas rift, which explains why Elizabeth Lake was "immediately on our right." Manly (1894:187) later recalled "the trail soon reached the summit from which we could see off to the east [northeast] a wonderful distance, probably 200 miles, of the dry and barren desert of hill and desolate valley over which we had come." Had they entered the rift via San Francisquito Canyon, they could not have seen the desert because Portal Ridge blocks the view.

69. They crossed Portal Ridge through Johnson Summit and made a beeline for the rainwater hole where they had camped a few days before. Here they found the Jayhawkers' trail, which they followed north to Desert Spring—Manly's willow corral.

70. Manly means two days travel from Indian Wells Spring at the base of Owens Peak in the Sierra Nevada to Indian Joe Spring at the base of Argus Peak on the east side of the Argus Range. There is conflict between this account and the 1894 account (p. 188) as to the exact location of camps T and U. They camped their 20th night (T) at or east of Indian Wells Spring and spent their 21st night (U) at or east of the saltwater hole at Paxton Ranch (map 5).

Kurt Diemberger and LeRoy Johnson descend Deadman Canyon, Argus Range. Manly described it as "well filled with boulders and hard for our weak animals to get over."

hard for our weak animals to get over.[71] Before we got to the summit our white mare seemed a little lame and walked head foremost against a bluff of rocks and fell down. We helped her up but she soon lay down again and would not get up, so we took off her saddle and left her. We were only half way to water and could not stop. We hurried on [down east Wilson Canyon] and got to the camp Doty told us of at about dark.[72] The horses could hardly be

71. The boys were now following the Jay-hawker trail. It ascended the west side of the Argus Range through Deadman Canyon, one canyon north of Burro Canyon, the one they used on their march for provisions (map 5). We have hiked all the canyons in this part of the Argus Range, and Deadman is the only one that fits the descriptions and mileages given in the various firsthand accounts (Brier JA 70; Manly 1894:228; Young in Long 1850:277). Historians wishing to explore this area must secure permission from the base commander, Naval Weapons Center, China Lake.

72. They camped at "Providence Spring"

(Manly 1894:227), which we have identified as Indian Joe Spring, 5 miles north of Trona (camp V, map 5). Historians (e.g., Chalfant 1936:37; Long 1950:244) have searched in vain for references documenting the location of Providence Spring. Wheat (1939b:94) suggested Peach Spring in Bruce Canyon 13 miles north of Trona as the location, and Long (1950:139), Ellenbecker (1938:44), and Belden (1956:41) have perpetuated Wheat's suggestion. Koenig (1984:140–151) concludes it is 6 miles northwest of Carricut (he calls it Carricart) Lake high in the Argus Range west of Shepherd Canyon.

The only known maps with Providence Spring

coaxed to get there, they seemed so weak. We saw they were not able to carry anything, so before we lay down for the night, we dug a hole in the sand, lined it with brush and put in it our bag of wheat. We covered it all over and slept on it to obliterate all signs of the deposit.

The next morning we put all we had on the mule and let the horses go loose. We camped beyond where Fish died [east side, Slate Range], without water or grass and left in the morning as soon as it was light enough to see to travel.[73]

The next day we had to try a new pass in the last range, for the way we came over could not be crossed by a dog, let alone our horses. We tried a canyon further south.[74] This was all new to us

drawn on them are Manly's Palmer and Jayhawker maps (HM 50895 & JA 1050). These maps show the routes the Jayhawkers and the Brier mess used to enter Searles Valley from the north and from the east, respectively. Both parties headed south for Searles Lake because they desperately needed fresh water, but when they arrived there they found the water too salty to drink. The Brier contingent arrived at the lake about midnight guided by the Jayhawker campfires.

In the morning the Briers moved west to the rocky outcrop now called Point of Rocks (a mile north of Trona) while some of the Jayhawkers went into the Argus Range to search for water. As "Mrs. Brier retired to the shadow of a great rock to pray," Deacon Richards brought word that he had discovered water (John Wells Brier 1911:4). The spring, 4 miles from the Brier camp (James Welsh Brier JA 70), was such a fortunate discovery that Mrs. Brier named it "Providence Spring."

Some of the Jayhawkers were still camped near the edge of Searles Lake about 2 miles from the Brier camp. Sheldon Young (in Long 1950:277) recorded in his log on January 13, "this day went six miles North to a spring in a deep rocky cañon." Asa Haynes (in Ellenbecker 1938:125) said, "north 6 miles. Water." Reverend Brier said the spring was "up a canyon" (JA 73) and "at the foot of the high peak [Argus Peak]" (JA 70). Manly (1894:189) described it as "a faint running stream which came out of a rocky ravine and sank almost immediately in the dry sand." Providence Spring as drawn by Manly on two of his maps fits the descriptions cited above and the location of Indian Joe Spring.

73. From Indian Joe Spring they crossed Searles Valley to the mouth of Isham Canyon. Manly (1894:190) described it: "There was now seven or eight miles of clean loose sand to go over, across a little valley which came to an end about ten miles north of us, and extended south to the lake [Searles Lake] where we went for water on our outward jour-

ney and found it red alkali. Near the Eastern edge of the valley we turned aside to visit the grave of Mr. Isham. . . . They had covered his remains with their hands as best they could, piling up a little mound of sand over it." The distance from Indian Joe Spring to the mouth of Isham Canyon is 7.5 miles. They had learned of Isham's death from Doty at Indian Wells Spring.

74. They chose Redlands Canyon, which is 6.5 miles south of Middle Park Canyon, the one they descended on their western trip (map 3). Manly's statement "We tried a canyon further south" did not appear in his book, but it is an important clue in unraveling the routes. His book (1894:191) said, "all things considered it seemed to be the quickest way to camp to try and get up a rough looking cañon which was nearly opposite us on the other side [of Panamint Valley]." Redlands Canyon is the only one "nearly opposite" Manly Pass. Koenig (1984:208) overlooks the "nearly opposite" evidence in his contention that the boys descended the Argus Range via Shepherd Canyon 14 miles north of Redlands Canyon. Had they exited Shepherd Canyon, they would have seen Pleasant Canyon "nearly opposite" them. It leads to the very point where they crossed the Panamint Range above Arrastre Spring. Koenig (1984:222) supports his Shepherd Canyon theory with the decided northern swing in Panamint Valley drawn on Manly's maps. However, Manly explained this northern swing in an article about his return trip to the Panamints in the winter of 1860–61 (in Woodward 1949b:61–72). He was asked to follow the '49er route as they traveled eastward from Providence Spring. Upon reaching Panamint Valley, they "had to go *some distance south* to get around a sluggish stream that ran north into a salt lake" (in Woodward 1949b:69, emphasis added). We, too, were forced south along the soft, salt-encrusted mud flats bordering the little stream when we hiked from Manly Pass to Redlands Canyon.

and we were anxious to see water. Our two horses moped along with their heads near the ground and looked awful sorry.

The canyon [Redlands Canyon] that we entered did not look very favorable, but there did not seem to be any other pass for a long ways, so we took it. As we went on between the rocky walls of the canyon, we came across a small fall of a couple of feet. The mule went up and over like a dog, but our two horses could not be made to go any farther. We had no time to lose so we took the mule and went on, after removing the horses' saddles and putting them on a rock. We told the horses goodbye; they turned around and looked after us, but would not try to follow.

About half a mile further up the canyon we came to an almost perpendicular fall of about ten feet. The wall on the north side was thousands of feet high and leaned over the canyon; the south side was sloped. The canyon represented a mammoth crevice. Now the question was what to do and how to do it. The horses were gone and there was a poor show to get the mule any further.

The last horses we had bought we had intended for the women and children to ride on and now they were gone. I thought the women and children could not walk where we had and their bones would be left to bleach on the desert. This prospect caused us to feel bad and we almost gave up in despair. We took the pack off the mule and looked the rocky walls over. How to save our mule was a puzzle. Finally, we decided on the only plan we could study out. We concluded to take the mule down the canyon a ways and help it

Lieutenant Charles E. Bendire, U.S. Army, also provided information to help pinpoint this canyon. In 1867, he led a scouting expedition into the region east of Owens Valley. On April 11, he camped "in Panamint Valley, on the west side near some small volcanic Buttes, and at the south end of a salt marsh" (Bendire 1867). This was south of the mouth of Redlands Canyon near the toe of Manly Peak. The next day Bendire went south 15 miles and sent Sergeant Neale back 16 miles to explore "Emigrant Cañon." Bendire gave Neale's description of his trip up "Emigrant Cañon": "Sergt. Neale and party left camp at 6 a.m. following up Emigrant Cañon and after working all day and night succeeded in getting his animals over the falls in the Cañons, four in number, one of them about 16 feet high, and camped in the morning near Candle Springs [Redlands Spring]. General direction N.47E.; distance traveled 16 miles; good water and grass." This "Emigrant Cañon" is not the canyon so named today. Redlands Canyon is the only one that fits the distances. Sergeant Neale had the benefit of the ramp constructed in 1860 by Bennett and companions, who searched here for gold (in Woodward 1949b:67).

Linda Greene (1981:139) provides corroborating evidence that Redlands Canyon was once named Emigrant Canyon. She surveyed the Inyo County *Land, Water and Mining Claims* records and discovered that D. R. Kimball and J. A. Mack located the "Emigrant Mining Claim" on January 9, 1893. They described the mine's location as being "situated about 3.5 miles west of Anvil Springs in Butte Valley [the spring is in Butte Valley, not the claim] and on North side of Emigrant Canyon." However, Greene says the "actual location [is] open to conjecture. Although it would seem to be located in the Redlands Canyon area, the reference to Emigrant Canyon adds a certain element of doubt." Greene did not have the unpublished field notes of Lieutenant Bendire; thus, she did not know Redlands Canyon was once named after the emigrants who traversed it in 1850. The Emigrant Canyon of today, southwest of Stove Pipe Wells, is not the same "Emigrant Cañon" mentioned in Neale's report or where Kimball and Mack located their "Emigrant Mining Claim." We hiked every major canyon between Pleasant Canyon and Goler Wash and conclude Redlands Canyon is the only one fitting Neale's description.

climb up the steep rocky mountain side as far as we could. We tried to fix the way for it as best we could by throwing loose rocks into the canyon, so the mule could have something solid to stand on. We succeeded in getting her, by a great deal of hard work, up to near the head of the falls. The mountain above here was perpendicular and we could climb no further. The rocks there were as smooth as if they had been washed by water and sloped down directly to the head of the fall. Now if our mule made a misstep here it would fall fifty feet to the bottom of the canyon, which would be sure death. I had the long pack rope around the mule and went ahead fixing the way as best I could and paying out the rope; I climbed across this smooth dangerous place, while the mule looked every way for a way out, but there was none. It could not turn around and there was no way for it only to try and cross this bad place, and the mule would have to take two jumps to do it.

"Now," Rogers said, "you pull on the rope and call her and I will take these big rocks in each hand and yell at the top of my voice, and make her think I am going to kill her." So he commenced swinging the rocks and yelling; Rogers was a Tennesseean, weighing about 180 pounds. I pulled and called, and Rogers' powerful voice echoed throughout the canyon, and thus the fearful venture began. The mule made one big jump and struck the smooth slanting rock about half way over; as she was not shod she did not slip and the next jump landed her safe above the falls.[75]

We had now accomplished what we thought impossible. If there had been listeners around before we succeeded they might have heard unusual sounds from the throats of two discouraged boys, who acted more like women than men, for we believed everybody and everything was lost, but now if no more falls were met, we might be able to do some body some good.

I would say here to anyone who takes the time to read these lines, that they must remember that this cannot be adequately described by an uneducated writer, and the story is very poorly told.

[August 1888; Volume V, Number VI, Page 94]

A short distance above the falls we found a small patch of willows and some good water. This was the first water we had found for two days and was a good find for man and mule. We

75. This is the uppermost fall in Redlands Canyon, 150 yards below Redlands Spring. Dr. Wolff (1931:28, photograph p. 21) first correctly identified and photographed it. The 180-foot vertical fall at the mouth of Redlands Canyon that now carries Manly's name is clearly not Wolff's Manly Fall. We now use "Ox-Jump Fall" to designate Wolff's Manly Fall (Ramsay 1979:166). Ironically, in 1850, Manly probably never saw the spectacular fall now bearing his name, because the Indian trails (still visible in places) circle to the north and south of it. The fall shown in Koenig (1984:215) is not Ox-Jump Fall, the fall immediately below the spring and the one pictured by Dr. Wolff.

talked of taking water down to the horses, but we had nothing to take it in, besides there was no chance of getting them across the falls, so we were forced to let them choke to death. Here we camped for the night.[76] This part of the canyon was so deep and dark that the sun never lighted it up. During the night we talked over our situation and future prospects, the miraculous feat we had just accomplished in getting our little pet mule over the falls alive. It was a mere stroke of good luck, but it seemed very hard to leave the good horses to perish, choke and starve without friends. Without them how could the women and children be saved? It seemed impossible, as our trail had been long, dry, rough and exceedingly hard to endure. It seemed to us as if they never could get out. Their prospect looked very dark. We thought they must walk and would die trying; they would have to ride or leave their bones to bleach, like others, in the hot burning sun of the desert, without coffin or grave.

The prospect was indeed dark. We had been gone far beyond the time allowed. Would we find anybody at the end of our journey alive? We were perhaps given up and they had all gone and tried to find their way out. This was a sad and dreary night and if the now happy readers of this narrative could have approached our camp undiscovered they would have seen two lone boys almost in despair. Many tears were shed here as well as at the falls where we expected to lose our poor little mule.

Rogers, after a little silence, just before the mule jumped, said, "Come Lewis, don't cry." I am not ashamed to own that as all here seemed to be going to destruction that I could not suppress my feelings and all for those innocent ones who, it seemed, must perish without assistance. These words are true and hard to write, for my eyes fill with water as I reflect and bring these trying times back to my memory. I have tried to forget the trying past of this trip ever since 1849 and have refused talking about it, and made up my mind to forget the worst, consequently the readers will never realize the troubles, trials and hardships we all endured.

Our moccasins were now worn out on the bottom, and our present path was the worst place in the whole Rocky mountains to travel barefoot. I took off my buckskin leggings and fixed them on our feet, for they were getting very sore and, if we had to look for soft places for our feet we could not watch for Indians, and might be taken advantage of.

In the morning we started up the canyon. It was a very steep grade and our worst fear was that we would meet a greater fall than the one past, before we reached the summit and be compelled to lose our little mule, but the road from this point to the summit

76. Redlands Spring, 150 yards above Ox-Jump Fall, now supplies water for the Southern Homestake Mine at the mouth of Redlands Canyon (camp X, map 3).

proved to be clear of these waterfalls, or what would be waterfalls in seasons of high water, and we experienced no difficulty on this account, but the entire bed of the canyon was covered with small hard rocks which were very hard on our feet.[77] The down grade [in Warm Spring Canyon] on the eastern side was much worse, as we were going down hill.

About sundown we got to the camp we left just 25 days before.[78] This was a poor camp. A little sulphury water hole on top of a small mound, and nothing but sage brush for the mule.

We were now awful glad we had got off of the sharp rocks, which had nearly worn our feet out. They had worn our moccasins entirely out and our feet were very sore, but we had the wagon road to follow to camp where we supposed all would be anxiously looking for us.

We started on barefoot and, as the road was somewhat sandy and free from rocks, we got along quite comfortable. The mule went ahead of us, turning out on first one side of the road and then on the other, hunting for the little bunches of dry grass that were scattered thinly among the sage brush. When we had gone about a mile or two, I stopped to fix something on my feet while Rogers went on ahead. When I started, I saw him standing with his gun on the ground looking very steadily at something. When I got near I asked, "What have you found?" He answered, "Capt. Culverwell here dead." We looked at him for some time. He lay on his back, one arm out at full length; his little canteen, like ours, lay empty by his side. He looked to us as if he had been dead but a short time; there was no sign of swelling or decay in the least. He had not been disturbed by bird or beast. We learned afterwards that he had been dead ten or twelve days. The climate was so void of malaria or wet weather and there is so much salt in the country that nothing decays.[79] Our

77. In Butte Valley they headed northeast to Warm Spring Canyon. Manly (1894:196) recalled they could see the "water hole" (Arrastre Spring) near where they camped the first night they left Death Valley.

78. They camped at or near Mesquite Well (camp Y, map 3). Only 24 days instead of 25 are accounted for by dovetailing both of Manly's accounts (appendix A). We think the day Manly does not mention was spent grinding wheat and corn at the Rancho San Francisco. In his book (1894:196) he said, "We at last got down and camped on some [the same] spot where we had set out twenty-five days before. . . . Here was the same little water hole in the sand plain, and the same strong sulphur water." The next day, the 26th day, they arrived at the long camp. Corroborating this, Manly also wrote on the Jayhawker map (JA 1050): "Bennetts camp [at Bennetts Well] while we ware gone to hunt a settle-

ment. We ware gone 26 days." Correlating Nusbaumer's journal with Manly's accounts, the boys left the sulphur water hole on January 15; thus, they returned to it on February 8 and arrived at the long camp on February 9 (appendix A).

79. According to our calculations, Rogers found Culverwell's body on February 9, and Rogers and Bennett buried him on February 11. Goldsborough Bruff (in Read and Gaines 1949:xlviii) wrote on his map "Death of Culverwell, Feby 10, 1850." Since no one knew what date Culverwell died, Bruff probably gave the approximate date he was buried. Apparently Culverwell left the long camp about January 26 with the Earharts, since Manly said (1894:202), "Capt. Culverwell went with the last party. I afterward learned that he could not keep up with them and turned to go back to the wagons again."

conversation was now of a serious nature, for we expected every moment to find the dead body of some one else. Perhaps many might have wandered away from camp while out of their right mind and had perished in the desert like Culverwell, all alone.

As we had been gone far beyond our allotted time all might have made the last desperate effort to get out and save the women and children. We now felt quite bad over the prospects, but the worst would be known soon, for we were within ten miles of the wagons. We now became very watchful. We could look around, for as the road was soft, we did not have to look for soft places to put our sore feet. We now knew the party was smaller than when we left and maybe they were all dead or gone. The Indians had an easy victory if they waged war on them, and a victory would give them quite a prize in cattle and blankets.

These were reasonable suppositions, we thought, and might occur, as the camp was not well protected, and those wandering night devils could capture all without much fear and gain a rich haul. Every possible misfortune that could occur came to our minds and what we would or could do seemed difficult to determine, as we walked slowly along and neared the end of our road. Our mule saw no danger and kept hunting grass, first on this and then on that side of the road. We paid little or no attention to her, but kept our eyes and ears open to watch for danger on both sides, for we did not expect to find a live person in camp with a white face. How did we know when the shower of arrows would come from a superior number lying in ambush for us, for they would know some one would come some time to those in the wagons.[80] We moved along cautiously and talked low until we were in sight of the wagons, but still quite a ways off. Thus far no more dead bodies had been found.

We now stood a long time and looked over the place [Bennetts Well], which was nearly level.[81] The wagons were in a little lower ground than the rest of the plain. We looked first carefully for cattle, but none could be seen; this looked bad for us. The covers were off the wagons; this looked like no one was in camp. The Indians might be hiding in ambush for us. Only four wagons could be counted and no signs of life about them. We now thought for sure that all were dead, but who, if anyone, had possession? Maybe they had given up our return and made an effort to get out while their oxen lived to afford them food, or the Indians had murdered them all and drove

80. Indian habitation sites are numerous in this portion of Death Valley (Alice Hunt 1960:310–313), so the boys assumed Indians were lurking nearby. In the 1800s, these sites were still used during the mesquite bean gathering season in June and July. Later, the wooden wickiup frames became a convenient source of firewood for the miners; only a few have survived to modern times. One was photographed by Ansel Adams (Corle 1941), and three others are shown in the Wallaces' (1978) booklet.

81. The families first went back to Eagle Borax Spring but later moved south to Bennetts Well, where better water and more grass were available.

the cattle off and put them to their use, and they might be waiting under the wagons for our return and were letting us come up close so as to make the battle short and sure.[82]

Finally, after looking over the place and all around for at least half an hour, Rogers said, "Let us go down to the camp and see and know what we have to do. No living creature seems to be anywhere around."

We, after our long reconnaissance, concluded to move on to camp. I had seven shots and Rogers two and we would get there or die trying, and learn, if we could, what had become of those we left. If there was a white person in sight they would certainly show themselves, as we and the mule were in plain sight, and not more than one hundred and fifty yards away.

We advanced slowly and when we got within a hundred yards we concluded to fire a shot and see if we could raise any one. If the enemy came we would have eight shots left with which we would do our best, for if beat, this valley would be our last resting place and our bones would bleach in the sun for all time. Still we were bound to go to the wagons and find out what had become of its occupants.

We put our guns at full cock, prepared to make the shot. To our surprise, soon after the report reached the wagons, Bennett and Arcane came from under them, and looking around in different directions, finally saw us. They, including Mrs. Bennett, came running to meet us, and here the pen of no man like myself can describe the scene. They were so overjoyed that they could not talk, but all eyes were moist and silence reigned for some time. Mrs. Bennett fell before me on her knees and clasped her hands around my lower limbs and wept, as we all stood with our tongues tied and holding each other by the hand. Mr. Bennett was the first to speak; he said,

82. Manly (1894:199) said they "surely left seven wagons" in camp when they departed on January 15. The movement of emigrant wagons in and about Death Valley can be compared to musical chairs. We are not always sure just whose wagons are together at any one time. Manly (1894:133) referred to seven wagons in the train before they reached Ash Meadows. We know Nusbaumer and company burned their wagon about 5 miles west of Death Valley Junction. We also know the Bennett-Arcan party had four wagons at least as far as Eagle Borax Spring. We know the Earharts had one, as did Anton Schlögel. The Wades had one wagon and maybe two. Ellenbecker (1938:52 & Supplement:5) tells us the Wades left Death Valley with two wagons and Earhart with one. That Wade had a hired driver would support the two-wagon supposition. Thus, at Travertine Springs there were seven (maybe eight)

wagons. We know, from Nusbaumer's journal (sheet 13), that one wagon was burned at Eagle Borax Spring before all the parties moved south to the sulphur water hole. The wagon belonged either to the Bennett-Arcan party or to the Wades. We agree with Read and Gaines (1944:1230) that Nusbaumer, Hadapp, and Schlögel were not at the water hole when Manly and Rogers left. Therefore, Manly would not have seen seven wagons when he and John left. There is a good possibility Manly's writing assistant used the only figure she had and inserted "surely left seven wagons" as a point of clarity.

The Earharts' wagon broke down, and Captain Culverwell, who was traveling with them, could not keep up on foot. He attempted to return to the Bennett-Arcan camp and managed to get within 6 miles of camp when he died.

"I know you have found some place, for you have got a mule." We now joined hands and walked to the wagons; here we now shook hands again and Mrs. Arcane joined in the happy event.[83]

"O, how glad I am," said Mrs. Bennett, "you got back! We had given you up for lost, you were gone so long. All the others got discouraged waiting for you, and as they were eating their cattle and would soon have nothing left to live on, they thought they had better go on and do their best while able and their cattle lasted." At this Bennett told them he had known Lewis (myself) a long time and he believed if I lived I would come back. "Well," they said, "all we have to say is, if he gets out he is a d——d fool to come back to help anybody out of such a God forsaken place as this. We are not going to wait and be helped by anybody. Every one is now for themselves. So they commenced leaving us. Some only staid in camp six or eight days, and Capt. Culverwell, that we found dead, had been gone about two weeks."

When we all got seated under the wagons we were more composed, and they were anxious to find out where they were.[84] We now told them, as well as we could, how far they were from a settlement. This surprised them. The women were silent, but our story had to be all told and it was near night before we thought to unload our mule. When this was done, what we had brought with us was shown and a little of the flour was used for food. We told them how the meal at the ranch served us so it was dealt out sparingly and our little cholera attack was avoided, that we experienced when we traded for meal at the ranch. We presented the oranges to the children, which was another proof that we had found a better place.

All were now anxious to know if they could possibly get out. We told them the distance to a settlement and that we had lost as little time as possible and had made the trip back in 9 or 10 days. We knew every water hole on the whole road and could tell them how many dry camps they were compelled to make. We gave a description of the country they would have to pass over, but we did not tell all, as we were afraid of the effect it might have on them if we told all as bad as it really was; how many animals we started with and how we lost them, and had to bury our wheat, and how much trouble we had getting the mule over the falls.

They seemed much interested in our narrative which was quite complete in a short way. We now began to inquire if they thought they could make such a trip.

83. Apparently Mrs. Arcan did not run out to welcome the boys. She was over five months pregnant with her second child, a daughter they named Julia, who was born on July 1, 1850, but died 19 days later (Johnson 1981).

84. The leafless mesquite trees provided poor shade, so they sat under the wagons.

The men answered emphatically, "Yes, we can now as you know the road. We know now just what we have to do and we will do it." "Can't we Sally?" said Mr. Bennett, addressing his wife. She answered with some hesitation, thinking, no doubt, her and the children's chances to ride were poor and oxen at any time were hard to ride on. But she seemed to have some courage left and had some hope of relief, if they could hold out long enough.

Our supper was late and had been forgotten, as all were very talkative as well as very interested. We now took a little [flour?] from our pack and added to their poor meat, and did not stop talking while eating. They said they had been afraid for some time, since the others had left them, that the Indians would surprise and massacre them, as they could not make much of a defence, as they had been alone for the last two weeks.

We had not been gone more than ten days when Capt. Culverwell started with some others and had probably given up and was left where we found him. He had likely died with no friend near to give him a drink of water.

They had about given up our return as we had been gone two weeks longer than the time agreed upon. They had taken the covers off their wagons, emptied their beds and tore them all in strips to make a kind of pack harness for the oxen, and as they had no rings or buckles, every cinch or surcingle had to be tied to fasten things on. This was a slow tedious job, but it was now nearly done. The oxen had had a good long rest, but as feed was scarce they had not gained in flesh. They had calculated two oxen for the women to ride, one for the children, one to carry 2 five-gallon kegs of water for dry camps, the other seven to take all the other camp equipage. The cattle had some range here and worked diligently among the sage for the scattering spears of grass and had to take some of the sage as food, as they browsed along among the worthless brush.

The Families Escape from Death Valley

[September 1888; Volume V, Number VII, page 110]

The climate in this place is a perpetual summer, and in the months of May, June, July and August this summer heat increases to so great an extent as to call out the expression from many a one that it must be very near the internal region, and many at this early day spoke better than they knew, for I have since then seen the reports of government surveyors and others that this portion of this terribly dry and heated valley is 377 feet below the level of the sea.[85]

The [Funeral] mountains on the eastern side of the valley are terribly rough and ragged, and the appearance is like that of an immense crater, and there are high, sharp peaks of various colors, so steep that it seems they must be completely inaccessible to man. They are evidently volcanic in their origin, and one can seem to trace in some places where the lava must have flowed, and since have been broken up in various ways. On the west side the [Panamint] mountains are a great deal higher, and the summit covered with snow. From where we were they seemed too steep to be ascended, and it seemed strange indeed as we lay in camp in a summer climate, in the month of January, to look up and see the snow in dusty clouds drifting over the summit, and in the clear pure air seeming only a short distance from us. Distances in this region are always twice as great as they seem to be, and sometimes more than that, for the atmosphere is perfectly clear, and everything is on so large a scale that to measure a distance by sight is sure deception. Many times a mirage is seen, and we are cheated again, and what

85. A depression 282 feet below sea level located 2.2 miles east of Tule Spring is the lowest spot in the western hemisphere. Death Valley's highest recorded air temperature is 134° F; the highest recorded ground temperature is 201° F. Average winter temperatures range from 52° to 67° F, and the average annual rainfall is 1.76 inches. Mr. McLeod, a member of the 1861 U.S. and California Boundary Commission, was probably the first person to take barometric readings in the valley, and his calculations seemed "to indicate a depression of nearly four hundred feet below the sea level" (Owen 1861). McLeod's field notes were later "carefully investigated and computed by Major Williamson . . . [who concluded] Death Valley is certainly over 100 feet below the sea-level, and that it may be as much as 250 feet below it" (Whitney 1865:473).

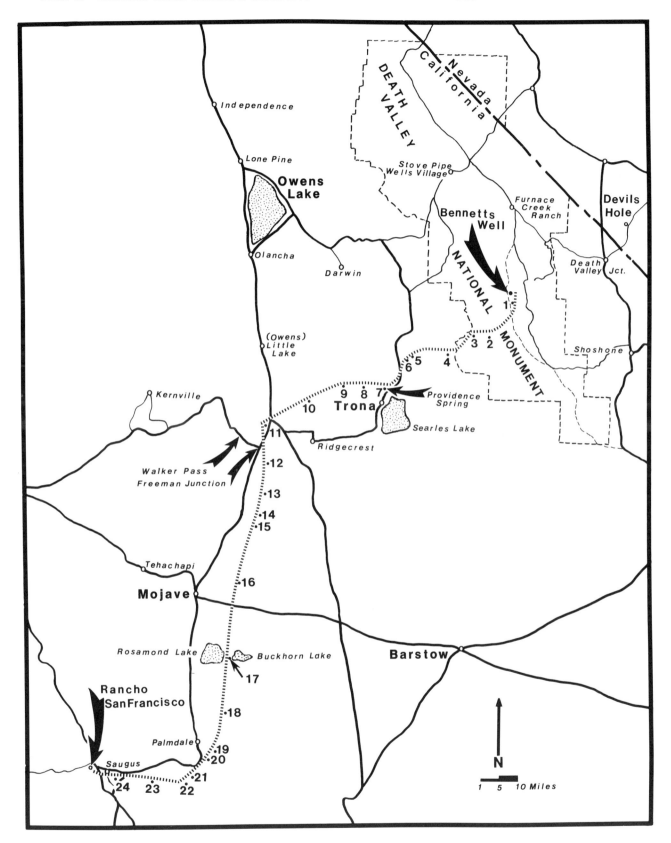

Route of Bennett-Arcan Party from Bennetts Well in Death Valley to Rancho San Francisco. Numbers refer to camps along the route, from February 10 through March 7, 1850 (see appendix B).

seems to be a clear lake of water not a mile away turns to dry shining sand.

The summit of this mountain here in this corner of the world seemed almost overhead and seemed truly to reach the sky clear and cold, while at its foot we found the shade much more comfortable than the sun, and as I think of it now it seems almost as if we were way down in the ground.

It was quite late that night when we lay down to sleep, but daylight saw us up again. The people who had waited so patiently for our return, said that they concluded, several days before, that they must make some effort to get out, and when they heard us relate the story of our journey for their relief, they were almost in despair. Said they, "When such men as you and John R. had all you could do to get out, what are we to do?" The two small children were not able to walk. Mr. Bennett's youngest, that a few months before scampered about camp as lively as a quail, was now helpless. It had been sick during our absence, and without medicine, it was saved only by careful nursing, making soup out of the choicest bits of meat and devoting to it every care. Indeed they once gave up that it must die, but it grew better and still lived, but unable to walk, and looked more like a big toad in shape than like a child.[86]

We decided we must start as soon as possible. Bennett and Rogers were to go to the Salt lake, and gather enough salt on its shore to last us through. Mrs. Bennett and I went to sewing as fast as ever we could on the pack harnesses, and as she talked the tears came in her eyes. She said, "I hope you are telling us all and no more. I began to firmly believe that you could not get back, and we must starve if you could not help us, and though there seemed hardly a shadow of hope, we have worked on for the last week fixing up for our almost hopeless journey as best we could, and as we worked all day we felt too bad to talk and hardly spoke the whole day long. Sometimes we told our plans, what we could do with these helpless children, and I could see them in my mind suffering for want of food and water which could not be got for them, and saw them gasp and die." It did indeed look dubious. Our only way of traveling was on foot, and as the two youngest children could not walk, they must be packed some way, and how these little helpless ones could be got through seemed indeed a question hard to answer. Her tears came too fast to talk and we both sat and worked in silence, and though I tried to be brave, the sorrow of that mother's heart, from which all hope had gone before we came, and

86. Little Martha Ann, 4 years old on January 21, 1850, displayed classic symptoms of malnutrition. "Her limbs had lost all the flesh and seemed nothing but skin and bones, while her body had grown corpu-lent and distended, and her face had a starved pinched and suffering look, with no healthy color in it" (Manly 1894:206).

with all the help that we could give seemed scarcely more hopeful, was too much for my bravery and my own thoughts and feelings were too much for words. Even now when forty years have almost passed, when I try to tell about those sad days, there are no words to tell our cheerlessness, and tears stop the story.

We sewed on and words came again, and I may not be blamed if my own eyes were red with weeping as were hers. But still our work seemed to inspire courage, for she said, "Since you have come back I may try and get up courage enough to walk some further than I expected, but I do not think I can ride an ox as we calculated to. This prospect seems to me to be almost beyond endurance for myself and children. Do you now think, honestly, that we can get out alive?" This was a hard question to answer by saying either "yes" or "no," so I told her all I could about the road we had to go over; the dry camps we would have to make; the desolate country we would have to pass through; the hardship the weak ones would have to endure in various ways. I said to her, "If you can muster up a little courage you may get through all these and to the fertile land on the other side." I told her of the one hard place we would have to get over, when we lost our horses at the falls, and that we knew no other pass. If we could get safely over this, we might hope to work our way over the balance of the road if no great misfortune over-takes us and you keep up the courage to hold out. I told her to try her best and we would make it as easy for her and the children as we could, and if she would be encouraged, and understand that our ultimate delivery from this desert and these mountains depended on keeping up the best you can. Courage and hope and the new provisions we have brought with us will help to build up your strength, and if you persevere and never give up we will get over the road, hard and rough as it is, even if you walk, and we will escape from this desert section, unknown it seems by the Lord himself at least his blessings are very scanty round about.

Mr. and Mrs. Arcane were near by under their wagons, as it was necessary to get in the shade in these clear days of January [about February 10]. They were busy at the same work, but were silent listeners to what we said, and grasping every word that might give hope to a sinking heart as they thought about the journey out of the desert.

Both the smaller children [Martha Bennett and Charlie Arcan] were in about the same physical condition, unable to walk and could not sit on an ox and hold on. We took two of our strongest hickory shirts and turned the sleeves inside, sewed up the necks and then sewed the two together by the flaps, making two large pockets, each large enough to hold a child, and these were thrown across the ox and a child in each, facing outward, while the two large children [George and Melissa Bennett] were strong enough to sit on the ox and hold on. To bear this precious load we selected the brindled ox, "Old Crump," for he was thought to have the best disposition, the gentlest, quietest old fellow in the lot, with one broken horn and to him we trusted this particular part of our deliverance.

Our experience in packing things on oxen was rather limited, as were the facilities and things we had to work with. The oxen were so poor their hides seemed too big for them and it was hard to make the packs stay on. We made strips of cloth from our wagon covers and from the ticks of our feather beds, and by passing these around we kept the packs from slipping forward or back, but with all these they were hard to keep in place.

One ox was set apart to carry two small kegs of water, so we could have a small supply when we had to make dry camps. Two more oxen were chosen for Mrs. Bennett and Mrs. Arcane to ride upon when they could. This took four oxen and seven were left out of the original sixteen. Five had been eaten. Our little mule was set apart to carry the most valuable of our property, our little bit of flour and a few beans. She could be trusted, would not run away nor throw off her pack and was well tried. She would follow on like a dog and would nip every spear of grass that showed along the trail or very near it. She needed no care or attention and was really as moral in her conduct as any one could be in a country where a man's morals are sometimes left as far east as the Missouri river. Our animals were now selected and their work determined.

Bennett and Rogers had returned with salt enough for our use. They said it was no trouble to get any amount, for there was a windrow of it clear around the lake made by the small waves on the shore.

We now talked over the route we should take. We told them about the bad place at the falls, and doubted if we could get the oxen over alive. Farther south the country looked black and barren, dry and unsafe for us to try to seek another pass in that direction. To go north and cross where those crossed who burned their wagons was to go 50 miles due north, then cross the mountains, and come 50 miles back again, to take us to the place only 30 miles from our present camp after traveling 130 miles.

After considering all the ways, Bennett and Arcane concluded to take the route Rogers and I had returned upon, and take the risk of getting the cattle over the falls alive in some way. It was now agreed that we had better make a start and see how things would work. We first loaded the mule; then all the oxen but three, the one for the children and the two for the women to ride, but as they must ride without saddles, it looked like a tiresome job. We had intended the three horses for them to ride, but these were lost, and though it seemed to me we could hardly get along without them, we must make the experiment even if it had to be abandoned afterward. We got the oxen loaded with small packs, loaded the children in their pockets on "Old Crump," and Mr. Arcane was to lead him with a cloth halter made out of some of our strips from the wagon covers, and take the entire charge of this part of our transportation.

Our cattle were very poor and thin, but had rested a month and seemed as gentle as ever. When the two women were mounted Rogers and I took the eight cattle and the mule and started on, taking the wagon road going south. The road was soft and sandy, and the feet of the oxen had much improved by their long rest, and we went along all right for a few miles on level ground, the oxen seeming to be as glad as we were that they were at last going somewhere. The women and children were behind, and the women seemed to be considerably exercised in holding on and bracing against the awkward motions of the ox, for they were clinging to the bands with a desperate grip and were on the point of giving up riding as a bad job and trying their own feet instead, when one of the oxen ahead happened to see his pack and got scared at it, and commenced to bawl and jump stiff legged, and soon had his pack under him and torn off entirely.

The other oxen stood and stared at this one a moment and then began to do likewise, even the ones the women were on, and when Rogers and I looked back to see what was going on, Mrs. Arcane's ox was jumping around his best and trying to throw Mrs. Arcane off. Now Mrs. Arcane, when she started off, had many fine things she hated to leave and had put on lots of her Chicago "best millinery," as it had little weight.[87] Among the finery was a lot of high colored ribbons, and many things hung loose. She did her best to hang on to her horned steed, which we had named "Old Brigham,"[88] and as he ran the ribbons stood straight out behind, and she hung on like a good rider for awhile, but finally was unoxed and came off, luckily not hurt at all. Mrs. Bennett was also thrown, but not hurt. When we turned to look back, Bennett was standing still in such a state of laughter he could not move, as he saw Mrs. Arcane taking her flying ride with streaming Chicago ribbons and

87. One of the "many fine things" Abigail Arcan took with her was a linen tablecloth she had woven. She wrapped it about her waist hoping to save it from loss or destruction. It is the only known article from their two wagon loads to survive the trip. The cloth was exhibited in Death Valley in 1942, and again in 1949, at the California Centennial Gold Rush Celebration. The tablecloth is "71 inches wide and 72 inches long. It was cut from a bolt of cloth [that Abigail wove] and the ends have hand sewn hems, with stitches that are unbelievably fine. It is of the delicate Dicer pattern with half-inch squares of slightly contrasting color" (Kevil in Johnson 1981:19).

88. Mr. Arcan purchased this ox in Salt Lake City and named him "in honor of the great Mormon Saint" (Manly 1894:209). It was a common practice among the emigrants to name their oxen after the leaders and elders of the Mormon Church. This practice was one of several that helped kindle the malevolence leading to the Mountain Meadow Massacre in 1857 (Brooks 1962:46).

fancy fixens in best circus style. Arcane stood holding on to "Old Crump," but the big children jumped off and Mrs. Bennett snatched the little ones out of the pockets for fear he would get frisky also, and she followed on, carrying the youngest, the perspiration running down her face, and soon compelled to stop and rest. After this performance we concluded we had better go in camp and repair damages.

We had to go back four or five miles for water, but we let the frisky oxen go without, mended our broken harness, gathered the things together, fixed and mended up while Bennett and Rogers took a shovel and went about a mile and covered the body of Capt. Culverwell with sand.[89]

"Old Crump" proved to be a good old christian ox, never offered to stampede as the others did, but stood quietly by Mr. Arcane's side and gazed at the others with surprise to see them spend their strength so foolishly. Our little mule was well behaved and stood through all the rumpus with perfect unconcern.

Bennett said he saw no other way than to make the nearest route to the falls, where we lost the horses, for we might find no other or better way, and as we now had new rawhide moccasins, all of us, we were well prepared to take a nearer route to the summit, even if it were rough and rocky, and it might be as well for us as to try to follow our wagon road. We thought best to take the shovel along, for it might be of use to us in preparing a way around the falls.

We started again early in the morning, the women on foot this time, as they had already had enough of riding oxen and were afraid to try it again. Arcane led the ox with the children, and while they worked slowly up the rough and rocky road, we took the others and crowded them on as best we could. Their feet soon got tender, and they did not seem so much inclined to buck off their loads as they

89. In 1861, Hugh McCormack found what may have been Captain Culverwell's grave. Spears (1892:22) recorded that McCormack "discovered a spring, known as McCormack's Wells on some of the maps of California, and near where Mesquite Well is now. At the lower end of the valley he found the skeleton of a woman, with part of an old calico dress wrapped about it. It had been buried in a shallow grave, but the wind had uncovered it." According to Hanks (1883:35), "At Mesquite Springs [Hugh McCormack] saw the shallow grave of a person supposed to be one of the emigrants, probably a woman, as a portion of a calico dress was found with the bones, left exposed by the drifting of the desert sands." Mesquite Well is labeled on old maps (e.g., USGS Furnace Creek, Calif.–Nev., 60 min., 1910, reprinted 1920) and was an important watering stop for

the 20-mule borax teams. It is 230 feet south of benchmark −246, 7.5 miles south of Bennetts Well, where bailing wire and tin cans still mark the old camp's location.

We calculate Culverwell's grave is east of the present road 5 or 6 miles south of Bennetts Well. McCormack's "At" may refer to the general area rather than specifically at the well. Material from a calico dress belonging to Mrs. Bennett or Mrs. Arcan or a few yards of calico cloth may have been used as his shroud or winding sheet, since wrapping bodies in cloth or blankets was a common practice for those who died on the trail (Evans 1945:127).

Their choice to go back 4 or 5 miles to get water at Bennetts Well rather than proceed south 2 or 3 miles to the sulphur water hole was based on the better quality and more plentiful water at the well.

The Bennett-Arcan party crossing the desert. When Manly drew this picture for *Death Valley in '49,* he said: "The sketches in my book are only to
show the reader how we worked our way from *purgatory to heaven.*"
Although it was originally titled "Leaving Death Valley," the picture de-
picts a scene later in their exodus. The women's skirts are tattered, Arcan
has thrown away his gun, the flora is typical of the Mojave Desert, and
there are no longer eleven oxen. The procession is lead by the one-eyed
mule followed by Lewis Manly, Cuff the dog, Asabel Bennett, big John
Rogers, John Arcan leading Old Crump the ox with Martha and Charlie in
the pockets and Melissa and George on his back, followed by Sarah
Bennett and Abigail Arcan (from *Death Valley in '49*).

did the day before. Arcane's gun was troublesome and he threw it
away. They had much trouble with the children, who complained
pitifully of being tired and hungry in their cramped position, and
much stopping and fixing was required for their comfort, and their
progress was slow. We hurried our cattle to a camping place, and
one watched them while two others took water and went back to
meet the ones behind.[90]

90. A definitive conclusion as to the exact
route the families used is not possible with the evidence at hand. But after studying the alternatives, we
decided the families exited via the main fork of Galena Canyon. We've identified four plausible routes
from this camp to Ox-Jump Fall in Redlands Canyon:
(1) up the south fork of Six Spring Canyon (a difficult
if not impossible route with oxen); (2) up the main
fork of Galena Canyon (our choice); (3) up the unnamed canyon just south of Queen of Sheba Mine
(Carbonate Canyon) and over its pass into Warm
Spring Canyon; and (4) a direct course up the alluvial
fan from Salt Well to the mouth of Warm Spring
Canyon (the way the boys went on January 15). The
first three routes are more direct than the fourth, and
they fit Bennett's "nearest route to the falls" statement.

Before making our decision as to which route

Our oxen were all lightly loaded except "Old Crump" with the children, and not one of us had the second garment to put on. The women came into camp somewhat late and almost dead from fatigue. Supper was ready, but they laid down and rested some time before they could be coaxed to eat. It looked as if they were not going to endure the trip, for we had to make fixed marches from camp to camp, and not less than twenty days of travel before us to take us through. They seemed much discouraged and could not believe they could endure twenty more such days as the last.

Mrs. Bennett said, "If the boys did not know all about the road I could never stand it." The camp here was at some small water holes [Arrastre Spring] where enough water could be got by patiently waiting for the holes to fill up, and is the same place where Rogers and I slept the first night when we set out for the settlements. We were now high on the mountain near what seemed to be a low pass, but it was not.

When morning came the women were somewhat rested and felt much better, but still looked as bad as if they had been on a big spree for a week. I now took Bennett and Arcane around the mountain, perhaps a quarter of a mile to the summit, and showed them the mountains they had talked about and looked for so anxiously for the last two or three months—the great Sierra Nevada.[91] They were

they took, we hiked each of these routes three times plus an oblique route from the valley floor, 1 mile south of Gravel Well, to the mouth of Galena Canyon. (The oblique route was some of the roughest country we have ever crossed in Death Valley.) This "nearest route" was tortuously difficult, and Manly pointedly credits Bennett with the decision to go this way. We feel Manly was not in favor of it, and may have recommended the longer but easier route up the Pleistocene fan to Warm Spring Canyon (route 4 above). They did not take the narrow "westerly fork" of Galena Canyon as Koenig suggests (1984:172). It is obviously a rougher canyon and also leads to a 4,940-foot pass, whereas the main fork ends on a pass we call "Galena Gap" at 3,720 feet.

The families could not have covered in one day the nearly 16 miles plus the vertical rise of 5,790 feet from the valley floor to Arrastre Spring, especially with "much stopping and fixing." We have done time-distance tests on the routes to see if it was possible and conclude they stopped for the night somewhere in Galena Canyon (camp 2, map 7). Manly appears to have left out this camp in both his accounts, although he later said (1894:214) their "camp was at a narrow pass in the range," and they hurried the oxen "so that we could reach the water." If someone had scouted the canyon while Manly and Rogers were gone, they would have found the spring the Park Service calls "Talc Mine Spring" (not shown on USGS quadrangle maps) just 50 yards south of the

main canyon at 2,680 feet elevation or the spring in the mesquite grove higher up the main canyon. Manly, or his writing assistant, mixed the descriptions of the Galena camp with the one at Arrastre Spring so they seem to be synonymous.

91. The "quarter of a mile" (1,320 feet) to the summit may refer to vertical rise, not horizontal distance. Mountaineers commonly use this terminology to document distances to passes or summits of peaks. The vertical rise from Arrastre Spring to Manly Lookout is 1,938 feet. We have hiked the 4-mile round trip to the Lookout in three hours at a leisurely pace and judge the men could have done it in considerably less time. The "quarter of a mile to the summit" was changed to "three or four hundred yards away" in Manly's book (1894:215), a rewording, possibly by Manly's writing assistant, that changed his meaning. An alternative explanation is that when Manly (1894:215) said, "the best point of view was near our camp, perhaps three or four hundred yards away," he may have been referring to the camp where he and Rogers slept above Arrastre Spring the first night on their trip for supplies. In the 1888 (April) account he said, "we built a fire and ate our supper of dried meat [at Arrastre Spring]. When it got dark we traveled on [toward the summit] some ways further. . . . Here we lay down." Thus, the vantage point to which he took Bennett and Arcan could be a quarter-mile beyond Manly and Rogers's first camp.

astonished at the sight and gazed with wonder, as they were ten times larger than they imagined. They thought it must be 100 miles from east to west over these mountains, and they were covered with untold depths of snow, and there were many peaks that seemed to reach the sky. After they had gazed a long time in wonderment they looked behind them and could look a hundred miles east over the country they had crossed, but the valley they had just left behind seemed but a little way across and away down in the ground. We stood here and talked a few minutes, and Bennett took off his hat, and Arcane and I did the same and said, "Goodbye Death Valley," and that locality has ever since borne the name.[92]

We went back to camp and soon packed up, but everything went hard and proved slow work, like an old, worn out, ungreased wagon, and our road was now down a steep grade [Redlands Canyon] and we were able to make camp at the falls before night.[93]

Here was the troublesome place we had looked for, and how to get over it and not kill the mule and cattle was the question of vital importance to us. We had water here and a little willow patch and some grass. The rocks on the north side hung over, more than perpendicular and seemed to be sky high, while those on the south side sloped back a little, but the gorge was so steep and narrow the sun never shone down into its depths, and the grass was weak and scattering. And now we set to work to pass the falls.

[October 1888; Volume V, Number VIII, page 126]

The first step in the preparation to pass this formidable obstacle to our progress was for us to go below the falls and move all the rocks away from the area directly below. Of course there was no water flowing over these falls to make a cataract, but the channel and the rocks told of plenty of water at certain times. Having moved away all the rocks we could, we shoveled up in their place as huge a pile of sand as we could, with a view to make as soft a landing place as possible for our animals, which would have to be forced over the perpendicular fall [Ox-Jump Fall].

We now set to work to get all our things over, not forgetting the two water kegs, as there were still two camps before us before we could get water. We got to work early, for we wanted to see how

92. One of the three men named Death Valley, not Mrs. Bennett, as is often written. The first place the name appeared in print was apparently in the Los Angeles *Star* on March 18, 1861 (Lingenfelter 1986:71); the same year Farley used the name on his map (redrawn in Long 1950:230). A map purportedly dated 1860 (in Preston 1974:20–21) named Death Valley "Dead-mans Valley," an apparent reference to Captain Culverwell, the only member of the 1849 emigrants to die in the valley. This map must be incorrectly dated in Preston's book because "McCormacks Spr" appears on the map, and Hugh McCormack did not visit Death Valley until 1861.

93. The trail from Arrastre Spring to Redlands Canyon is still traceable; however, it is used now only by wild burros. It contours southward, "along the foot of the high peak" (Manly 1894:219), passes north of Striped Butte, and curves west into the canyon. They camped at Redlands Spring 150 yards above Ox-Jump Fall (camp 4, map 3).

much stock we would lose, and what sort of condition we would be in when we got over this troublesome place.

We now gathered our ropes together and fastened a good strong one to an ox's head; one went below to be prepared to pull at the proper time, while the rest of us stayed above to keep him straight and in a good position to give him a final push over the fall. There was a sort of steep slope for a little way, and then an abrupt fall of ten feet or more, and we wanted to look out so he would not strike on his head and break his neck. When all was ready one gave the signal, and with a pull and a push away the old fellow went and landed all right on the sand pile, somewhat bruised and shaken up but able to get up and walk off, indeed much better than we expected. After this one came the rest and the little mule, with pretty good luck for all.

The animals and packs over, the next anxiety was for the women and children and in this my memory is refreshed by a conversation with Mrs. Arcane, who still lives in Santa Cruz. It

Ezra Hornibrook and Dick Bush inspect Ox-Jump Fall in Redlands Canyon, Panamint Range. Rubble at the base of the fall was blasted from the walls to make a ramp. Manly said: "an abrupt fall of ten feet of more. . . . with a pull and a push away the old fellow [ox] went and landed all right."

seemed the best way for them to try to pass along the little ledge, a trail which we used when we brought the mule up, and this proved very difficult. They went gradually along, their feet on a projection of only a few inches, clinging on with their hands to any little roughness in the rocks that gave a chance to cling to, keeping their backs to the falls, and with strict injunctions not to look down, lest they become dizzy and fall to the bottom of the canyon, which would surely kill them.

Bennett and Arcane each took his wife next to him, and they slowly climbed and hitched along the side of the rough, steep, rocky cliff, looking only for a place to put their fingers, and feeling out the narrow path for their feet, afraid to tremble lest they lose their hold. But they were brave and came through all right. And now the children; one at a time they were tied to the end of a rope and lowered away to their anxious mothers, who clasped them to their hearts with love and thankfulness.

We loaded up and got in marching order as soon as possible and moved on slowly down the canyon. We noticed the bodies of the two horses we were obliged to leave when we came up; they had been dead some time, but their bodies had not been disturbed by beast or bird, and showed no signs of decay.[94] We passed the south end of a narrow valley [Panamint Valley], and a little farther north we could see a large salt lake. The range before us which we must cross looked black, rocky and barren, without vegetation or water; but on we passed and were pretty well toward the summit by night. The women complained bitterly of the hard, rocky road, and we had many fears that their strength might fail them. This night's camp [upper Fish Canyon, Slate Range] was a cheerless one—no feed for our animals; no water except what we carried with us. We tied the mule to a big rock, and the cattle lay down where they were and never moved till morning. Their moccasins, which we had prepared to protect their feet, were getting worn and their feet tender.[95]

In the morning when we had moved up the ravine nearer the summit, we passed the dead body of Mr. Fish, only slightly covered with a few little sage brush, and probably his bones remain today unburied.[96] We had still two short drives to make, and one dry

94. We conclude the Indians were not following Manly and Rogers during this portion of the trip because the horses were not butchered and eaten. Since Indians in this area often suffered from food shortages during the winter months (Steward 1938), the two abandoned horses would have been a welcome addition to their larder.

95. This camp (camp 5, maps 4 & 7) in Fish Canyon was at Brier's "Silent Sepulcre," a short box

canyon 1 mile northeast of Manly Pass, where the Brier mess and later Manly and Rogers had camped about a month earlier (Manly 1894:155).

96. On Manly's return to the Death Valley area in 1860, he noted "Mr. Fish's bones scattered around among the rocks" (in Woodward 1949b:69). We searched several times for some vestige (e.g., teeth, a belt buckle) of his exposed grave but found nothing.

camp [lower Isham Canyon] before we could reach any water. Each man and woman carried some sort of a canteen for water, some regular ones, and some made out of a couple of powder cans tied together and covered with cloth. It was now thought best for Bennett, Rogers and I to push on with the oxen as fast as we could, and get to the next camping place, put over a kettle of meat for soup and have it cooking, make the beds and have everything ready when "Old Crump" and the children should come along. The women did not improve in walking and complained bitterly; the children, cramped up in their pockets, were tired and hungry and dry.

As soon as we got to the camping place, Bennett filled his two canteens and hurried back to assist the weak ones, finding them out of water and crying for it, and the demand seemed more and more urgent to hurry on to where we could get water, with as little delay as possible.[97]

We started early the next morning, and just after we reached the level sandy valley on the other side, we passed Mr. Isham's body, scarcely covered in a little pile of sand their comrades had scraped together with their bare hands, for they had no shovel. It was now only a few miles to our next camp where there was water—a small weak stream, but very good, that came from the rocky cliffs [Providence Spring]—but there was no feed for the cattle, except now and then a bunch of sage. We're in hopes to find here the little bag of wheat we had buried on our return from the south, and which contained 30 or 40 pounds.

As we were now in the trail of those who had gone before, our road was not so bad, though it was soft and sandy. Our meat was all gone and at the next stopping place we would have to kill one of the oxen, but we felt that we were now fairly on our way, and were in a much better position than those who had preceded us, for we well knew every camp we had to make, and every water hole on the whole route, so we could make calculations for our march, and besides this, we had something of a trail to follow, which was an advantage, as we no longer had to look out a route, hunt for water and feed, and then make the first track over a rough and rocky road as we had done for some time in the past, when our oxen would only creep along, picking out the way so as to favor their sore feet.

97. This account, with which we agree, mentions two camps in the Slate Range—the book mentions one (Manly 1894:222). We conclude this second camp was on the west side of the range at the dogleg bend of Isham Canyon where the middle branch joins it (camps 5 & 6, maps 4 & 7). The distance between the "Silent Sepulcre" and this camp is just over 2 miles. Factors contributing to this short drive were the arduous descent of the Panamint Range the day before, the difficult terrain in the Slate Range, and the jaded condition of oxen and humans. Mrs. Arcan was five months pregnant, which may also have been a contributing factor.

Providence Spring, Argus Range. Fred Camphausen and LeRoy Johnson sample water from the stream in Indian Joe Canyon. Manly said it was "a small weak stream, but very good, that came from the rocky cliffs."

We of the advance reached the camping place about noon, and two of us hurried back with water to meet the women and children, for we well knew their little canteens were empty, and the day was very warm.[98] We knew they must be nearly choked, and might do as the man, Isham, did, sit down to rest, as we were told, while his companions hurried on to find water, and though they went back to his relief as fast as ever they could, they found him too far gone to swallow, and he soon breathed his last. His burial was without

98. The hike across Searles Valley to their camp at Indian Joe Spring was strenuous because firm footing is hard to find in the loose sand. The women collapsed when they arrived at camp and questioned their ability to "endure . . . another five day's work like the last" (Manly 1894:226). Actually, they had been on the road seven days from Bennetts Well. We agree with the camps chronicled in this account rather than the book. They are: camp 1—dry camp 4 or 5 miles south of Bennetts Well (map 7); camp 2—Galena Canyon, Panamint Range; camp 3—Arrastre Spring, Panamint Range; camp 4—Redlands Spring in Redlands Canyon, Panamint Range (maps 3 & 7); camp 5—"Silent Sepulcre" in Fish Canyon, Slate Range; camp 6—lower Isham Canyon, Slate Range (maps 4 & 7); and camp 7—Indian Joe (Providence) Spring, Argus Range (maps 5 & 7).

ceremony, and their hands the only tools to make the shallow grave. When we met our party the children were crying loud for water, and the silent ones were just as dry. Even Old Crump kept his mouth shut and grated his teeth.

We had water enough to slake the thirst of the human beings, but the poor old ox, who seemed almost human in his faithfulness, for he had done his part better than any of us, human or otherwise, as he bore his load of four children safe thus far, had to go without. We have often praised this good old beast and speak highly of his good sense and amiable disposition, sensible ways and almost reasoning intelligence. And he deserved all the praise we, or any one, could give him, and we thought of how calm he stood and gazed in amazement at his companions when they showed their lack of good sense in tearing off their packs and wasting their strength in a foolish stampede. We praised and petted the old fellow as if he could understand, and wished we had a bountiful supply of water and fresh grass for the good old Christian.[99]

We were not so very long in bringing all to camp, and then we killed an ox as soon as we could and got the meat over the fire drying, while we caught and cooked the blood, but it made a dry and tasteless dish. We used the hide to make new moccasins for the cattle and ourselves, and broke up the bones for soup. The marrow in these bones did not seem much like the firm and healthy marrow of a well fed ox, but was thin and could be poured out from them, and looked streaked and discolored, more like corruption than healthy material. We dug up our little bag of wheat which was undisturbed, but attracted moisture to itself even from the dry sand, and had swelled a great deal, but not so much as to injure it. We boiled some for the children and put a little in our soup, and it made a good and strengthening meal for all of us.

The women when they reached camp lay down at once, for their work in walking was almost more than they could endure, and when they got up toward night to eat they looked bad enough and could hardly stand upon their sore feet and tired limbs. They would say every night that they would not try to worry through, and would stop and die right here but for the faith they had in Rogers and myself who knew the road, and speaking so confidently of it gave them courage to make another effort. We men were convinced and fully understood that we must hurry on with all the diligence at

99. About 1856, Manly (1894:472) found Old Crump "near French Camp on the east side of the San Joaquin Valley. . . . He was now fat and sleek and as kind and gentle as when so poor upon the terrible journey. I got off my horse and went up to him, and patted my old friend. I was glad to find him so contented and happy." Old Crump's new owner would not allow him to be worked—a just reward for his faithful duty during the escape from the cursed hole.

our command to save our oxen, and every bit must be saved and used, even if we suffered with hunger ourselves. When we left camp the whole carcass was used up except the meat we had dried and packed along. We knew that when we got through that an ox or two would be a good thing to have, for there was not a cent of money left and we would be perfectly destitute, in a strange land and among strangers, 500 miles from the mines, which seemed our only hope. We could not talk Spanish with the Spaniards who occupied the country ahead of us. These were some of the topics that forced themselves into our thoughts and conversation in camp. We might be delayed; the Indians could easily capture Old Crump and his load, for he was always behind all the rest, and no one with them had anything to protect themselves with. As yet we had seen no Indian signs and did not think there was much danger.

Morning came, and when we got the cattle together Arcane's

LeRoy Johnson and Dick Bush follow the Bennett-Arcan trail near dry Sweetwater Creek, Argus Range. Manly said: "We passed down the western slope, and in a broad, shallow, sage brush, valley-shaped place we made our dry camp, and could see ahead of us our road as far as we could travel in the next two weeks." (Official U.S. Navy Photograph.)

old ox, Brigham, was missing. We started on, following his track, expecting the Indians had stolen him, but when we found no track of anything but the ox, we felt relieved, and soon overtook him and brought him back and loaded up again. One ox carried the full water kegs, our canteens were all full, and we took a parting drink of as much as we could hold, for we knew that a four day's march was ahead of us, and no water except a small hole of quite salt water, no grass except salt grass that the cattle would eat, for they always chose sage brush when no other grass could easily be found.

We had now a long canyon [east Wilson Canyon] to go up to cross this our last range, and another one the other side, and we worried up to the summit, where we were in full view of the wonderful snow-capped Sierra Nevada, the father of all the mountains we had ever seen. We passed down the western slope, and in a broad, shallow, sage brush, valley-shaped place we made our dry camp, and could see ahead of us our road as far as we could travel in the next two weeks, it seemed.[100] To the north there seemed to be everlasting snow fields, all mountains, and sky high, and so clear and steep and cold it seemed no man could live in them. These grand old mountains seemed to come to an end near here, and quite suddenly going south, widening out into a seeming level country compared with them, but it looked black, rocky and barren, and what mountains we could see seemed like low buttes, without fertility enough to support a living creature, and they extended as far south as we could see.

At these camps we rested our cattle, and that was about all we could do for them, except a little sage brush, and hurried on as fast as we could. As we passed down this canyon [Deadman Canyon] we passed the body of our beautiful white mare that died here on our way back from the south. She was as white as snow and very fat, and lay there just as we left her—not a hair disturbed by wild bird or animal. We made the foot of the mountain over a rough, rocky trail, and camped near sundown at the salt water hole, and not very far from the place where Rogers and I melted the thin skim of ice that had saved us a month before from choking to death. This was in plain sight of the unending fields of snow, but they were 30 miles away.

The water here [pond at Paxton Ranch, Indian Wells Valley] was almost too salt for good soup, but we used it. The cattle would not drink it at all.

100. They ascended the Argus Range via the east branch of Wilson Canyon and camped on the plateau near the junction of Moscow Canyon and Sweetwater Creek (camp 8, maps 5 & 7). Most likely they camped at the large pile of granite boulders near the dry wash. We have traversed this area 3 times; from the pass between east and west Wilson Canyons there is a magnificent panoramic view of the Sierra Nevada (cf. Koenig 1978:223).

Dick Bush and LeRoy Johnson at the saltwater pond, Paxton Ranch site, in Indian Wells Valley, with Owens Peak on the western horizon. Of this place Manly said: "The water here was almost too salt for good soup, but we used it. The cattle would not drink it at all."

We now had an ascending plain before us, 30 miles wide [Indian Wells Valley], and a dry camp to make again. The women seemed to get along better now they could see the country ahead of them, but they would have to hold out pretty well to make camp. They did not forget to complain, which they could hardly help, but they, as well as the cattle, were newly shod and in the very best walking condition it was possible to fix them. We did not permit them to do any camp duty, knowing they were not able, and it took them about all the time to straighten out the children's legs that were cramped up so badly by riding all day in a sack, in a position that would have crippled a grown person, not to say a poor half famished child.

We left the wheat for the women and children. For ourselves we cut our meat up small and made a kettle of soup every time we could get a chance, and our stock of meat soon ran out. As to nourishment, it was little better than basswood chips, and it took only two or three days to clean out our kitchen, which must be replenished, and only a poor ox to do it with. We filled our kegs with the brackish water, for it was all we could get to last us to our next camp, which will be 15 miles from water, and we had two days hard work before us, up grade all the way, to the base of the snow mountains [Sierra Nevada], which lie all to the right, or north, and to the south is a level desert plain for miles.[101]

When we got ready to start we agreed to take all the cattle and go ahead, and not stop until the camp was made, which was about one half the way across [Indian Wells Valley], and then return to assist Old Crump & Co., as they were usually a few miles behind the others. The women that night were late; the day was hot as summer, although it was February, and much water was required and called for by the little ones, and they drank freely and their thirst was only partially quenched. Old folks knew better than to drink much. We make our kettle of soup, but this time needed no salt in it, for the water was salt enough, but it had a disagreeable taste.

That night it was with great difficulty that the women reached camp at all, and as usual, went immediately to bed. We carried them and the two small children soup, and they remained in bed while they ate, not rising till morning, and then with the usual complaints, and they said that every step forward was at least one step nearer heaven, if not nearer to the settled land, but thought they might reach that if they could only hold out long enough.

We left the next morning very early so as to travel in the cool morning air before the sun got too high, and the air too hot for comfort. The camping place ahead of us now was the same one Rogers and I crept up to after dark, supposing it might be Indians, more than a month before, and found it to be E. Doty and his mess. We hurried to get to this place of quite good water in a hole that did not run [Indian Wells Spring], and besides a little sulphury.[102]

We were now entirely out of food and had to kill an ox and replenish all around. Our feet needed new protection as well as those of the oxen. We dried the meat, made soup of the bones, and a sort of pudding out of the blood.

101. Manly (1894:229) said, "From this camp to the next water holes at the base of the great snow mountain . . . was at least 30 miles." The "30 miles" is from Paxton Ranch (camp 9, maps 5 & 7) to Indian Wells Spring (camp 11, map 7) at the base of the Sierra Nevada. Reverend Brier (JA 70) remembered the distance as being 25 miles; it is actually 19 miles. We assume the dry camp was about halfway to Indian Wells Spring which would explain Manly's reference to the dry camp being 15 miles from the next water (camp 10, map 7). Although the valley is now part of the Naval Weapons Center, China Lake, it is almost as the pioneers first saw it.

102. Indian Wells Spring is at Homestead on Highway 395 (camp 11, map 7). The sulphur smell came from decaying organic matter in the spring. Although Manly's book (1894:230) said they "were now nine days from the wagons," it was the eleventh day. We feel the inaccurate day-counts in the book were insertions made by Manly's writing assistant, who did not reconcile the number of camps in this account with those in the book.

Arcane's little boy, Charley, now became quite troublesome and cried a great deal; indeed he soon broke out all over with a sort of rash like the measles, and was so uneasy that he could hardly be quieted.[103]

The women came into camp more worn out than ever, for they had to be helped along during the last of the journey, and on reaching camp fell down as if they had taken their last step, and went to bed at once, rousing up long enough to be fed a little soup, and sleeping then til morning. We all, indeed, were getting worn down in body as well as feet, but our road was growing shorter every day, and as all were sensible of this, it gave us more courage. The women sometimes said they believed the road was longer than we told them, and they never could endure this hardship long enough to see the west end of it, where themselves and children could once more get bread to eat.

They did not seem to be much refreshed by a night's rest, and got up slowly and with some difficulty, but by starting time had improved a little.

[November 1888; Volume V, Number IX, page 142]

From here we had to take all the water we could carry again for another dry camp out on the level plain, and at this place the wind came down raw and cold from the mountain snows, so that we had to gather brush and make a wind break around our bed, and tie our animals to bushes to keep them from running away, as there was no water or grass for them. We tied them close to camp and they seemed to enjoy our brush fire as well as we did ourselves.[104] We had a level road from here until nearly night, when we suddenly came to a canyon [Last Chance Canyon] which we started down, and when we got fairly at the bottom there was a weak running stream, but no grass, and but little sage or anything else that cattle could eat, and our cattle were getting terribly hungry for some good food, as well as ourselves, and looked as if they would not live much longer without it. This was the same place where Capt. Haynes and party were when they told Rogers and I that they could never endure much more, but would die on the desert. The women now felt like these men, but did not conclude to die on the desert, for this was the last one to cross, and that next night brought us out of the canyon with a 75 mile plain before us on our left. Here was a

103. Charlie's ailment appears to be an allergic reaction, probably caused either by the mineralized water he was forced to drink or by the close and prolonged association with Old Crump, the ox he was riding.

104. They probably filled their water kegs and canteens at Coyote Holes (about 1 mile southwest of Freeman Junction) then camped on the open plain 3 or 4 miles southeast of the spring (camp 12, map 7).

partly dry alkali lake, and on or near it was some grass and fresh water.[105]

Night came on; the stars were hidden by clouds, and for the first time in two months it began to rain. We tried to stack our guns and fix some sort of shelter, but the wind was too strong against us, and we had to stand the fury of the storm without. We were now almost out of meat again, and had to go without a fire, eat a cold, poor supper, and then lie down on the ground as close together as we could, so as to have as many blankets as possible to put over us; and to keep our guns dry we put them between us and covered up head and ears much like a lot of pigs. When we crawled out in the morning there was two inches of snow, everything wet, poor sage brush for a fire, and nothing to eat till an ox could be killed.

They all staid in bed until we had gathered brush and got a fire started, and in point of fact I remember very distinctly that the weather was very uncomfortable for all of us, with our bare feet and thin clothes.

We led one of the oxen up near the fire and shot him, and by the time he was fairly dead we had a piece of meat already on the fire and just a few minutes afterward took the women and children as good a piece of broiled steak as we were able, under the circumstances to procure, which they ate in bed. We cooked the blood into a sort of thick mush, with no addition but salt—a very poor dish.

The sun soon came up and with it the snow vanished, and as we had about 4 miles to go to reach the willow corral, we loaded up the wet and heavy things and they all but I marched ahead. I staid to watch the meat, and as soon as Rogers came back with the mule we had the whole ox cut up and loaded, hide and all, on the one little mule, for the ox was not very fat, and joined the rest at the willow corral [Desert Spring], which was a pretty good camp, with some wood and water, and a little grass for the stock.

We now went to work, all hands at drying meat and making raw hide moccasins, both for ourselves and the oxen, and by night we considered ourselves pretty well shod again, and our preparations made for an early start in the morning. We now had our last stretch of desert before us and if the women could only hold out for four or five days longer we could reach the mountains of the Coast Range, where water, wood and grass were plenty, which would be a great improvement on our last three months experience.

105. Camp was on a small playa in the low hills 2 miles southwest of the mouth of Last Chance Canyon (camp 14, maps 6 & 7). The old trail from the canyon to Desert Spring is still visible here. Manly (1894:235) later described the camp's location as "at the mouth of the cañon . . . on an elevated plain, with a lake near by [Koehn Dry Lake]." They found enough water on the playa for cooking and drinking. On January 23, 1973, we also found potable water here.

The women seemed glad to know that our bad road was getting shorter, and they seemed to feel much better for the day's rest, but poor little Charley Arcane broke out with a rash all over his body, like the measles in appearance, and when taken out of his pocket on the ox he cried by the hour, but we had no way to help him and he lay on a blanket and seemed to suffer terribly.

As our next camp would be a dry one we loaded up the ox with water early in the morning, and with a new start on a bright sunny day, we continued our pilgrimage. As we passed along we passed the bones of numerous horses that lay bleaching on the ground, some of which seemed as if they might have laid there for the last hundred years, and others that were left there, perhaps, a year ago. This was the most pleasant day's walk we had experienced since we left Death Valley.

There seemed to be a slight rise in our trail across this big plain, and though our path seemed somewhat crooked, it seemed best to follow it, for the soil was light and floury on either side and had blown away a great deal, leaving the trail like a narrow hardened ridge, and on the sides so soft as to let the cattle down six inches at every step, making it very hard walking for them or us in any other place.

Our night camp was in the midst of this genuine desert, and as we had traveled up a gentle ascent all day we could see off in the northwest a large dry lake, and still farther north, our unmeasurable snow mountain, covered with everlasting winter, yet no water seemed to come out of it on the south side. It seemed as if, in the early days of creation, some ponderous giant had set his heavy feet down very hard upon this end of the mountains and flattened them out into this desert plain. We could see backward nearly to the place where we worked the mule over the falls, and to the south the plain seemed to go down into a misty distance, that required but little imagination to picture as the very infernal regions themselves.

We tied our animals to some little low bushes of brush and they staid there all night. The women were not as tired as the night before and their faces looked more cheerful [Mohave Desert near California City].

As soon as we could get ready in the morning we packed up, to march again over our desert road, and all day we traveled over that desolation, reaching at night the rain water holes which, fortunately for us, had been replenished by the recent rains, since we were there before. Our poor cattle seemed glad enough to get a drink after two days of fasting and thirsting, and looked pretty sorry, poor fellows, for they had fared hard.

We were now exactly south [southeast] of the dry lake and had to cross its outlet, which, instead of being a single channel, seemed to be divided up into a hundred little ones, only a few inches wide,

Rainwater on a small playa between Rosamond and Buckhorn dry lakes, Edwards Air Force Base. The families found "rain water holes which, fortunately . . . had been replenished by the recent rains."

which did not look as if water ran in them more than once a year, and between these channels were islands of small brush. The cabbage trees were plenty and a good many dry ones that made good firewood, and the cattle filled their stomachs, a little at least, with some poor grass and dry brush.

Before the women got to camp they were pretty well worn out again, and Charley cried continually. Bennett went back with water to meet them and helped the party, with Old Crump as a central figure, into camp [between Rosamond and Buckhorn dry lakes, Edwards AFB]. We tried to cheer them the best we could, telling them that if they could hold out another day we would reach the western shore of this great desert and be safe ever more.

We made an early start next morning, thinking if we started in good season and made a forced march, we could reach water again in a single day, but after going on awhile we came to a place where this soft and dust-like soil was wet and slippery, sticking to our feet and loading them down so heavily that we were soon very tired and the women soon gave clear out, for the moccasins were smooth and wet and the hardest sort of foot gear to walk in. In this predicament

we were forced to go into camp before we were half way over the
distance we expected to travel when we started out in the morning.
We had but little water, but stop we must, for the women could not
go another step, and this was the driest camp of all, for our canteens
held but a small amount for camp use. Our wheat and beans
had been gone a week or more. We chewed a little of our poor dried
beef to satisfy our hunger as best we could without water, and
slept.

The next night we reached the water holes in the foot-hills
[Barrel Springs] and breathed with much more freedom when we
knew we had at last left the horrible desert behind us. We were not
in so much of a hurry when that next morning came, but we went
about a quarter of a mile to the top of a hill and looked back over the
plains and mountains we had crossed and worried over so long; we
could see the high snow peak near where we left our wagons, and
with thankful hearts we said, "Goodbye to desolation."[106]

In this camp our cattle fared very well, as they found some
grass and water, and there was plenty of wood for our fires. The
next day we went on a little farther to the edge of the snow and here
we camped [near Soledad Pass] and melted snow for ourselves and
cattle, and here we killed an ox, hoping it would be the last it might
be necessary to kill. We now had only five oxen out of the eleven we
had when we left the wagons. This was the coldest place we had
found for a long time, and we gathered brush and built fires on the
ground to warm places for our beds, for we should have suffered
much without this precaution. This was something I had learned to
do, and had often done when traveling without blankets.

We made a blood pudding for supper, but this ox was no fatter
than the others, and the dish was not any improvement on the last.
By morning we had the meat well dried, and when we started our
train the load was light even if our animals were less, for we did not
now need to take any water with us, and doubling up the loads did
not make the burden very heavy. We were up in the morning early
so we could cross the snow before the sun softened it much, for if
we failed to get clear across we should have a cold camp again, and
the oxen might not stand such a night. The women seemed very

106. Barrel Springs (camp 19, map 7) "has
been a watering place for many years" (Johnson
1911:54). It fits Manly's description better than does
Una Lake, which we had earlier thought to be the
location of this camp (Johnson 1981:14). The vantage
point was the hill just north of Barrel Springs, 4 miles
southeast of Palmdale. From the hill, on a clear day,
the tip of Telescope Peak looms above the intervening
mountains. There is also a fine view of the Panamint
Range from the freeway viewpoint near Soledad
Pass and the hills north of Una Lake. Van Dorn (in
Woodward 1961:51), of the U.S. and California
boundary survey party, 1861, said of the Panamint
Range: "They were the first objects to attract our
attention on emerging from Lieut. Williamson's
[Soledad] Pass, on our journey from Los Angeles to
Fort Mohave, and shone, conspicuous in their garb of
white, against the eastern horizon, one hundred and
fifty miles away."

happy to get out of the desert, even if it was colder, and kept up better than at any time before.

Just before we got out of the snow some old tracks crossed our trail, but we did not know what made them. We kept on down to the little brook where Rogers and I tried the experiment of "eating crow," and made camp.[107] I took my gun and mule and went back to the tracks and followed them; they went out of the snow pretty soon and into a bushy place for a mile or two and then went down a steep short hill into the creek bottom. I stood here and watched awhile, and finally saw some animal, some ways off, looking through the top of the trees that grew in the creek bottom. I now led the mule down a side ravine into the creek and tied her and then followed the creek along till I came to a little half-acre meadow, where I crawled up the bank, and there saw before me three head of cattle, a cow and two yearlings. I killed the cow the first shot, and the others did not seem to know where the report came from and stood still while I loaded again. I saw one's face between two trees, and killed it in its tracks. I thought now I had enough but if they were any of them poor I wanted a choice, and as the third stood just a little too long waiting for the others to move, I took aim and killed that one also. When I went to them I found I had done a good thing, for the last one I killed was the only fat one. I now went for my mule and brought him over on the grass, then skinned out the hind quarters and took all the fat, for I was particular to take that to camp, for with all our slaughtering we had not seen a particle of tallow for months.

I now concluded I was on the same creek the camp was on, but the creek bottom, as well as the hills, was terribly brushy, but it seemed the best way for me to follow down the stream. I put the two hind quarters on the mule and started, and soon the brush became so thick I had to go in the bed of the creek itself, which was full of big boulders, on which I often fell and got wet all over. It now came on dark; thick clouds came over the mountain and it looked like rain. I found a little open spot and thought I would stay all night, but I was so wet I could not make a fire, and I started on again and worked down through the brush for three hours or more, and it seemed to me there would never be an end of that field of brush. Some way in the darkness I got one side of the bottom and there seemed to be a second bench, and I concluded I would try to get on

107. Thousand Trails recreation park, 2 miles south of Acton, is now located on this campsite (camp 21, map 7). The florid description in Manly's book (1894:247) is picturesque, but not typical of his writing. We think this embellished description was written by his writing assistant: "The blessed water! There it danced and jumped over the rocks singing the merriest song one ever heard, as it said—Drink, drink ye thirsty ones your fill—the happiest sweetest music to the poor starved, thirsty souls, wasted down almost to haggard skeletons."

top of that. So I started up along the side hill which was rather steep, and when we got nearly to the top the mule slipped and went back down to the foot again, a distance of 50 yards. I went down and got him and tied the load over better, and at the next trial we gained the top, and soon got in a kind of trail where we could go much better.

We had not gone far on this trail when the mule, which was ahead of me, stopped suddenly, and when I had crowded past her in the brush to see what the matter was, behold there was our old camp dog who had come to meet us. I was glad to see him and after he had sniffed at our load a little he started on toward camp and we followed. We were not so very long in getting there, and when we walked up to the fire they were all asleep and did not hear us till I called out, and they were out of bed in a minute, for they did not have to dress to get up. I took the load off the mule and went immediately to cutting meat and throwing it on the fire to roast, and would hold up pieces and say, "Look at the fat."

I now lay down, for it was nearly morning, and the others roasted and ate meat till after sunrise, and it was a rare treat, for we had seen no nice fat meat since we began killing our own cattle. Each one cooked for himself and ate till he was satisfied.

When I awoke the sun shone brightly and the wet clothes I had taken off and hung by the fire were dry, a nice breakfast of roasted meat all cooked and ready for me, and you may be sure I ate it with a relish, for I had gone through a hard night's work, and supperless at that. This was truly a heavenly situation compared with our position two weeks ago, for now we could feed and water both ourselves and stock any time we liked, and we felt we could go more slowly and not have the women and children get so very tired, and look so sorry and worn out as they did in the days when we were struggling with the terrors of the desert that nearly overcame us.

We were ready to move on again at ten o'clock and missed the mule's saddle blanket which I went back to seek and found it where the mule slipped down the hill. I overtook them about noon as they had camped, for Mrs. Bennett had been taken sick with violent vomiting, probably on account of eating too much fresh fat meat, after partial starvation in eating the poorly nourished beef our poor oxen had furnished. She was able to go on next day, however, and our trail led down the brushy canyon. Some one had passed through it with oxen since Rogers and I first went through it on foot, and they had broken down the brush so much that it was much easier traveling now than then.

At night Mr. Arcane said, "I wonder if these boys won't surprise us by getting to the Spanish house sooner than we expect to." I told him to wait a few days and see if we told the truth about it. This was the camp where I was taken lame on our first trip out, but I did not get lame this time, and they all said this lameness was what saved them, for if I had been well I might have gone on west and found no assistance, and thus not be able to get back in time to save a single one from starving to death, for we were convinced they never could have got out without help, so that we were really getting the benefit of a fortunate misfortune.

Here we could see tracks of bear and deer and we could soon supply our table, for Bennett and I were both good hunters, and we felt sure we could kill something if we tried. We kept working on down through the brush, and on this last day had to cross the creek perhaps twenty times, and pack the women over, and in places there was no other place to go but in the creek bed itself, wading through the water, and the women often fell over the rough stones and got completely wet all over which made them look like drowned rats or wet chickens, but for all this it was better than the rocky, sandy, dry trails of the desert, for when we got to camp [lower Soledad Canyon] we had plenty of wood and a good fire, and standing up near that, and turning round pretty often, somewhat after the manner of a roasting goose, we managed to get our clothes dry by bedtime.[108]

[December 1888; Volume V, Number X, page 158]

From this rough and brushy canyon we came suddenly out into a broad treeless bottom, and the stream sank below the surface in the porous sand, leaving no obstructions to our movements as we passed along. The next morning the dry creek bed had water in it again for an hour or two, when it all sank again. We thought there had probably been a shower near the summit which had sent the water down.

We were within seven or eight miles of the Spanish house, which we would reach before night. The creek bottom, which formed our road that day, was bare of vegetation except sage, and as we slowly wound along its course we led the party up on a small point which came up from the south and obstructed the view in that direction, and when we were fairly on the highest part the most beautiful natural picture a human being ever saw burst out before our eyes, and lay before us.

108. This was the last day of difficult travel, but two more days elapsed (one more camp) before they reached the adobe hacienda at the Rancho San Francisco. The next night they camped 7 or 8 miles short of the hacienda (camp 24, map 7). And on the last day, March 7, 1850, they climbed the ridge im- mediately east of the present town of Saugus, "tar- ried here perhaps two hours," and finally "reached our camping place . . . about a hundred yards from the house we have so long striven to reach" (Manly 1894:258 & 260).

There was a thousand-acre green meadow, speckled with cattle of all sizes and colors, some lying down and some standing to crop the rich green grass. What a contrast between this scene we now looked forward to, and the desolate Death Valley we looked back upon a few days before!

We stopped here to rest and let our cattle eat, and we looked at the beautiful landscape over and over again, and wondered what the vast waste we had passed over was made for, and we thought of what the man said at the place where the large wagon train was burned; "That this must be the place where all the dregs of creation were dumped, and everything bad since then, including Lot's wife."

This beautiful and charming picture was the same one Rogers and I had seen a month before, and it was even more pleasing now than then, and now as we sat and rested, one's thoughts went back over the whole journey and the happy homes we had left about a year ago, with plenty to eat and drink, and how many times since then strong doubts had come to us if we should ever see a fertile land again. But we had found it at last and we all agreed never to try another "cut-off." Now that we were out we would stay out and at least try to keep full stomachs hereafter.[109]

When we were all well rested we arranged our things once more, and, traveling on, we soon came to the foot of a hill near the house, where we camped under a large willow. Here we took the packs off the animals and let them have a good feed once more. The people at the house soon saw us and came down—the lady and her child—and, taking an orange from her pocket, asked us by sign-talk if we had given the others she had given us to the children. We made her understand that we had done as she had wished us to do, and she seemed much pleased.

This was now the 7th day of March, 1850, and we had been traveling twenty-two days since we left Death Valley.[110]

---

109. In 1860 (not 1862), Manly and Bennett did return to the Panamint mountains (in Woodward 1949b:61–72). With Caesar Twitchell they returned to rescue Charles Alvord, whom Bennett had abandoned there. Alvord stumbled into their camp at Redlands Spring, and the foursome decided to stay in the area and prospect. When their provisions ran low, Bennett and Twitchell returned to the coast for more. Manly and Alvord waited the agreed upon time, but their two partners never returned. Without food and mules, Manly and Alvord made a forced march out of Panamint Valley. Alvord was lame, and it was only with great fortitude that the pair reached Indian Wells Spring at the base of Owens Peak. Here they were rescued by Dr. George and party, who had been searching for the lost Gunsight Mine (George 1875 & in Ray 1966). In 1892, Manly learned from Twitchell that a snowstorm had blocked the passes. Twitchell and Bennett had been caught in the storm and nearly perished; thus, they could not return with the provisions.

110. We've determined the families made 24 overnight camps between Bennetts Well and the Rancho San Francisco; thus, they were on the road 25 days, but traveled 22 days after leaving Death Valley proper (i.e., from Arrastre Spring). Manly's various accounts (in Woodward 1949b:18, 52 & Manly 1894:266) give 17, 21, and 22 days of travel from Death Valley to the ranch house. However, at the very last of this chronicle he says 25 days. We have

These people looked curiously at us all, and seemed to realize how poor and destitute we were. They began to ask us questions as best they could, and we tried as hard to understand. They wanted to know how many days since we had left our wagons; if the Indians were bad, and how the road was. By studying over and committing to memory the little memorandum of Spanish words which I had made on our first visit to these people, we could talk a little, and as they seemed very anxious to know all about us, we told them the wagons could not be got out except in pieces, and at this they shook their heads.

We now made them understand that we were out of everything to eat, and that the man French who sent us to them for assistance, had said they would provide us with something to eat. They soon mounted their horses and rode away, and very soon came back again leading a two-year-old, which they threw near our camp and killed, and then made signs for us to help ourselves. We dressed it and took a quarter, and then they came and took the rest.

Arcane tried to talk to them in French, but did not succeed in making himself at all understood, but by signs and motions told them he was a Catholic, which seemed to please them, and they became more friendly.[111]

Near night they came down to camp again and made Bennett and Arcane and their wives and children go up to the house with them. They then went out and drove a lot of cattle into the corral, and then lassoed the calves and put them into a sort of side pen and kept them there all night. The families were kept at the house all night and furnished with a good supper of a kind of pancake and baked squash, with good meat and the best they had in the house. When they came down to camp in the morning they said the children had cried most of the night with a sort of colic or cholera morbus, being affected about the same as Rogers and I were when we ate our first corn meal as we came from off the desert.

The older Spaniards seemed to be religious people. Before retiring for the night they kneeled as if for prayers, which they seemed to say, and they remained in this position for an hour or more, which seemed strange to us, but, no doubt, they meant well by it.

In the morning the cows were lassoed, their hind legs tied, and

carefully analyzed the number and location of camps (appendix B) and conclude one camp was forgotten or not specifically mentioned—the second night's camp in Galena Canyon. We accept Manly's recollection in this account of two camps in the Slate Range because it best fits all the data and because of the great amount of time it would take to get animals through the rugged canyons in the Slate Range.

111. We (Johnson 1981) find no evidence that John Arcan was a Catholic. To the contrary, he was not buried in the Santa Cruz Catholic Cemetery, his children were not married in the Catholic Church, and his funeral was in the Methodist Church. He was active in the Santa Cruz Masonic Lodge, of which he was a charter member, and his gravestone in Evergreen Cemetery, Santa Cruz, California, bears the Masonic symbol.

in this condition they were milked. We all went out to see how dairy cows were handled in this new country, and their way of operating was all new to us, this lassoing business, and after the milking was done, they practiced some for our benefit with their rawhide ropes, catching an animal by either head or feet as they wished, and throwing down the rope on the ground and picking it up again without dismounting and on a keen run. This was as good as a show for us.

The calves and cows were now turned together, and let out to pasture again, to be driven in and the process repeated when they needed some milk for any purpose.

They put a little kind of a gourd shell dipper into the bucket of milk and told us to help ourselves, which we did, and it was a drink we poor half starved ones relished and probably the best nourishment we could have in our condition.

The Spanish lady, one time after this again, when she was in camp, showed an orange and seemed to want to know if we had carried the two [four] she had given us before clear through to the children, and when she was sure they had received them she said *"buenos muchachos"* (good boys) and expressed much pleasure that we had been so thoughtful in such a thing.

Arcane now tried our new friends to see if they might not be free masons, but none of his signs were recognized or answered, but with the help of Rogers and I, who seemed to be more ready with the sign language and a few words we had picked up, he made a bargain with them to take himself and wife and child to San Pedro, the nearest sea port, about 60 miles away, and they were to have his two oxen for pay.

The next morning they left on horseback, after many good wishes were given and taken. Before parting, Mr. Arcane gave me a small gold ring worth about $1.50 and to Rogers a silver watch worth a little more, and then they jointly gave me the little black mule that had served us so faithfully, this being all the compensation they could make us for our services.[112] They acknowledged that to us they owed their own lives and those of the family and that we would never be forgotten for the services we had done them, even at the risk of starving ourselves. They expected to get a passage by sea to San Francisco, and get along faster than they had been doing. Mrs. Arcane seemed to be an inexperienced rider, and as they started off we thought she might have the same unpleasant experience Rogers and I had on the same road a month before and would find walking quite as pleasant as riding, if, indeed, she were not as

112. Manly kept the one-eyed mule during the summer of 1850 while mining in the Mother Lode. Before returning east he sold the mule and his gun to Davenport Helms for twelve ounces of gold (Manly 1894:406 & 471).

unfortunate as when she tried to ride "Old Brigham" in Death Valley. All the capital which Arcane had now was his field glass, which he thought he might be able to trade off for a passage, and this and their blankets was all their baggage. We were all, indeed, in a poor and penniless situation.[113]

Our party was now broken up; our train was reduced to three oxen and the little black mule. These people we had met were as good friends and as kind as any I ever met, and had done nearly all without thought of pay. The lady, though dark skinned, had very pleasant features, indeed almost like my own mother, and she seemed so kind and benevolent that I really liked her.

About this time a lone man came to us and by signs wanted to know how many leagues it was back to the place where we left our wagons. We told him, by counting on our fingers, seventy-five leagues [about 225 miles], and that we had been twenty-two days in coming. He then inquired about the Indians; how they treated us, and from his manner, he seemed to fear them considerably. He then asked about the roads, and we told him as well as we could the "sleeps" without water, and the difficult road for horses; how we had lost all we took with us and that the wagons could not be got out except by taking them to pieces and packing them on animals at least a part of the way. At this he shook his head and seemed to give them up. Wagons such as we had were very highly prized by them and badly wanted, but when he heard of the perils of the trip he moved slowly away, thinking the wagons would be dear even if they could get them.

We now got our cattle up for a start, and these kind people gathered round us as we put our scanty supply of this world's goods on our poor, worn-out oxen, which, though much refreshed by food and rest, yet staggered as they walked, they were so poor, and we ourselves as poorly off in body, not so much as a single dollar amongst us all, not a piece of clothing except that which, patched and darned, badly worn and dusty, covered our own bodies, and upon our feet only the rawhide moccasins we had made in haste as we came along. We were in a strange country and could not talk common language, the journey to San Francisco would take us more than a month, and our only prospect for food such game as we could hunt and kill, or beg as we went along. Such an outlook was not very conducive to good courage or high spirits, and we seemed to be behind all the rest, for those who had turned back on Mt.

113. The Arcans obtained passage as far as Santa Cruz. Apparently Mrs. Arcan remained there—Julia was born July 1, 1850, in Santa Cruz (Johnson 1981) while Mr. Arcan went to the mines (in Woodward 1949b:28) and obtained enough gold to buy property. He built a combined home-gunsmith shop with a hall upstairs where the Masonic Lodge met; the Arcans remained in Santa Cruz the rest of their lives.

Misery and followed Hunt, the guide, must have been gone at least a month. We talked over the situations freely, and discussed various plans and decided to move on and do our best and trust to Providence for the result. So we bade our kind friends good bye, putting on as pleasant and agreeable faces as we could, for we wanted to make them know that we had been glad of their friendship, and with "adios, adios," many times repeated we parted as good friends, and, with our little train, started on, and by night we had reached the foot of San Fernando mountain, where we camped.

In the morning as we sat by the fire, a flock of quails came marching by, close to us—proud little fellows—the first flock we had seen. We kept very still while they stopped to look at us and we at them, and we never made a motion to shoot them, but enjoyed their graceful beauty and watched them as they went away on a run.

This mountain was not wide, but steep on both sides, and, although not rocky, it was still tiresome to cross. We reached the San Fernando Mission shortly after noon, when we stopped for a short time, and a man came out and gave the children each an orange, but we saw no one else, and as this one gave us no invitation either by word or sign to rest awhile, we kept on till nearly night, when we came to a stream and made our camp.

When we went on again our road was through grass-covered hills for some miles, and when we were nearly through we could see a large level plain expanding south and west, and no mountains in sight that way, and a little farther on we came in sight of the City of the Angels, and this, to us, was worth standing to look at for some time. We had never seen anything like it; houses all one story, made of mud, and with a flat roof covered with tar.[114] The streets seemed irregular and unimproved, and not a team or vehicle to be seen around. It seemed to us to be like a deserted city—it might be an Indian city.

As there was neither water nor wood here we could not well camp and explore to see what could be found. So we concluded to move down and see how we would be received. When we got to the first street we met a man who proved to be an American, and when we inquired for a suitable place to camp, he told us there were two men on the creek bottom and we could go down to their camp, to which he pointed the way, and we went on as soon as possible, for we were anxious to get into camp as soon as we could conveniently, for we were not dressed up very nice to be seen by city folks, and I

114. Tar for the roofs came from the tar pits on Rancho La Brea. Whitney (1865:175) said the "brea is used almost exclusively for covering roofs at Los Angeles." He said the tar sold for one dollar per barrel in 1861 if "the purchaser collected it himself." These pits are part of the Hancock Park Scientific Area near the heart of Los Angeles.

assure you our clothes were in a very sad state of repair. Mrs. Bennett's dress was badly worn off at the bottom and hung with ragged edges about as high as her knees, and besides this extreme and irregular fringed shortness, it was otherwise somewhat out of fix. Then we all had on rawhide moccasins that were made up in a terrible hurry while the hide was very raw indeed, and I expect we had more the aspect of digger Indians than of respectable white people. And then our train; one ox with three children in pockets made out of hickory shirts, and two others loaded down with odd traps and things, and a few better things on the little mule, made up a caravan that might look very strange to see today. We cast a few odd glances at the place and then ventured down the hill toward the river bottom, every one coming out of their houses to gaze at the curious looking company. They were all Spanish and talked pretty fast, but we could not understand very many of their words.

When we got in sight of the two camps, two men rose up from their seats and stood in wonder at the sight, as we moved on slowly, and when we got near their wagon, they rushed up to us and said, "Why this is Bennett; Is it really you?" Then they clasped hands and walked to camp in silence and in tears.

Bennett and his wife were taken into the tent, while Rogers and I, who were strangers to them, unpacked the animals under a big willow tree and sat down with the children. After a little they all came out and we were all introduced. It was R. G. Moody and H. C. Skinner, and they and Mr. Bennett had been traveling companions from the Missouri River to Salt Lake, and were old acquaintances.[115] They knew the route we had taken and were anxious to know what had become of us, and had staid in that camp six weeks to learn our fate, if possible. All the others who came with Hunt had gone up the coast toward the mines.

After a little while Mrs. Bennett came out of the tent with a clean dress on, hair combed and face washed, and I assure you she looked much more pleasant than she did before. We sat there in the shade and told our troubles and hard times, tears stopping the tale many times, but after a little rest the narration would go on again,

---

115. The reminiscences of Ransom G. Moody were published in 1877 (in Hafen and Hafen 1961: 108–116). His family and that of his brother-in-law, Henry C. Skinner, traveled together from Wisconsin to Salt Lake City. Skinner joined the Hunt train the same time the Bennett and Arcan families did; however, they continued with Hunt and arrived in California via the Old Spanish Trail. The Moody family left Salt Lake City about two weeks after the Hunt train left and followed it to Los Angeles. Skinner told Moody that "Louis Manly and R. Kane [John Rogers, not Arcan] had succeeded in reaching the settlements and after obtaining food and horses for the remainder of the train, which had been left in Death Valley, had nobly gone back to their rescue" (in Hafen and Hafen 1961:115). After waiting a month and a half in Los Angeles, Moody and Skinner decided "to go after them. But, very much to their gratification the men arrived that afternoon after enduring most terrible sufferings" (in Hafen and Hafen 1961:115).

and midnight was upon us before we could stop telling the sad stories of our suffering and the trials we had endured. They listened with great interest, and wondered how we could endure such labor and such food and live; and especially how Mrs. Bennett and Mrs. Arcane could walk so far over such a dry and barren desert for twenty-five days and still be alive.

Bennett's youngest child was an object of pity, as it was as helpless as it was a month ago. Mr. Moody and Mr. Skinner took much interest in our welfare, and the next day were busy trying to find for Mr. Bennett an ox yoke, chains and a wagon, which they finally did, out of those that had been sold or left by those who had gone on before us. Bennett traded off his repeating rifle, which had helped him to make out his outfit, and by being liberally assisted he got several things together and went on up the coast with them.

Rogers and I went over to town to see the sights, and among them found the Rev. Mr. Brier, one of our way travelers, whom we last saw on the virge of Death Valley, delivering a lecture to his boys on education, which, to us, under the circumstances, seemed very strange advice. He was now in partnership with Mr. Granger, the man who read the preamble and resolutions when our big train first started, sixty miles south of Salt Lake.[116] They had started a boarding house and had done well while hungry immigrants wanted a square meal.

As I was without a cent I hired out to them for $50 per month, hauling water with a pair of oxen and a cart, for the use of the house, and when not so employed, I hoed weeds out of a vineyard which they had jumped and claimed as their own, on the ground that Uncle Sam's soldiers had occupied it during the war with Mexico.

116. Lewis Granger was a proponent of the shortcut, but he returned to follow Hunt's wagon train and traveled the Old Spanish Trail to California. After his party reached California, he wrote his father, "we crossed the mountain range, [via Cajon Pass] . . . in the early part of January. The grass was fresh and green. . . . Nothing could exceed the beauty of the valley spreading out before us" (in Hafen and Hafen 1961:63). What a contrast to the suffering and anxiety of his companions still struggling in the California deserts.

Part III

John Rogers's Account—
"On the Plains," 1849

From Hobble Creek, Utah,
to Los Angeles, California.
Written for the *Merced Star*, 1894

Introduction

John Haney Rogers was a burly man from Tennessee who stood 6 feet 2 inches tall and weighed over 200 pounds. He was a quiet, gentle man with a dark complexion and gray eyes. Manly said, "he has a heart as big as the oxen we picked the bones of on the Desert" (JA 647). We know nothing about his life before 1849 except Manly's comment that he was a capable butcher. John was 24 or 25 when he ventured to California, where he remained after his harrowing trek through the desert. He began his migration west as a wagon driver for Mr. Dallas. When the train reached the Missouri River, Manly also hired on as an ox driver.

After Mr. Dallas announced he would set the men adrift in Salt Lake City to fend for themselves all winter, seven of them decided to navigate the Green River to the Pacific Ocean. After a nearly disastrous trip down the turbulent river, five of them took the advice of the Ute chief Walkara and hiked cross-country toward Salt Lake City. Manly and Rogers grew to respect one another as the trials of their Green River trip and the cross-country trek exposed the strengths and weaknesses of each. At Hobble Creek, 45 miles south of Salt Lake City, the men came across the large train of wagons preparing to travel south into California via part of the Old Spanish Trail. In this train Manly found the Bennett family, his dear friends from Wisconsin, whom he was supposed to have met at the Missouri River several months before. Manly joined the Bennetts and asked John to travel with them.

After arriving at Los Angeles with Manly and the Bennett family, John stayed with the Bennett, Skinner, and Moody families as they made their way north toward the mines. John mined up and down the Mother Lode but returned to the mines in the Merced River area and remained in Mariposa County the rest of his life, where he worked as a carpenter, mechanic, and separator on threshing machines. He was well respected in the community, and lived to be over 75 years old. We know he was still alive in January 1900 because Manly comments in a letter (JA 651) that John had just written to him.

Frank Latta provides information about John's later years in *Death Valley '49ers* (1979:346). He quotes his conversations with John Flanagan (84 years old in 1941), who knew Rogers after 1880. Flana-

gan said Rogers had been a bachelor as long as he knew him and
had high praise for the old pioneer, calling him a "generous old
fellow and a square shooter." We know nothing of Rogers's where-
abouts between 1854, when Manly saw him on a steamboat at
Benicia, California, and April 1894, when John wrote the following
article for the *Merced Star*. On January 14, 1895, a man visited Manly,
at John's request, to let him know his compadre was still alive. Big
John Rogers, as he was called, invited Manly to visit him, and in
1895 Manly went to Merced for a reunion, where he found that John
"like myself was an old man with a hairy face and walked with a
cane. He had in retorting gold inhaled so much quicksilver that it
had settled down and came out at his feet and both were off at the
instep" (JA 651). We feel it is unlikely Rogers's feet were amputated
because of mercurial poisoning, commonly called the "Mad Hatter's
Disease," because it affects the nervous system and causes the limbs
to tremble and teeth to fall out—symptoms John did not have. John
was still able to hobble around with a cane, but he could no longer
work. He lived with an old friend, Mr. Ellis, and had to depend on
his friends for a livelihood. Manly told the touching story of their
reunion in his article for the *Pioneer* (in Woodward 1949b:43). John
apparently never married, and his death record has not been found.

Rogers's account was written shortly before Manly's book was
released. Manly (JA 624) wrote John Colton on April 4, 1894, that he
was having trouble getting the binding material from New York and
that "the first book finished will be mailed to you." Since the book
had been advertised in newspapers before its release (Manly told
Colton he had numerous advance orders), John's account may have
been solicited by the newspaper in response to the advertisement.
Because there are many abrupt transitions in his account, we feel
the article may have been heavily edited from a longer narrative.
John's account starts as the wagon train leaves Hobble Creek.

Rogers's Account

[Merced Star, April 26, 1894]

I have often thought that I would give my history of crossing the plains in 1849. I will give only part of it as it would be entirely too long if given in full.

I will give my experience from Cobble [Hobble] Creek, Utah, to Los Angeles.

When we left Green River we struck across to Cobble Creek, Utah. There we fell in with a company coming to Los Angeles. We bought provisions from a man by the name of Ahart [Earhart] who had just come in from Iowa City. My partner's name was Manley. We were joined by a man named Bennett from Wisconsin. The company consisted of 110 wagons. We hired a guide by the name of Hunt to pilot us through to Los Angeles. We broke camp on the 1st of October and started on our journey, traveling on the rim of Salt Lake Basin. There was one man in our party who claimed to have a "waybill" through the mountains to the mines in two weeks. The train left the guide [6 miles northeast of Enterprise, Utah] except thirty wagons and followed this man who had the "waybill" to the mountains. The guide told us when we left that no man ever went through there. Still we went on. We traveled for three days in the mountains and brought up in a canyon [Beaver Dam Wash], where we came to a halt. From there we sent out scouts to find a way to continue our journey. They were gone two days and came back, one of the parties reporting that he had found a way through. We hitched up to start. Twenty wagons turned back to follow the guide. Sixty wagons started with the man who made the report, and we followed him sometimes north and then south and traveled on til about the 1st of December.

The company being dissatisfied sixteen wagons were piled up and burned. Next morning the owners of the wagons packed their traps on their cattle and drove off. The rest of the party hitched up and continued their journey in that way for about ten days when another split up occurred [Emigrant Valley, Nevada]. They all left except three wagons. The latter party comprised Ahart from Iowa City, Bennett from Wisconsin and a man from Chicago named Arcane, the two latter having families. Manley and myself stopped with them.

We traveled on as nearly west as we could on account of the mountains. Our greatest trouble was to find feed and water for our stock. We would have to send ahead from one place to another to find a camping ground before we would start.

We struck an Indian rancheria [at Cane Spring, Nevada]. The Indians were very much frightened. They had a garden and raised corn and squashes. Our train being behind we told the Indians that we had to go back. We went back and met the wagons. Our teams were so nearly given out that we had to camp without feed or water for our stock. The next morning we hitched up and drove to the rancheria. All had left when we got there. Being good feed and water we camped there eight days. During that time we ate a good many of those squashes. We explored ahead and found that it was two days' travel before we could strike water and feed for our stock. We hauled water so as to give our cattle drink the first night. The next day we struck water [Ash Meadows, Nevada] and the cattle were turned loose, being two days from where we ate the squashes.

The next morning [actually four days later at Travertine Springs] we went out to drive our cattle in. We found three of them shot with arrows, two of them with only one arrow in each, and the third was filled with them. We killed and skinned him and jerked the meat. We also found about twenty arrows sticking in the ground as if they had been shot upwards and dropped down.

We had never stood guard since the train had bursted up. I suppose the Indians shot our cattle out of revenge for eating their squashes.

Next morning Manley and myself started down the creek exploring. We went down to the mouth of the creek where it emptied out into the plains. There we found a big Indian camp [at the mouth of Furnace Creek Wash]. Their fires were still burning and the Indians gone, except an old man who was blind. He was crawling around on the ground. He had a little willow basket full of muddy water and had a sharp stick which he was using in digging up roots. Manley said that he had a notion to shoot him. Says I, "The deuce you would. I would as leave shoot my father."[117] I took his willow basket and went to the creek and rinsed it out and gave him some clean water. I gave him some meat and he raised his head and grunted as if he didn't know who was there. We started down into the valley. We traveled about ten miles and struck a bunch of

117. Manly (1894:139) saw the old man while scouting a possible route to the north. This hostile attitude was not in keeping with Manly's personality. He did not accompany Rogers on the scouting trip into the southern part of the valley; Rogers's scouting partner on this occasion was probably Asabel Bennett. Manly wrote (in Woodward 1949b:30) of Bennett that any "idea of treating an Indian other than as a wild beast, vanished from his mind, and he looked to his trusty rifle and his ability to take care of himself, as the only safe method to pursue."

willows and a spring of fresh water [Tule Spring].[118] In prospecting ten miles farther we struck a lake, after which we retraced our steps to camp.[119]

When we struck the Indian camp again the old Indian was gone. I think that he was left there for a purpose—to see what we would do with him. I think the kind treatment we gave that Indian saved our party. We moved camp to the spring at the willows. The ground was covered three or four inches deep with something like saltpetre or borax. We then traveled down the valley till we struck the lake [before they camped at Eagle Borax Spring], and down the lake, some fifteen or twenty miles where we concluded to cross at a point not over 25 or 30 yards wide.[120] We got three of our wagons across all right and the fourth one broke through. Underneath the water was a crust of salt some six to eight inches thick. We struck then to the foot of the mountain, it being difficult to find drinking water, as it was all salt. We found a spring we could use. We left the families there and went up the mountain to spy out a route that would lead us to the other side. Finding that we could cross it we went back to camp.[121] Next morning we started up the mountain to make the crossing and when about half way up the mountain our teams gave out. We retreated to the valley again.

We had all this time been maneuvering in what is called Death Valley! and didn't know it. We then saw that there was no use trying to get the wagons out of the valley. And having two women and four children (two of them babies) we couldn't pack our cattle and go on foot.

We told the families if they would wait for us for three weeks we would try to get through and get some relief. So the next day we went to work and killed two oxen and jerked the meat of one ox and a half. We had 22 pounds after it was dried, eleven pounds apiece.

118. Tule Spring, 15 miles south of Furnace Creek, is the first freshwater spring they encountered. Willows do not grow there, and it is unlikely they did in 1850. Although Indians were known to plant willows around springs where they had camps so they could have a convenient supply of raw material for weaving baskets, willows would not survive in the alkaline soil around Tule Spring. Arrow weed, which looks much like willows in the winter, is most likely the plant he saw (see also note 19).

119. He is not saying the lake is 10 miles from the spring, but he is saying they found a lake during the scouting trip that took them 10 miles south of Tule Spring. The lake was either the pond at Eagle Borax Spring or the ephemeral salt lake in the middle of the valley. It was on the basis of Rogers's scouting trip that Bennett decided to move the train to Eagle

Borax Spring. Ample grass for the oxen around Eagle Borax Spring and the fear of more Indian attacks at Travertine Springs were compelling reasons to move.

120. Rogers's mileages from Travertine Springs to the valley crossing cannot be reconciled with Manly's and Nusbaumer's accounts. This lake is not the lake referred to in the preceding paragraph. During the wet winter of 1849–50, Death Valley's salt pan would have been covered with water, giving it the appearance of an extremely large lake.

121. Rogers and his scouting companion (not Manly) felt they could get wagons across the Panamint Range via Warm Spring Canyon. It is possible they scouted up all the way to Butte Valley and thought there was a way across the mountain by going south through Butte Valley (see also note 25).

We put it in our knapsacks, shouldered our guns and started out, bidding them good-by, not knowing whether we would ever see them again.

We got pretty near the top of the mountain the first day, near a spring [Arrastre Spring]. Next day we started on and crossed the mountain and traveled that day till late in the evening. We passed a hole of water in some rocks, having nothing but a quart canteen, which we filled with water and traveled on, with nothing to eat but jerked meat. The next morning, with but a teacupful of water we started and traveled all day and found no water, and continued on until ten o'clock at night. Struck an Indian camp and expected to find water there [southern Argus Range]. We stopped there that night and found no water.[122] Next morning struck out down the mountain. The weather being very cold we traveled on to the plains [Indian Wells Valley]. We found a little place covered with ice which we scraped up into a kettle and melted it over a fire. We then made a cup of tea. Enough ice was melted to fill our kettle and canteen. We then started for the foot of the mountain [Owens Peak] and when within three miles of the mountain we saw a smoke raise. Manley thought it was an Indian camp. He proposed to wait till it got dark and if there were not too many of them make them divide grub. As we got near them we found that it was the same party [Doty's contingent of the Jayhawkers] that had burned their wagons before we had struck Death Valley. The place they were camped is known now as Indian Wells. We camped with them that night and the next morning we struck out on a trail. We followed the trail all that day, and so on the next day. In the evening it clouded up and commenced snowing.[123] We kept the same trail until we struck the Mojave. There we lost it and hunted all day for it. The mountains ahead of us [San Gabriel Mountains] were covered with snow and we were afraid we couldn't cross. We picked out the lowest place we could see and started for it [Soledad Pass]. Before we got to the edge of the snow I shot two little hawks and a raven, being the first birds we saw. The mountains were crossed in a low pass without any trouble. We then camped for the night, and while I was building a fire Manley took my shotgun, went up the creek and shot two quail. We dressed them, and putting them in a camp kettle, cooked and ate them all.

122. The first night they camped above Arrastre Spring (map 3). In the morning they ascended Manly Lookout and descended the western flank of the Panamint Range via Middle Park Canyon, where they found water in "some rocks." The second night was spent at the "Silent Sepulcre" in Fish Canyon, Slate Range, and the third night was in Burro Canyon, Argus Range, west of Trona.

123. It did not snow when the boys went for and returned with provisions. It did snow when they guided the families to the rancho (Manly 1894:235).

We traveled down the creek all next day till about three o'clock in the afternoon when we came out into the valley and five miles [east] from where Newhall now stands.[124] Being lots of cattle there we shot a yearling on the bank of the creek, skinned and roasted it. We ate all night. In the morning we filled our knapsacks with roast beef. Hearing a dog bark we went down to the Spanish ranch [Rancho San Francisco] where we were given breakfast. I bought some corn and had it ground in a hand-mill. Started up the valley, Manley getting lame in the knee. Soon after making camp I went to baking cornbread on the camp kettle lid. A man rode into camp and wanted to know where we were going. I told him our business. He told us to go back to the ranch and stay all night. He said that we were going the wrong way, and that he would tell the Spaniard to keep us all night. Next morning he sent up two horses to ride down to the camp where a party of emigrants were cutting a road up through to Tulare Valley from Los Angeles.

There we bought three horses and a mule.[125] Also flour, coffee, sugar and tea and then went to the ranch and purchased beans and corn, the latter being ground. We packed two animals and mounting the other two started on our return.

We traveled too fast for our horses, they giving out, but the mule stood it. It lacked 75 miles of camp.[126] We then packed our mule, filled our knapsacks and struck out. When we got within ten miles of camp [Bennetts Well, Death Valley] we found [the body of] an old man by the [name of] Culberwell [Culverwell] from Washington City. He was with the Aharts [Earharts]. After we had left the families they packed their cattle and left alone. Culverwell was sick and died at the spring.[127] We went on to camp and found the two families all right. They were glad to see us back, and it wasn't long before they had some bread baked. It was the first they had had in two months.

We got ready and packed our cattle with bedding and clothing. We put two children on the mule [actually on Old Crump the ox] with the pack, and packed the two babies time about on our backs.[128] We camped the first night on the mountain at a little

124. The creek was the upper part of the Santa Clara River, which flows down Soledad Canyon.

125. They bought two horses at the rancho. The white mare and the faithful one-eyed mule were purchased from the road construction crew in San Francisquito Canyon.

126. The white mare died in Deadman Canyon, Argus Range, and the other two horses were abandoned and died in Redlands Canyon, Panamint Range.

127. Culverwell did not die "at," but north of the sulphur water hole 5 or 6 miles south of Bennetts Well (see also note 89).

128. Apparently all the men took turns carrying the two small children. When Charlie broke out with his rash and cried incessantly, it was extremely unpleasant to carry him; no wonder Rogers remembered doing so. Very possibly Rogers devised a better pocket for the cramped children after they were on the trail awhile.

spring.[129] We got tired packing the babies so I took a long sack and fixed it so that it could be fastened on the ox. A hole was cut on each side like a pair of saddlebags and a baby was placed in each end. The little fellows would ride thus and sleep half of their time. Having plenty of grub we took our time in traveling. Arriving at the places where we left our horses we found all three dead. We got the balance of our provisions that were left there [Indian Joe Spring, not where horses were left] and traveled on without anything happening of any note till we got to the Spanish ranch. The old Spaniard sent out his vaqueros who brought in a beef and killed it. The old Spanish lady took the two families to the house and kept them there two days.

We camped there eight days and then packed up our cattle, put the babies in the sack and started for Los Angeles, where we arrived on the 7th day of March, 1850, dead broke.[130] I went to work in a blacksmith shop at $1 per day, and after earning a few dollars all hands started for the mines.[131] We struck the mines at Sonora. I then drifted down into Mariposa County. And here I am, a cripple for life.

Arcane went to Santa Cruz and settled. The boy I packed is there yet. The last I heard of Bennett he was at San Bernardino, but do not know where he is now.

This was my trip from Cobble Creek, Utah, through Death Valley to Los Angeles.

John H. Rodgers

Merced, Cal., 1894

129. Because of Bennett's decision to take a shorter route (which we feel Manly disagreed with), the families exited from Death Valley via Galena Canyon (see also note 90). Manly (1888:September) recalled that "Bennett said he saw no other way than to make the nearer route to the falls . . . even if it were rough and rocky, and it might be as well for us as to try to follow our wagon road," which went up the Pleistocene fan to the mouth of Warm Spring Canyon. The little spring is either Talc Mine Spring or the nearby spring in Galena Canyon, neither of which are shown on the USGS Bennetts Well, Calif., 15 min., 1952 quadrangle map.

130. They arrived at the Rancho San Francisco on March 7, 1850. Only one baby was packed "in the sack," since the Arcans left for San Pedro before the rest started for Los Angeles.

131. Rogers traveled north with Bennett, Moody, and Skinner. Manly (1894:275) stayed in Los Angeles a few weeks longer.

Part IV

Louis Nusbaumer's Journal—
1849–1850

A New Translation of the
California Desert Portion,
From Ash Meadows, Nevada,
to Los Angeles, California

Louis Nusbaumer's portrait from *History of Alameda County, California* (1883). (Courtesy of California State Library, Sacramento.)

Introduction

Louis Nusbaumer was born in southeastern Germany in 1819. He received a good education and wide experience in business and farming before coming to America. Elizabeth Roth became Louis's bride in 1842, five years before they ventured across the Atlantic to America. When they arrived in New York in 1847, they had already suffered the travails of business reverses in Germany and the birth of a stillborn child on their Atlantic crossing. Elizabeth was pregnant again when Louis started for California in March 1849. He traveled west with about sixty men from New York, many of whom were German. At Salt Lake he teamed up with Hadapp, probably of his original group; Culverwell, who had been with Bruff's group but was delayed due to illness (note 16); Fish, an older man from Indiana; Isham, who apparently drove for Fish; and Smith, a black man from Missouri. Nusbaumer struggled out of the desert in the company of only one of his original group ten days short of a year after leaving his home.

According to the *History of Alameda County, California,* Louis was "below medium height" and wore glasses ([Alameda County] 1883:953). He had great abilities as a hunter—he was hardy, an excellent shot, and a fine horseman. He was also "an entertaining companion, warm hearted and generous . . . always ready to forgive." Excerpts from his journal indicate he was also a romantic and very much in love with his wife: "My heart, my all, my star, when will I again look into your faithful eyes?" He called her "my dear, good, beloved, sweet wife who is my all in the world" and wrote that "a year without love . . . is time lost."

On June 13, 1850, Louis arrived on the Merced River, where he mined for gold. Instead of returning to the East as he had vowed in his journal, he sent for his wife to join him. Apparently he sent her money for the trip sometime in December 1850, but did not hear from her. He wrote her a poignant letter in his journal on March 30, 1851, wondering where she was and if she still loved him (in Koenig 1967:66). Certainly her arrival in San Francisco on April 5, just six days after his entry, must have come as a great surprise. They had been separated for two years.

The Nusbaumers stayed in San Francisco for five years, where three sons were born to them; George Louis, January 5, 1852, exactly nine months after Elizabeth arrived in California; Albert, date of birth unknown; and Emil, February 13, 1856 ([San Francisco] 1892:347, 648). A daughter, Bertha, presumably was born after their move to the Pleasanton area. In 1862, the Nusbaumers bought a joint interest in the 3,000-acre Rancho el Valle de San Jose.

Elizabeth died May 25, 1876 (not 1878, as Koenig [1967:66] says), and Louis died two years later on July 10, 1878 ([San Francisco] 1892:641). All four children continued to reside in Alameda County. George Louis became the county surveyor, Albert remained on the farm, Emil became deputy district attorney, and Bertha married and remained in the area.

In 1933, Bertha translated her father's journal for her son, Welles Whitmore, Jr. Her translation is incomplete; where pages were torn from the journal, she wrote "pages missing." The original journal, Bertha's translation, and a copy of the journal typed by Max E. Knight in 1948 are in The Bancroft Library.

The original journal is comprised of two small notebooks written in German script—sometimes in pen, sometimes in pencil. The changes from pen to pencil and the changes in style and quality of penmanship indicate how much of the journal was written at a sitting. Although the entries appear to have been made daily through the Death Valley area, they were not. He labeled them as to what happened on which date, but he often wrote several days' entries at one time. For example, sheet 13 is in rust-colored ink and covers January 8 through about January 18. Sheet 14 is in pencil, but there is a definite change in his writing about two-thirds down the page starting with February 7, 1850.

Nusbaumer wrote across the left and right pages as though they were one sheet; thus two facing pages are called a sheet. Unfortunately, some pages are missing, which means the left or right half of a sheet is gone. We adopted Knight's numbering system for sheets 9 through 14, but for clarity we renumbered the remaining sheets as if pages were not missing. We did not have sheets 1 through 8 translated because they do not apply to our research. We have included a translation of the words from the surviving pages (half sheets) where the adjoining page was torn out even though this may lead to speculation—or pure conjecture—on the part of readers as to what words were on the missing page.

The first published translation of parts of the journal was in Margaret Long's *Shadow of the Arrow* (1950 edition). George Koenig edited and annotated the journal in 1967. He says (1967:9) he checked Bertha's translation against the original journal and "corrected and completed" her work, but when we saw "100 mls" at the bottom of an illustration of the original journal in Koenig's book and could not find

it in the translation, we suspected there might be other mistakes—
and there were. Therefore, we had another translation made of the
Ash Meadows to Los Angeles portion of the journal. Barbara Johnson, who had been a translator for the Central Intelligence Agency,
worked with a photocopy of the original journal and Max E.
Knight's typed transcription. Sometimes there was a question about
what a certain word was because an *e* might look like an *i*. Anton
Schlö[a?]gel was spelled several different ways; we use *Schlögel*.
Barbara translated as literally as possible; verb tenses were translated as written unless they were part of an idiomatic phrase.

Barbara's translation was checked by Gela Hunt, a native of
Germany, who learned German handwriting in grade school. She
was able to check Knight's typed transcription against the photocopy of the journal. She also used German handwriting samples in
E. Steiger's 1890 *Colloquial Method of Learning the German Language* to
confirm her interpretation of Nusbaumer's handwriting. Unfortunately, neither Barbara nor Gela was able to check the translation against the original journal in The Bancroft Library.

Nusbaumer's Journal

[Sheet 9; entire page written in pencil]

The 23rd 13 mls southwesterly. We arrived at a beautiful valley [Ash Meadows] considerably lower than we had been before and quite a warm region so that we encountered flies, butterflies, beetles, etc. At the entrance to the valley to the right is a hole in the rocks [Devils Hole] which contains magnificent warm water and in which Hadapp and I enjoyed an extremely refreshing bath. The temperature of the water is about 24–26° [75–79° F] and the saline cavity itself presents a magical appearance.[132] It seems the Christ child will show us the right way. # (24th) Our prospects begin to become more dismal again, since one of our oxen is about to die, though we will not lose courage on the eve of the day on which our Savior was born. We came about (# 12 mls) 15 mls[133] the same day through horrible alkali marshes and had to camp the night without water and grass. We had [to go] 2 hours further back to get water for our supper.[134]

[Sheet 10; entire page written in blue ink, obviously at one writing]

The 25th December 1849. Christmas in the mountains of California. (Written at the campsite before leaving it.) This day was in general a day of sorrow for us, since the previously mentioned ox was no longer in a condition to go on and we were forced to throw away all our possessions in order to lighten the wagon enough that 1 yoke of oxen can pull it. I left here at the camp site 5 good linen shirts, boots, handkerchieves, 1 basket, friend Adolph's hat, stockings, 1 buffalo hide, etc., and took only 3 shirts, my little cashmere [lined?] basket, 1 pair stockings, 1 pair boots and 1 pair shoes, 1

132. Camp the night of December 23 was at Collins Spring, 0.75 mile south of Devils Hole, where there was firewood, grass, and water. Nusbaumer and his friend Hadapp hiked back to Devils Hole for a private bath (see also note 1).

133. They progressed 12 miles west, but they traveled a total of 15 miles on December 24, which included a total of 3 miles back and forth to get water. In his journal the "(# 12 mls)" notation is in brackets just before the "15 mls." He then indicated with "#" and an arrow that the 12-mile entry should be inserted just before the "24th," which indicates a westward progress of 12 miles that day.

134. After a day of difficult passage through Carson Slough, they camped near where Death Valley Junction now stands. The nearest potable water was the runoff from Big Spring.

buffalo hide and my cloak and so each one of us. Friend Hadapp is sick and also had to give up his best things. If we are able to reach the company which has gone ahead, we intend to load one ox with provisions and then to go further, if our strength, which is diminished through poor nourishment, permits us. But courage has not yet left us, and we hope with the help of God to still reach our destination. That is the difference between the Christmas days in God's states. In one you receive gifts, and in the other you have to throw [things] away. (What fun!) I hope my dear wife has a happier Christmas day at home than I [am having] here. May the one God keep her healthy and if I am never to return to her and fortune should bring my journal into her hands, then she may see from it, that she was not forgotten and that my heart beats for her to the last moment.

[Sheet 11; entire page written in pencil on December 28 and January 2]

(Continuation of 25/12/49) As just said we started out from the camp site and with heavy hearts traveled further and when we were scarcely 6 miles further on the one ox lay down on the trail and wouldn't get up again and then we were forced into killing it. We went to work immediately; in one hour's time it was skinned and cut up, and we erected a smokehouse and dried its meat the whole following night.[135] The morning of the 26th loaded our other 3 oxen with the meat and with our clothes and blankets and began to travel after the company that had gone ahead. We had to travel 2 days and night without water and without forage for the cattle, until we caught up with the company on a steep mountain slope where there was however enough water and forage [Travertine Springs]. As we were traveling to them, the Indians had shot 3 of their oxen in one night.[136] Here on the 28th our other fellow travelers left us, all but Culverwell who is too ill to go further with the others, and Hadapp and I kept one ox in reserve, which, after it has recovered somewhat, we will load and see if we can travel further with it.[137] The 29,

135. They camped 5.5 or 6 miles west of Death Valley Junction. Here the Nusbaumer group dismantled their wagon to make a smokehouse in which they dried the meat of the fallen ox. In 1906, Herman Jones of Shoshone, Nevada, found an old camp at this location. He built a stone monument at the site that was still there in 1938 when Dr. Long (1950:126 & 330) visited it. She said there were faint traces of three camps within 0.5 mile of each other, and this spot became known as "Burnt Wagons." This camping spot coincides with Nusbaumer's mileages from Collins Spring. Coolidge (1937:29–37) quotes Dad Fairbanks's fabulous story of an Indian attack on the '49er emigrants who camped here. The yarn, which in-

cluded buried treasure and the killing of a few emigrants, is not corroborated by facts. There is no guarantee the sites mentioned by Long and Coolidge date from 1849, but the location fits the mileage figures given by Nusbaumer.

136. The oxen were shot the night of December 27. John Rogers was in camp, but Manly was at McLean Spring—both mention this incident (see also note 18).

137. Hadapp, Culverwell, and Nusbaumer remained at Travertine Springs while Fish, Isham (called Graham in Nusbaumer's journal), and Smith followed the Jayhawkers north and left Death Valley via Towne Pass.

30 and 31st we spent drying and preparing meat and a Happy New Year 1st January 1850. We received split beans from 2 Alsatians who sympathized with our situation, and so we began the new year quite happily, whereas 2 or 3 days ago we were almost in despair. We exchanged beans and coffee for one pistol, etc., and so now we live in luxury. Today, 2nd January we had an excellent soup. We boiled ox feet and mouth a whole night with beans, etc., and so the next morning we had a good jelly that really strengthened us. Our Lord does not forsake us Germans. *Blessed New Year, dear wife and perhaps child.*[138] Splendid weather *favors* us!

[Sheet 12; entire page written in pencil]

6th January 1850. We have camped here now about 10 days and tomorrow intend to follow an Indian trail about 4 miles west and then south from here and intend, if our supposition in reference to Walker's Pass does not deceive us again, to arrive in a short time at the diggings.[139] W[*illegible*] Hadapp is not in a good mood toward me and only God knows what [*illegible*] condition there burdens [*illegible*], that the friendship of a man was never more suited to me than his and it shall then not waver [*illegible*]. 7th January. We started out and [traveled] without water about 8 miles but did not know beforehand that we should find no water since from up on the mountain we saw the whole valley filled with water. On approaching, we found clear salt water and had to wade through salt marshes and walk over pure boulders of salt. The 8th it went the same and both Hadapp and I were so thirsty that we even tried to drink the salt water. It was there where I offered a coat and 2 shirts for a drink from one of the two wagons that were ahead and they both had enough and [we] could get no water. The same man refused me water [left] an ox behind, which because of sickness could no longer walk and the two of us shot it, caught the blood in a pail and being so thirsty drank it all and regretted that the ox had no more blood.[140]

138. Unfortunately, this child was either still-born, as was their first child, or died before Elizabeth joined Louis in California. George Louis, born January 5, 1852 was their first child to survive to adulthood ([San Francisco] 1892:347).

139. This is one of the few references in all the Death Valley '49er writings that mentions following an Indian trail—a practice that strongly influenced where they traveled. These trails inevitably led to water, so they were logical routes to follow. This statement also reveals that some of the emigrants thought the lofty Panamint Range before them was the Sierra Nevada; if so, Walker Pass would be to the south.

140. Who left the ox behind? Who, with water in a wagon, would refuse it to men on the verge of fatal dehydration? These are burning questions to which we have no satisfactory answers. This seemingly ruthless act is particularly difficult to understand because the wagon was carrying plenty of water. But as Reid (1980:144) points out in his definitive treatise on personal property rights of emigrants along the trail, "there was no item of private property that an owner had to share," and water was considered personal property. Koenig (1967:49 & 1984:104) reasons it was one of the Bennett-Arcan drivers. However, these drivers cannot be implicated, because they had already left Eagle Borax Spring on foot to follow the Jayhawkers (see also note 22). It is not likely this heartless man was Anton Schlögel, with whom Nusbaumer teamed up a week later and to whom he swore eternal friendship. We reject the

Mark and Eric Johnson, the authors' sons, stand beside an ancient Indian trail in Death Valley. Nusbaumer wrote in his journal, "We intended to follow an Indian trail"; and it was along this trail that he and Hadapp drove their ox.

It made us thirstier however and we started out and traveled by night—1 o'clock when we lay down in a bush and tried to forget our thirst by sleeping. The 9th of January we started out at daybreak and with increased thirst and thank God after wandering about 2 mls we came to a warm sweet spring [Tule Spring] where we just boiled coffee for the 4th time to drive away the result of drinking the blood yesterday, since the ox was sick.

[Sheet 13; entire page written in rust ink]

The next day [January 10] we wandered further [and] reached a place [Eagle Borax Spring] where the company that had gone before us had burned a wagon and slaughtered oxen and dried meat. They

Earhart brothers as the culprits because these Jewish emigrants treated the Nusbaumer mess so kindly a few weeks later that Nusbaumer wrote he would like to settle near Jews the rest of his life. We know of only one other mess that had a wagon (or wagons) that took the southern route—the Wades. Maybe it is just as well that history will not allow us to single out this cruel person.

with their families also are in a sorry condition, since their provisions also dwindle each day and still no prospect of passing through these mountains.[141] The 12th and 13th we traveled with our old Brins as we had christened our ox without water and feed and reached the company just as they were turning westward.[142] We remained here a day to rest up and [intended] to follow them the next day the 14th, which we did, and left in the company of a wagon. The owner of the wagon, an Alsatian by the name of Ant. Schlögel from Ergersheim [district] of Molsheim near Strasbourg, settled in Quincy in Illinois. He had 3 yoke of oxen on his wagon and after he had traveled with us a little while one of his oxen became sick and it could not go any further. Whereupon we both joined with him and pledged mutually never to forsake one another.[143] We threw our provisions together and slaughtered the ox; took the tongue, heart, and liver and traveled after the company when we suddenly saw them coming back and so also turned around. We decided among ourselves to see if we could not find a way out in a southerly direction.[144] Shortly before our departure from there [sulphur water hole] the 14th, I felt a swelling in my legs and saw that my hands were greatly swollen. Paid no further attention to it however since friend Hadapp complained about the same trouble. But today the 4th day after we again are traveling on the trail back since we could not get through.[145] My feet are so swollen that I could not get into my stockings, had to cut my boots down to the toes to put them on and can walk only with the greatest effort, since my body up to my chest and my thighs, everything is swollen

141. "They with their families" applied to the Bennett-Arcan party and probably the Wades, who camped at Eagle Borax Spring. The burned wagon may have been one of the four belonging to the Bennett-Arcan mess or one of the Wades' two wagons.

142. They caught up with the Bennett-Arcan group at the sulphur water hole, which we think was at or near Mesquite Well about 10 miles south of Eagle Borax Spring (see also note 23). Mesquite Well is shown on the USGS Furnace Creek, Calif.–Nev., 60 min., 1910, reprinted 1920, quadrangle map.

143. It should be noted that Culverwell was not mentioned as traveling with Nusbaumer south of Travertine Springs. Nusbaumer said he and Hadapp "both joined with" Schlögel—not *we three*, which would have been the case if Culverwell had been with them. Since Culverwell was at the sulphur water hole on January 15 when Manly and Rogers left, he traveled from Travertine Springs with the Bennett-Arcan mess, the Wades, or the Earharts—the latter being the most likely.

144. This sentence is missing from the Koenig translation (1967:50). It is important because it makes

clear that Nusbaumer, Hadapp, and Schlögel were not among the 11 adults mentioned by Manly (1894:153) as being at the sulphur water hole when he and Rogers left (see also note 30). When Nusbaumer, Hadapp, and Schlögel saw the Bennett and Arcan wagons returning to the sulphur water hole after their abortive attempt to cross the Panamint Range via the Pleistocene fan and Warm Spring Canyon, the threesome continued southwestward—possibly up Wingate Wash. They were forced to abandon this route, most likely because their jaded oxen could not pull the wagon, and they returned to Eagle Borax Spring, where the Bennett, Arcan, Earhart, and Wade families plus at least three other unnamed emigrants were camped. Because Koenig (1967:53) did not translate this sentence, he assumed that Nusbaumer, Hadapp, and Schlögel were at the sulphur water hole on January 15. We agree with Read and Gaines (1944:1230) that they were not there when Manly and Rogers left.

145. It is not clear if the "4th day" is counted from January 14 when they left the sulphur water hole or from the day they turned around because they could not get through.

to abnormal proportions. What the cause of this illness is is in-comprehensible to me. Whether it is the water, the way of living, or the air and whether I survive it or whether I will succumb to it still causes doubt.

[Sheet 14; entire page written in pencil]

I restricted myself in eating and drinking water 1 or 2 days and now feel much better. The swelling went down and after we had lost still another ox with 3 still remaining [we reached a camp] where we found sweet water [Saratoga Spring] and before that [encountered] Schaub and Wade in the trail who told us they had found a trail and a lake [Leach Lake] to the west and thought [they] could be at the diggings or settlement in 6 days.[146] Man proposes and God disposes. At said camp [Saratoga Spring] we had to slaughter one ox to provide food and so we 3 men now have 2 oxen, about 30 lbs. dried meat, and some grain-salt and pepper and this ought to suffice at least until the diggings. This evening, the 1st of February, we await a signal from one of the scouts sent out. Whether he can recommend the pass that Wade traveled and if he happens to find water and grass, then the day after tomorrow finds us also on the way. Schlögel and I have sworn friendship to each other forever and if I happen to make my fortune at the diggings then I am determined to go with him to Quincy, buy a farm there or establish some other business and to take my whole family there and provide a happy life for them. *The 7th of February, 1850.* Six men from the above mentioned company decided to go with us[147] and follow the aforementioned trail Wade had taken and they joined us today with 4 oxen and as soon as we had also loaded our two again had to leave behind a good portion of our clothing and other be-longings we moved on further to the west, the 1st evening about 7 miles.

[Sheet 15; right page missing; written in pencil]

Feb. 8th From there . . .
stony and very bad . . .
to these however in . . .

146. Schaub and Wade probably scouted west from Saratoga Spring. The lake would have been on Leach Lake playa nestled in a basin surrounded by the Owlshead, Avawatz, Granite, and Quail moun-tains. From Saratoga Spring they should have gone southeast 10 miles to Salt Spring on the Old Spanish Trail, but of course they did not know this. Alas, logic prevailed, and they went west through the pass be-tween the Owlshead and Avawatz mountains. They may have thought this was Walker Pass.

147. The "above mentioned company" refers to the Bennetts, Arcans, Earharts, and other men who were camped at Eagle Borax Spring on January 10. The six men were the three Earharts plus three unnamed men. Captain Culverwell left the Bennett-Arcan camp about January 26 with the Earhart bro-thers (Manly 1894:202). Their wagon broke down and was abandoned somewhere in the southern reaches of Death Valley (Ellenbecker 1938:52; Latta 1979:195). Culverwell could not keep up with the six men, so he turned back and died north of the sulphur water hole (see also notes 23 & 79).

could I see him in the beginning . . .
Culverwell from Washing[ton] . . .
other man of . . .
a little out of the . . .
sometime before 5 p.m. . . .
remained behind because [?] . . .
his near break up . . .
for this reason . . .
without anything to eat . . .
the other day I went . . .
where the remainder of our . . .
struck us. As I . . .
I almost died of thirst . . .
Schlögel very cordially . . .
canteen with water . . .
to my dismay I heard [?] . . .
did not arrive at the camp . . .
all attempts through . . .
were and we have . . .
without going further . . .
after Hadapp and the old one . . .
very poor condition . . .
Brins [the ox] was butchered . . .
liver and some meat . . .

[Sheet 16; left page missing; written in pencil]

. . . Devils or Teufels
. . . about the thing was that
. . . found water there. The 14th
. . . as we all assumed
. . . [W]ade we had worried [about?]. The 15th
. . . passed a spring and at night
. . . the 16th. Again without water
. . . hope since we are now near
. . . Indians or other
. . . moving west and [gave?] us hope
. . . end of our year's journey
. . . I went into the mountains
. . . and all of the thirst almost
. . . found only two pieces of ice
. . . put in leather trousers
. . . where we such
. . . on the 17th. From there on
. . . on which we had our
. . . uphill always along the Indian trail
. . . led to a high plateau

. . . without water and lost
. . . and that from thirst and fatigue
. . . already saw nothing more
. . . not to sleep and plowed [ahead?]

[Sheet 17; written in pencil]

in the middle of the night in order to get to water and feed and
reached [it] thank God after about 4 miles traveling where we then
remained the 19th and 20th of February. Slaughtered another ox
and dried its meat. The 21st we left late since our oxen had run away
and made only 5 miles where we otherwise are able to cover usually
20–25 miles in a day. Since oxen travel with packs on their backs as
well as horses and if we had followed this plan long before we could
have reached our destination without [having] to sacrifice all our
oxen. It is the best luck for us 3, Schlögel, Hadapp and me that we
have gone with these people since if we had traveled alone, [we
would] not have been able to carry our provisions and water and to
go so far each day. Hadapp and I reserved 30 dollars if we are lucky
enough to earn it and I will [give it to] the man whose name is Jack
Ehrhardt from Iowa and settle in the vicinity of Jews all the rest of
my life [*illegible*] know how to thank that he treated me so kindly
and I want to try to pay him back in every other way too for what he
[has] done for me. The 22nd from there to a river [Mojave River], the
first

[Sheet 18; written in pencil]

that we see since we left the little Salt Lake and at which [we] see
hoof prints of horses and the snow covered mountains of the Sierra
Nevada [San Gabriel] in the west, and so it seems that the good
Lord who protected us until now, will permit us to reach our
destination shortly, and I believe that most of us have changed
greatly in mind as well as body, and no longer desire great wealth
but after this [desire] to lead a quiet happy life in the bosom of their
families, and mention returning home with a much smaller amount
than they had [planned] in the beginning.

Hurrah for California

Just now J. Ehrhardt returns and informs us that a few steps from us
lies a road and that we are now certain that we will be at our
destination in a few days. God be thanked! And as said, so it was
too. The river was the Mojave, the road Capt. Hunt's trail, and we
were about 100 miles away from the Spanish settlements

[Sheet 19; written in pencil]

which we then reached in 4 days after we had traveled through the
Sierras [San Gabriel Mountains] in 2 days, and at which we now
[*illegible*] it recruit, and from there will be able to go to the Pueblo

and San Francisco. And today, the 1st of March, 20 days earlier than I left my dear wife a year ago, we are here on a Spanish rancho and are eating beef and Welsh corn, the best meat that I [have] eaten in my life so that it almost takes our breath away and intend tomorrow or the next day to go to the Pueblo and work there until we have the means to set out to Francisco and now suddenly we have to try begging, which we also go through [in] all schools, may my dear wife forgive me if the wedding ring must be used for credit. With this I will close my journal since the rest now

[Sheet 20; written in pencil]

takes place in an inhabited land and familiar region and will be of little interest for the reader.

FINIS

March 10 started as a government teamster, 2 1/2 dollars and expenses per day. In the Pueblo of Los Angeles news received that Fish and Isham starved to death and Smith was killed by the Piutes and so from six of us that leaves no one but Hadapp and I myself.

Part V

The Reverend James Brier's Letters—1876–1898

From Death Valley to Rancho San Francisco

This Brier family portrait was taken in Marysville, California, 1852. Shown
are Juliet, Columbus, Kirke (in front), James, and John (Brier 1903:327).
(Courtesy of California State Library, Sacramento.)

Introduction

James Welsh Brier was a circuit-riding Methodist minister from Covington, Indiana, when at the age of 25 he married a well-bred and educated young lady, Juliet Wells, in her father's parlor in Mottville, Michigan, on September 23, 1839. He was descended from rugged Scotch and Irish (McBrayer— McBrier—Brier) stock that often produced "fluent and successful politicians and preachers" (Leadingham 1964:19). James did love to preach. He stood 5 feet 11 inches tall with blond hair and gray eyes. A newspaper from 1887 reported James as "a tall, raw boned man of intelligent face and natural eloquence, whose countenance bears many a graving of hardship." Grace Leadingham (1964:19) describes him as "tactless, idealistic, somewhat impractical, honest, courageous, venturesome, more than a little egotistical, tender in his own way."

Reverend Brier was remembered with mixed emotions. His son, John Wells Brier (1903:335), proudly said, "My father had always been active, enterprising and irrepressible. He had spent his manhood in self-sacrificing labor, and had never known what it meant to be discouraged. Now, however [while in the desert on the way to California] we could see that he was failing, while, under an acute disorder, it was hard for him to perform the ordinary duties of the camp. Still he continued to explore as he had always done, until his infirmity forced him to the rear." On the other hand, E. I. Edwards (1940:44) said, "The Jayhawker letters in the Huntington Library exhibit expressions that reject all semblance of pretense and denote a marked aversion for this comrade of the trail." Manly conveyed similar impressions from the Jayhawkers.

Juliet Brier was born in Bennington, Vermont, on April 8, 1814 (JA 69, 105, & 106), of hardy New England stock, as was Lewis Manly. Her family moved to Michigan in the 1820s; while there, Juliet probably taught school. She was small, never weighing more than 115 pounds, and of dark complexion with hazel-brown eyes and red highlights in her auburn hair. She possessed a spirit that bloomed and grew in the heat of adversity; those who traveled with her through the Great American Desert remembered her as hardworking and generous. "All agreed that she was by far the best man of the party. She was the one who put the packs on the oxen in the morning. She it was who took them off at night, built the fires, cooked the food, helped the children, and did all sorts of work. . . . It seemed almost impossible that one little woman could do so much. It was entirely to her untiring devotion that her husband and children lived" (Manly 1894:342). Her faith was always a comfort to her, and her keen mind and memory brought forth Scripture at will.

The Briers' first son, Christopher Columbus, was born in 1841, two years after they were married. John Wells followed two years later. In 1845, when Kirke White was born, they were in Iowa, where they remained until they left for California. Juliet had been teaching school the winter before and wrote to her brother that gold fever ran high in the neighborhood. When she was able, she rode circuit with James. She loved her husband very much and respected and supported him in every way she could.

James caught the fever for gold, and the family of five traveled across the plains and Rocky Mountains as part of the San Francisco wagon train. Apparently James held a prominent position in the train of about forty-five wagons that turned west before reaching Salt Lake City. For some reason he became disenchanted with the group and left them to go on to Salt Lake City alone. The Briers joined the caravan of over one hundred wagons preparing to head south to Los Angeles that included the Bennett, Arcan, and Wade families, among others.

At Mount Misery, on the brink of Beaver Dam Wash west of Enterprise, Utah, the Brier family joined a group of forty-two men from Georgia and Mississippi led by Captain Townsend (Town) and James Martin (Ellenbecker 1938:supp. 2). A few days later, when about twenty-eight wagons were committed to the cutoff route, the single men made it clear they did not want to be encumbered by or responsible for women and children. However, Brier did not band together with the other families; he doggedly followed the companies of single men.

The Briers were forced to abandon their wagon, as were James Martin's men, in the vicinity of Forty Mile Canyon, Nevada. As they hiked out of the mouth of Forty Mile Canyon, the mountains ahead forced them south along the Amargosa River bed until they found a pass heading west—near Death Valley Junction. Fifty-six years later, in a letter written in 1905, Juliet (JA 106) described her climb over the pass and down Furnace Creek Wash to Travertine Springs—a fearsome ordeal.

> We were then on foot having left our wagons several days previous—The train stretched along leaving space between so the foremost division was a long distance from the last—Ours

was next the last—Capt. Town's the last—Night came and no
water—All day long we walked in silence, not in sight or hearing of a soul except my little ones. There was no moon and the
stars shone faintly. My little 4 year old boy gave out and said Oh
Mother! could you carry me a little? Taking him on my back—[I]
carried him until my breath almost left me setting him down he
says, Now I can walk—I took his hand and went on for a minute
or two when again he says Oh! I am too tired! cant walk, and
again time after time I carried him—The ground was hard,
composed of small pieces of broken rock and the feet of the oxen
made but little impression and I sometimes was obliged to get
down and hunt for the track. Hapily this state of things did not
last all night. Suddenly we came round the point of a high rock,
a fire was burning and Mr. Brier was setting by it—I said is this
the camp. He answered No. They have found water six miles
ahead—Now I will take Kirke on my back and hasten on—leave
2 oxen with you and the boys. He did so, and I was greatly
relieved. . . . When we reached the camp it was 3 o'clock A.M.
Christmas morning [actually the day before]. . . . On Christmas
eve there were no illuminations. . . . An ox was butchered, and
having some bread with plenty of coffee we feasted and rested.
. . . Our company was from the southern states and called the
Mississippi Boys. They called Mr. B. Parson   Toward evening
one came to him and said, Parson we would like to have you
give a lecture this evening. He complied and gave them one on
Educ[ation] . . .

Manly caught up with the Brier family at Travertine Springs
before they turned north, still following the trail of the Jayhawkers
and Georgia-Mississippi boys. At McLean Spring, the latter gave
their remaining oxen to Brier after they dried meat to pack on their
backs so they might travel west more quickly. Several unattached
men, such as Fish, Gould, and Isham, joined the large group at
McLean Spring and later, in Panamint Valley, traveled with the
Briers. From Post Office Spring just south of Ballarat in Panamint
Valley, Reverend Brier crossed the valley and scouted south along
the eastern edge of the Slate Range. One of his letters describes his
journey. Most of the Jayhawkers chose not to follow Brier's lead, but
the men who did left their tracks in Fish Canyon, where Manly and
Rogers found them. Mr. Fish perished as he tried to scale the Slate
Range, and Manly and Rogers found his scarcely covered body. He
had lived in the Midwest a short distance from the Briers and had
heard Reverend Brier preach (JA 107). Isham died of thirst in Searles
Valley after crawling several miles in his attempt to reach the lake.
He was the brother of Dr. Ezra Isham, who had been Juliet's doctor
and Sunday school teacher in Manchester, Vermont. The Brier contingent rejoined the Jayhawkers near Searles Lake. From there to

the Rancho San Francisco they followed the Jayhawkers—sometimes a day or two behind, sometimes catching up.

After the Briers arrived in Los Angeles, they stayed a short time with Dr. John G. Nichols and his wife. During this time Reverend Brier gave the first Protestant sermon in southern California. He exchanged a half-dozen oxen for a half interest in a boardinghouse where Mrs. Brier was doing the cooking, washing, and cleaning when Manly arrived and applied for work.

The Briers were in Marysville by 1852 (Latta 1979:336), and during the next few years three daughters were born to them (Long 1950:215). However, the girls are not mentioned in Reverend Brier's letters or in a brief, undated biography by Charles T. Brier of Sacramento. Christopher Columbus Brier ran a private school in the San Francisco Bay area and John Wells Brier became a respected Congregational clergyman. Kirke White Brier was principal of Sacramento High School before he died at age 43 in 1888.

In the spring of 1873, Brier returned to the Panamint Range as a guide for some miners. He became active in Republican politics and stumped the state for presidents Lincoln, Grant, Garfield, and Harrison (Long 1950:215). The 1887 newspaper article said he had been "keeping up financially by occasional lectures" and "for nine or ten years he has been an evangelist taking no pay for his services."

Reverend Brier died in Lodi, California, in 1898. After his death, Juliet graciously hosted the Jayhawker reunion in 1902. She died May 26, 1913, just four months before she reached her 100th birthday, at the home of her second son, John Wells, who died two years later.

It is interesting that Brier did not write anything about the hundreds of desert miles east of Death Valley in his various letters to the Jayhawkers. There are several possible explanations for this: (1) their situation may not have become truly critical until they reached the Death Valley region; (2) Brier retraced his trail from near Walker Pass into the Panamint Range in 1873 so he was more familiar with this area; and (3) he associated with the Jayhawkers after the Georgia-Mississippi boys parted from him in Panamint Valley.

The five letters included here span twenty-two years—1876 to 1898. They were written in response to John B. Colton's invitations to attend the Jayhawker reunions held each February 4, the anniversary of the day they first viewed the pastoral expanses of the Rancho San Francisco. By the end of the trek, the Jayhawkers had accepted the Briers as deserving participants in the celebration and invited them to attend or at least send a letter to be read at their annual gathering. These five letters help pinpoint the Manly-Rogers routes through the Slate and Argus ranges and are, therefore, of particular value to our analysis of those routes.

We have not included Juliet's accounts because they are easily found in Long (1950), Belden (1954), and Latta (1979). John Wells Brier wrote two flowery accounts that add color and feeling to the trek, but they abound with literary license. He was 6 years old when he walked some 400 miles across mountains and deserts, and most of his narration is based on what his parents remembered and spoke of so often.

Reverend Brier also wrote an account in 1854 (in Hafen and Hafen 1957:277–281), but it is geographically inaccurate and of little value. He mentions writing a manuscript about the 1849–50 journey, but apparently it was never published.

We have retained Reverend Brier's spelling, capitalization, and form, but added paragraphs for clarity. Many sentences have no ending punctuation; we have left spaces where there should be periods.

Brier's Letters

[JA 70]

Grass Valley California, Jan 17th 76

Mr Charles B Mecum
Dear Sir

Your letter of invitation is before me & I am sorry that I find it impossible to be present at your dwelling on the 4th of Feb.[148] Your invitation brings vividly before me the sufferings & sorrows of that fearful winter of peril in the Deserts. How often we have gone back over the journey almost inch by inch recounting all our hungerings & thirstings & weary wanderings

Two years ago I was induced to go back as far as Death Valley (where you burnt your waggons) as a guide to a Company of Miners. The first place that I struck our old trail was at the Indian Springs where we first reached the Siera Nevada Mts.[149] There is a Hotel now at the spot. From there to Death Valley (as it is now called) every rod of the way looked as familiar to me as though I been there but a day before

Let me take you all back. From Indian Springs to the 1st range of Owen's Mt is 25 miles. We crossed this Desert [Indian Wells Valley] in 50 you all remember, in a little less than 2 days   From the spring at the mouth of the Canon [Deadman Canyon] that we came down to the top of the Mt [Argus Range] where we camped is 10 miles[150]   from the summit camp to the spring branch found by Deacon Richards at the foot of the high peak is 10 miles   That Spring Branch is now called Providence Spring [Indian Joe Spring

---

148. February 4, 1850, was the date the Jayhawkers reached Rancho San Francisco. Beginning in 1872, they celebrated their deliverance from the desert on this date annually (Manly in Woodward 1949b:52). John B. Colton was the self-appointed secretary and historian for the reunions, which were held at the homes of various Jayhawkers. The Bennett-Arcan party arrived at the Rancho on March 7, 1850.

149. Reverend Brier returned to the Death Valley area in spring 1873 to look for the Gunsight lead (Lingenfelter 1986:113). Indian Springs is now called Indian Wells Spring (see also note 47). The place name does not appear on USGS Inyokern, Calif., 15 min., 1943, quadrangle map, but the spring is at Homestead, 5 miles north of Freeman Junction.

150. The spring is the salty one at Paxton Ranch at the mouth of Deadman Canyon. While crossing the Argus Range, they camped in a dry wash called Sweetwater Creek, where water flows only after infrequent cloudbursts. The Bennett-Arcan group also camped here during their exit march (see also note 100).

north of Trona] on account of the number of lives saved by it since our day. From there to the Lake [is] 4 miles south   The Lake [Searles Lake] was not salt but Borax   It is now famous for that Mineral. From the Lake to the spring in Panamint Valley [Post Office Spring 0.5 mile south of Ballarat] where Capt. Town & Co left me & I joined the Jayhawkers is 25 miles. You all remember the Muskeet Swamps & Indian Springs & Wickeups[151]   You remember the very high Mt. [Telescope Peak] East of this spot   That Mt. is the location of the Celebrated Panamint Mines that were discovered since my trip back as a guide & as a result, there is now a populous mining town at this point & a good stage road to it all done, since I was there[152]   From the Muskeet Swamp to the head of the valley where the Mississippi Boys left us is 20 miles & 20 more to Death Valley   The pass over is called Town's Pass.[153] I had no difficulty in going directly to all these points although 23 years had elapsed.

At Providence Spring I found a Jayhawke ox shoe which I brought home as a memento. At our old Camp in Town's Pass where we melted snow I found a Butcher Knife. At most of these points I wept over the rememberences of our sufferings   Capt Culverwell one of the 4 white men & the Negro who overtook us in Utah, sleeps over the summit of Panamint Mt. near to where the mines are located[154]   Old Father Fish fell to rise no more on the Mt. this side [of] Panamint Valley that is west of the valley [in the Slate Range] & Isham his driver was buried 3 or 4 miles south [southeast] of Providence Spring   The Jayhawks voted me his watch & pocket book   His Brother came on from Michigan in '51 & found me in Marysville   to him I delivered the property

Robinson died near the Coast Range at a Spring [Barrel Springs]   The Old French Man that took the wrong path near to where your oxen took their final stampede & who was not found was discovered east of Death Valley 15 years afterward in slavery to

151. This camp, commonly called "horse bones camp," was so named because John Wells Brier (1911:4 & 1903:334) and Mrs. Brier (1898) mentioned there were horse bones scattered throughout the Indian village. The horses were stolen from Spanish ranches 250 miles away, driven here, and slaughtered for food. Wheat (1939b:90) places this camp in the center of Panamint Valley, but it was on the eastern edge of the valley near the mouth of Hall Canyon at Warm Sulphur Springs. Steward (1938:84) says, "The principal and probably only village within the northern part of the valley was at Warm Springs [Warm Sulphur Springs] . . . called Ha:uta." He shows it as a winter village (fig. 7, village 42).

152. Panamint City in Surprise Canyon sprang up after silver was discovered there in 1873, shortly before Brier led prospectors into the Panamints. But its glory was short lived (Coolidge 1937:77–84; Levy 1969:101); by 1877, the main veins were depleted, and it quickly became a ghost town.

153. The Brier mess camped on and exited from Death Valley over Towne Pass. Some historians (e.g., Southworth 1978:46; Koenig 1984:127) place this camp on the shoulder of Pinto Peak, but it was on Towne Pass (spelled now with an *e*). Further confirmation that Brier's "Town's Pass" is the current Towne Pass is found on Farley's 1861 map and Wheeler's 1877 map (atlas sheet 65D). On these maps the pass is clearly shown where the current road now goes.

154. Culverwell died in Death Valley about 6 miles south of Bennetts Well (see also notes 79 & 89).

the relentless Diggers & was redeemed by our Surveyors of the boundary lines of the state

The Lady who used to tighten the girths of your oxen is still alive   The 3 boys are all alive   The Eldest lives in Oakland & doing well   the second is a Congregational Minister & Pastor at Grass Valley   the youngest Kirke is a Teacher in Oakland

I will give you the names of all the Jayhawkes that I can recollect   Capt Doty, Haines, Richards, Allen, who now lives in Chico   John Groscup, Carter, Robinson who died   Abbot of the New York boys & I think 2 brothers named Herrison   The names of most have passed from my mind. I have met but few of them since we parted   There is one of the company near me, a silversmith, but cannot call his name

My second son has published a Series of Poems on our trip which he may send to your meeting[155]   The names of the dead are Culverwell, Fish, Isham & Robinson   The old French[man] turned up and was not dead as we supposed. I hope you will have a delightful reunion & each a blessed life & a glorious immortality   Please answer this & give some account of your meeting

Your fellow traveler
JWBrier Sr

I am much pressed for time & have written this carelessly so says Mrs B—— but I hope that you can make it out

JWB

[JA 71]

Glen Dale Farm Nevada Co Jan 23 '79

Mr Leuther A Richards & Comrades of the Desert
Dear Friends

I rec yours via Dacotey which has never been my residence. It is the residence of my brother W W Brier

Twenty-nine years have rolled away since we separated. Alas! how time flies. Soon, we shall all follow our old companions, to the land from which there is no return. Mrs B—— & myself are dwelling alone, on our farm in Nevada Co   Our children are scattered. Columbus, the eldest son, resides in Oakland, & teaches in San

---

155. We have not found John's published poems. They may be in a Congregational Church publication or a newspaper from the Eureka, California, area. He was asked to write an article for *Death Valley Magazine* in 1908, but the publisher "vehemently called for facts; and I told him that I was dealing with facts and not fictions; hence the absence of those sensational features that capture a certain class of readers. . . . I requested him to return my manuscript and photos, which he declined to do, stating that he would publish, in the original form and intact. He called my production a beautiful poem; but a poem was not what he wanted" (Brier JA 88). This article may be what Reverend Brier was referring to.

Francisco. John W. is a Congreational Minister, & is stationed, for the present, at Eureka Humbolt Co. He is called "the Beecher of the Pacific" by many.[156] Kirke White, is teaching in Sacramento, & is Vice Principle of the High School with a salary of $2500.00 per annum. So much for the three lads who were in your Company.

Two years ago, I gave you some account of a flying trip that I made as a guide, back over our old track, to "Death Valley," as it is now called—the valley, in which you burned your waggons. Perhaps some account of this region will interest you more than any thing that I can write. You all remember the first Alkali pond to which we came, & you remember just where we caught the first Indians [in Nevada]. From that point you sent two or three men in a west course to explore, & they returned with an unfavorable report, when we all turned south. Well, it is now certain that we were then within 40 or 50 miles of White Mt, where there is a beautiful stream of pure water running down into the head of Death Valley, where it sinks in the sand.[157] Grass, at that point is plenty From there, through a gentle pass [Westgard Pass], it is about 25 miles to Owens River. So you see how we missed it.

You all remember the snow Mt that we crossed after you left your waggons. The name, is Panamint, & the valley into which we descended on New Years day, is Panamint Valley. You recollect when some of the Mississippi boys, with little West, & Tom & Joe the darkies, left us & steered for a Cannon on the west side of the valley. The Cannon, is now called Darwin's, and at the mouth of it, is a large mining town, called Darwin City. You remember, that we traveled down Panamint Valley 25 miles to some Indian Springs, where the Mountains were very high on the East side. Well, right up in the top of those high Mts, stands Panamint City. Here are great Silver Mines. You remember that after leaving Panamint Valley, you crossed a rough mountain & came to a Salt Lake [Searles Lake], where I & my family, with Carter & Groscup found you at mid night—but was not that a time! Well that lake is not salt as we supposed, but is Borax. Here are the great Borax Mines or washings. That Glorious Spring brook, discovered on the next morning by Deacon Richards, is now called "Providence Spring" on account of the many lives it has saved. You remember, at the foot of the Sierra Nevada, some Indian Springs, walled up with rock, well, at this point stands, now, a Hotel. I rode up to the door, & told the Land

156. Henry Ward Beecher (1813–1887), brother of Harriet Beecher Stowe, was a noted Congregational preacher and pulpit orator known for his enthusiasm, dramatic sense, and wit. He published many volumes of sermons and lectures on preaching, religion, and evolution.

157. He is referring to Wyman Creek, which flows down the eastern slope of the White Mountains from the Ancient Bristlecone Pine Forest and terminates in Deep Spring Valley. This stream is 100 miles northeast of Travertine Springs, where the Briers spent Christmas eve.

Lord, that I held a claim on the ground, for I had slept there 25 years ago with my family. He looked stunned & could scarcely believe me.

I go back, in mind, over this whole trip, about 200 times per annum, & at this distant day, can describe every mile of the way with every camp, & every incident of the journey. When I went out as a guide, the old pioneers told me, that every thing would seem strange, & that I would recognise nothing, but so soon as we struck our old trail it seemed to me, that it was but yesterday when we passed   The journey was one of intense interest, and deep solemnity. At many a point where we suffered most I went alone into the rocks & sage & wept & thanked God for our deliverance.

My son JW has written, & published a poem on our journey, which I intended to send, but he is 300 miles away & has it with him, & it is now too late to get it for you. I should esteem it a great pleasure to drop down amongst you & share in your enjoyments, But I must close for I am blind with tears. How the past rises up before my thoughts! & then our diminishing numbers, who were stalwart men! Soon there will be but one of all that number left, & he will be old & bent & grey.

Wife joins in love   God bless you all   farewell

Yours fraternally
and affectionately
JWBrier Sr

[JA 69]

Lodi Jan 10th 93

Mr. John. B. Colton
Dear Sir & Comrade

Rec^d yours last night & in reply would say that we are still alive, & for old people pretty strong. I live on my little farm of 3 Acres in the Suburb of Lodi   I do all my own work, & preach frequently, though not in charge of any Church at present. Mrs B—— is still able to do her own work   My eldest son is Prof of Mathematics & Natural Sciences in the Urban Academy San Francisco. My second son is Pastor of the Congregational Church in Lodi & stands at the head, as a Pulpit Orator on this Coast. My wife & I were born in the year 1814 & are therefore in our 79 year. We still hold fast to our Christian faith & the hope of an endless life beyond the deserts of time & Earth. I was in Southern Cal not long since & lectured in many places on "Death Valley" as the great salt valley is now called where you burned your waggons.[158]

The rail road runs right along where we jerked Horse Meat & goes up the valley on the route taken by your Stampede Oxen   The great sage plain, where we buried poor Robinson, is called Antelope Valley

I send our love to all who remain & would greatly enjoy your meeting but our age, & want of means makes it impossible   The account of our trip is in manuscript, but not yet published.[159] We were in hopes of giving it to the public before this time, but the want of means has blocked the wheels   I have not met any of the old comrades for years although I often hear of them. Our prayer is, that we may all meet at last an unbroken Company in Heaven.

Your Unworthy Comrades,

JWBrier Sr

Mrs JWBrier

JWBrier Jr

On the reception of yours I went to the Gallery & had the negative of myself & wife & son taken but for 6 weeks a dense fog has overspread the whole country, so that up to the last moment, they could not be finished

JWB

[JA 76]

Antiock California Jan 16th 96

Dear Old Comrads,

Forty and six years have passed since we reached the San Francisco Ranch and a few of us are still on this side of the river. *We* are in our 82nd year both being born in 1814   Neither of us expect to see another anniversary. Well we are ready to go, and are only waiting for the tide that will bear us out to sea   Death has not come in to our homes the past year.

---

158. Reverend Brier was 73 years old when he went on this lecture tour, during which he captivated his audiences. The tour was reported in the *Los Angeles Times* under the title "Death Valley. Its Ghastly Story as Told by an Aged Survivor" (Brier 1887?). Charles F. Lummis (1911:38) met the Reverend on this trip and commented that his story was "one of the most interesting and graphic stories I ever listened to."

159. His manuscripts were never published, nor have they been found. In 1882, John Brier (in Belden 1954:46) wrote the *Inyo Independent* that "to send you my ms. at present is quite impossible, for it is not complete, nor have I my father's consent." John was 6 years old when he trekked through Death Valley in winter 1849–50; certainly most of the details in his two articles were supplied by his parents.

You all remember that we went down Panamint Valley 2 days journey when we reached the great Mesqueete Swamp [Warm Sulphur Springs] and camped 2 or 3 days at a pool where there were a number of Indian Wickiups   then we went down some 5 or 6 miles farther South to other Springs [Post Office Spring] where we all tarried a few days longer. While here Capt Town & I explored the West rim of Panamint [Valley] where we found an Indian Trail over a very steep pass which I condemned as impassable.[160] The Captain differed & turned back to camp   I went on south many miles farther & discovered a large canyon [Fish Canyon, Slate Range]. I then returned to camp which I reached about 10 p.m.[161]

I found my wife baking up the last of the flour which belonged to my companions. We had no ownership in it whatever   Old Capt. Haines sat by looking wistfully on, & a boy, I think his nephew or grandson was all the evening gathering fuel. At last the work was done & at midnight Mr Maston [Masterson] & Crumpton asked myself & family to eat one biscuit each & that was to be the last for us.[162] All was silent as the grave   Capt Haynes took out a five dollar gold piece & offered it to the men for one biscuit but they refused it. The Captain wept & said to me "I have the best 160 acres in Knox Co. Ill. 100 stock hogs, & 2000 bushels of old corn in crib & here I cannot get one biscuit for love or money," and the boy looked sad & disappointed & went away to his blankets.

Next morning the Jayhawks packed up & started for the condemned pass, but we remained until noon to assist our two comrads to pack up—not one word was spoken all that forenoon (all too full)   When ready, they turned their faces away & reached out their hands   Not a word was said. As they receded my little group stood with eyes dimmed with tears, & bitterly thought of the morrow. Well we gathered up our oxen & packed up & wearily followed on. At sunset we came to a part of the Jay Hawks & other stragglers who were waiting for us   These were Carter John Groscup, Harry Vance, M Gould, Father Fish, & Isham   Well we slept at that point.[163]

160. Based on Sheldon Young's mileages (in Long 1950:276), it would seem the Jayhawkers attempted to cross the Argus Range through Water Canyon, but turned back at or before reaching Snooky Spring and backtracked to near the mouth of the canyon where they took the Indian trail south into Searles Valley (see also note 42).

161. Reverend Brier is often criticized for not holding up his share of the labors during these trying times. This solo scouting trip in Indian country speaks highly for his bravery and stamina. His health rapidly declined about this time, and his wife assumed the leadership role. According to Mrs. Brier (1898), her husband became so ill he had to walk with two canes. Lummis (1911:41) tells us that, during the last three weeks of their ordeal, Mrs. Brier had to lift her husband to his feet in the morning and steady him before he could walk. Reverend Brier lost 100 pounds along this "short cut" and wasted away to 75 pounds.

162. Mrs. Brier (1898) said Masterson and Crumpton had all the flour, but they gave her "a small piece, which I made into twenty-two little crackers and put away for an emergency."

163. This was a dry camp in the rolling hills on the west side of Panamint Valley 2 miles northeast of

Next morning I started to explore the big Canyon [Fish Canyon] some 12 or 15 miles away leaving the rest to follow   Mrs B—— was taken that morning with sick headache & spent a most suffering day   I reached the mouth of the Canyon about 2 PM went up 2 or 3 miles untill it closed up to 20 feet in width, with walls on either side overhanging or perpendicular—*A Silent Sepulcre.*[164] Here I found a little damp sand & scooping out a hole a little water arose   Slakeing my thirst I went on 2 or 3 hundred yards when I found the Canyon walled in but the kind wind of long ages had blown sand enough from the hills above, at a low point of some 50 feet, to make a windrow of sand to the bottom of the pass.[165] With my hands I tore off the apex of this windrow & made a way out on to good ground   I reached the top of the pass & seeing our way clear I returned & met the Company at the mouth of the Canyon about sunset. We reached the sepe of water about dark driving our poor famished oxen up the Canyon above us & then we spread our blankets on the sand in this silent & desolate place, & gave ourselves over in the hands of the great God for protection. The place was not only dismal in the extreme, but dangerous. Indians were watching us from the heights of that I was aware, because I saw there fresh tracks in the wet sand in the Canyon in the morning. They could have rolled rocks on us from above & have buried us. I was aware of the danger but said nothing.

In the morning we found that about one half of our oxen had quietly passed us & as we supposed, had returned to the last water. The oxen of Carter, Vance, Gould Fish with 2 of mine were missing   Carter went back for the runaway oxen. I left Father Fish in the care of Harry Vance, for he was too weak to travel, & I took with me John Groscup & Isham. Before leaving Father Fish came to me weeping & said I have this morning been guilty of a great sin   Will God forgive me? I said what is it? He said the boiler turned over & spilled the coffee. Isham said where is the coffee? & I said it is gone to the Devil I suppose   Oh! said he   I have not said such a thing before in 40 years   It showed the reality of the old man   This was his last talk with me. Well I started on with my family, Groscup &

Water Canyon. Reverend Brier was correct in condemning a possible route over the Argus Range via Water Canyon, but he did not know there is a relatively easy trail, still traceable about a mile west of the paved road, over the pass into Searles Valley. The Jayhawkers took this trail after abandoning their attempt to cross the range via Water Canyon and entered Searles Valley via Jayhawker Pass (see also note 42).

164. The "Silent Sepulcre" is in the dogleg bend (a box canyon) almost 2 miles above the mouth of Fish Canyon. Finding this spot was important to

our research project because it provided an explanation why the Brier mess found water where Manly and Rogers, who camped at the same spot a few days later, found none. Descriptions given by the Briers and those given by Manly had to dovetail, and they did (see also note 38).

165. Similar windrows of sand still exist here. Beck (1940) first identified them during his quest to trace the Briers' route over the range. Faint traces of an Indian trail are still visible in this part of the canyon.

Isham. With much effort we got out of the Canyon on my windrow of sand in an hour we were on top of the pass.

After going down the western slope in another Canyon [middle fork of Isham Canyon] about 300 yards we suddenly came to a jumping off place of about 6 feet   Groscup & I built a stone Bridge down to the level over which all passed in safety. Groscup then took the lead with his one ox, & mine followed. He soon found other jump offs but the madcap did not wait for a Bridge but forced his Ox to jump & mine followed suit. So on we went until about 3 PM we found ourselves faceing what is now known as Borax Lake & right East of your camp.[166] It [Searles Lake] looked to be about 3 miles away, but it was Midnight when we reached the Jay Hawks camp   Isham being weary stoped to rest some 4 or 5 miles back, but did not come to camp.

I now go back to our last camp in big Canyon [Fish Canyon]. Well, Carter found all the oxen near the mouth of the Canyon   They packed up by noon & started   Father Fish took hold on the tail of his ox & was helped up the windrow out of the dismal Canyon. He held on to the tail 3 or 4 hundred yards when he reeled & fell to rise no more   The boys were so excited that they forgot to leave him his blankets   I sent back for him the next day but he was found dead. The story of Isham's death you all remember

I have given you this little narative of 2 days in which we were separated. I am now giving to the public the whole narative from where we took the cutoff to the San Fransketo Rancho   It draws an audience & holds it spellbound for 2 hours. I would go east & give it but cannot now. We have not yet put our Book to the press, but still intend to do so.[167] Now my Dear old Comrades, this may be my last communication so fare you well. Meet us in Heaven where there will be no hunger or thirst or pain forever

Yours truly

Jas W Brier & Wife

166. They reached the Jayhawker camp on the edge of Searles Lake at midnight; thus, Brier means they reached the mouth of Isham Canyon at 3 P.M. The Brier mess should have followed the Indian trail west 5 miles across Searles Valley to the springs in Great Falls Basin, but the lure of what appeared to be a freshwater lake enticed them to head south to it. The Jayhawker narrative in Manly's book (1894:340) tells us that some of the Jayhawkers steered "toward a pile of tremendous rocks, [and] found a little stream of good water." This is a perfect description of the water flowing from Great Falls Basin. When Brier said he was "right East of your camp" he may have been referring to a separate Jayhawkers' camp at the toe of Great Fall Basin.

167. Apparently Reverend Brier and Juliet never published their manuscript.

[JA 73]

Lodi Jan 20th 98

Mr Deacon Richards
Dear Sir

We are still alive though old & feeble both being in our 84th year. This will likely be our last letter   I request that no part of it shall be published & I further request that our names may no longer appear in the list of Jayhawkers, for we never had any connexion with that Company.[168] We were members of the Mississippi Boys untill we reached the head of Panamint Valley.[169] Here most of my company packed their backs & left us. Now my family Capt Town, Mr Mastin [Masterson] & Compton [Crumpton] & the 2 Turner boys went with the Jayhawks down to Mesquit swamp. *Here* these 5 men left us & struck off west [these men left the Brier mess at Post Office Spring, 6 miles south of Warm Sulphur Springs].

My family now fell in with the Jayhawks. We traveled with them a part of the time & generally camped with them on the same ground but were no part of their Company   My family was then composed of myself, wife & 3 boys, & Father Fish of Leima Indiana & Isham of Michigan [New York] Mr. Gould of Newyork though not in my family yet camped with us   Father Fish fell in the Mt west of Panamint & Isham in Borax Valley, (as now called)   further on Patrick & Lummis St John overtook us, & were utterly destitute.[170]   I took them in to my family & shared with them & brought them in. I remember you well as the discoverer of Providence Spring up a Canyon & as the man who climbed to the top of the highest peak of Inyo [southern Argus] Mts & found there a camp of Diggers who showed you our way out & how many sleeps. You found there a bason & cedar trees & a spring of water *(Many thanks)*   I remember Capt Haines & a boy that I suppose was John B. Colton   The Capt was a good man. I remember the 2 Achison

168. This letter was written after Reverend Brier read the "Story of the Jayhawkers" chapter in *Death Valley in '49* in which Manly recorded the negative feelings some Jayhawkers felt toward Brier. One comment (1894:342) was that Brier "had fallen out with any work but that of the tongue, and seemed perfectly willing for someone else to do the work."

169. The Mississippi boys, as they were called, made it to the gold fields through Walker Pass (Walker 1961). They left Panamint Valley about January 9, and twelve of them arrived at the Mariposa mines on January 29. According to Evans (1945:254 & 259), after crossing Walker Pass they subsisted "upon acorns, mule meat, and a few fish obtained from the Indians, [and] they happily reach these mines without the loss of a man, after having suffered intensely." He goes on to say that on February 9, "ten [more] men, be-

longing to the train mentioned as being yet in the desert beyond the mountains arrived here last night, having left the main body some three hundred miles from here, all in starving, and some in a perishing condition."

170. According to Mrs. Brier (1898), "St. John and Patrick" were with the Briers at Post Office Spring in Panamint Valley. We do not think they were Arcan's drivers as Wheat suggests (1939b:107, fn. 45) because Manly (1894:162) said he "met Bennett and Arcane's teamsters" with Asa Haynes's group in Last Chance Canyon. Since Mrs. Brier's chronology is very poor, it is possible St. John and Patrick were two of the six men Sheldon Young (in Long 1950:277) said came into camp at Providence Spring on January 14, the other four being the Bennett-Arcan drivers.

Brothers—good men   I remember Capt Doty, &, as a matter [of] course I recollect Carter & John Groscup & I further remember that when your old stampeded oxen left you in a bad fix that I lent you 3 or 4 of mine to help you on & I further remember that I sold to Capt Doty, as a favor, my 7 splendid oxen for $115 when on the same day I could have taken $200 in coin   I did this little act to help the Jayhawks but Tom Shannon that blackard of your company has paid me in full for my little unselfish acts of kinddness. This *Tom* of the Jayhawks has paid me in vile slander—*unmitigated falsehoods*   While I was helping the Jayhawks I suppose these slanders were being bandied through the Jayhawk camp *(poor, wicked selfish humbug) (See Louis Manley's Book. So called)*   And *who* is Louis Manley. He was one of Bennet's ox drivers   I did not know him but I recollect that he & John Rodgers passed us on the desert & that they filled themselves with my jerk[171]   This same ox driver came to me at Los Angeles strapped & I took him into my home, gave him employment & wages & by recommending him highly got him in with two of our friends who took him to the mines.[172] *Well* he has paid me—*the vile ingrate.*

As a matter of course, we do [not?] hold any of you accountable for the doings of these wicked men   I was a Minister & that was sufficient for them. I am not ashamed of [my] reputation in Iowa, on the plains, or in Cal   I hope these facts will not dampen the joy of your meeting   A few more winds will cover our tracks. Please drop our names from your list for I never belonged to your company & we do not want our names identified with such a lying scoundrel as Tom Shannon   I took Capt Doty's note for the oxen   I sold it to a Dr. Earl   I do not know whether it was ever paid. After I left you at the Spanish ranch I went to Los Angeles with just 2 bits in pocket & your company had the oxen.[173] This would have been a joy to me to this day had I not since learned of the dirty scoundrelism that was,

171. Manly was not one of Bennett's drivers. He was an experienced teamster who later drove for Brier in Los Angeles. Manly and Rogers did not encounter Brier either going for or returning with provisions. Possibly Silas Helmer and S. S. Abbott, Bennett's two wagon drivers who left the families in Death Valley in company with Arcan's two drivers, stopped by Brier's camp.

172. These two friends of Brier were certainly not friends of Manly. He traveled with them from Los Angeles to San Jose, and at their request rode one of their horses "as they said it would keep it more gentle to ride it" (Manly 1894:377). Manly's mule carried the provisions. However, as they neared San Jose, the owners of the horses demanded payment for the privilege of riding but "refused to allow me anything

for the use of the mule." They demanded and got one ounce of gold, almost all the money he had (Manly 1894:384).

173. Brier may have had only "2 bits" in his pocket, but he was hardly destitute. The gamblers collected and gave him $10, "a fortune to a minister in those days" (Brier 1887?), and he had Doty's note for $115 plus enough oxen to dispose of seven more to obtain a half interest in a hotel at the southwest corner of the Plaza. These trained animals were used for freighting to the mines and were not the seven sold to Doty or the oxen Manly used to haul water while in Brier's employ. The oxen could not be called "splendid oxen." Mrs. Brier said, "there was not an ounce of fat on one and the marrow in their bones had turned to blood and water" (Brier 1898).

at that very time being prac[t]iced in your camp   It is painful for me
to name these things but you should know them

                    Farewell
                        JWBrier Sr

            L[etter] to Tom Shannon Feby 17 '98.

[This note, in different handwriting, was apparently added by
Richards after he wrote a letter to Shannon.]

Epilogue

William Lewis Manly

After escaping from the Great American Desert, Manly worked in Los Angeles about a month, earning enough money to travel north to the mines. He caught up with the Bennett party including John Rogers near San Jose, and together they all proceeded to the mines in the Merced River area and worked their way north through Placerville, Coloma, and Georgetown. It was in Georgetown that Cuff, Bennett's ever faithful dog, was stolen and never seen again. The large white mastiff had suffered hunger and thirst along with his masters, the Bennett family, and had served them well. Manly later recalled that "a redskin never approached without warning from the intelligent brute. He seemed willing to die for his friends" (in Woodward 1949b:54). With three young children in the family, he was undoubtedly a family pet in addition to being a valuable watchdog.

In December 1850, Manly headed home via Panama. He traveled up the Mississippi and overland as far as Mineral Point, Wisconsin, before bad weather prevented his return to the parental farm in Michigan. He stayed the winter with E. A. Hall in Mineral Point, where he wrote a 300-page letter to his parents based on his diary. This letter was much read by his parents, but unfortunately it was destroyed when their home burned.

In the spring of 1851, Manly was talked into returning to California with a trapping friend, Robert McCloud. They traveled down the Mississippi River, across the isthmus of Panama, and up the coast of California. They tried their luck north of the Mother Lode, where Manly had been in 1850, and mined the middle and south forks of the Yuba River for two years. When the cold season arrived, Manly leased his share of the venture and set out for southern California, where a mining partner of 1850, W. M. Stockton, had a pear orchard near Mission San Gabriel. Stockton also ran cattle, and Manly bought half of his stock. However, in 1853, rustlers were siphoning off his profits, so he sold his cattle and helped the buyers drive them north.

After visiting his mine at Moore's Flat, Manly saw Rogers, apparently in 1855, who told him where the Bennetts and Arcans had settled (Manly 1894:469; Belden 1954:54). Since his mine was doing well and the lease was not yet up, he went to Watsonville to visit the Bennetts and to Santa Cruz to see the Arcans, who gave him a hero's welcome. From there he traveled north to San Jose and helped build Mr. Moody's gristmill. The Moodys had waited at Los Angeles for the Bennetts to come out of the desert and had helped outfit them to continue to the mines (Hafen and Hafen 1961:108). In the spring of 1856, while returning to his mine, Manly saw Old Crump, the ox who carried the children out of Death Valley. He was fat and well cared for.

At Moore's Flat he found the town had expanded to include two hotels and a post office. He was encouraged to enter the mercantile business, which he did. For two years, while working the Paradise claims, he also bought gold dust from other miners.

In the fall of 1859, he looked for a place to settle and chose a farm near Hillsdale, San Jose township. He was familiar with the area, having worked on Moody's gristmill and having visited the Bennett family in San Jose at the time of Sarah's death in 1857.

About this time Stockton again asked Manly to visit him in southern California. While there, he saw Bennett and his four children, who had recently moved to southern California from Utah. Bennett told Manly and Stockton how Charles Alvord and Bennett were in a party that prospected for silver in the Panamint Range during the summer of 1860. Alvord picked up samples containing gold; when the news leaked out, the company insisted Alvord return to the desert to show them the location. Alvord was unable to find the lode, and in anger the others, including Bennett, left Alvord to die. After Bennett told this story, they decided Alvord must be rescued. In the winter of 1860–61 Manly, Bennett, and Caesar Twitchell loaded five mules with provisions and retraced the '49er route back to the Panamints (Manly in Woodward 1949b:61 [incorrect date] & 72 [correct date]). They camped at Redlands Spring above Ox-Jump Fall, where Bennett and Alvord had built a ramp for the mules during their first prospecting trip. Quite by accident, Alvord found their camp; since he was well, they prepared to prospect further. Their meager provisions were soon exhausted, so Bennett and Twitchell took the mules to the coast for provisions while Manly and Alvord stayed in the mountains. A heavy storm smothered the mountain passes with snow for six weeks, and after that time Bennett and Twitchell assumed the other two were either dead or had made their way to civilization. In camp, however, grub was down to a bit of flour that Manly and Alvord made into biscuits. They left a note in case the other two should return for them and headed for Walker Pass. At Indian Wells Spring they met a group of five or six men led by Dr. George returning to Visalia from a prospecting trip to the Panamints, where they had also been hunting for the Alvord Lead. According to George (in Ray 1966 & George 1875), he found "Manley sustaining himself and Alvord on jack rabbits. Our party, having enough bread to sustain the sick man [Alvord] until an arrival at Kingsville, we put him on my riding horse and took him in."

In March 1861, Manly, Alvord, and Hickman (a Moore's Flat friend) took a wagon across Walker Pass and into the Coso Range, where they prospected in the newly established Coso mining district. While there they heard about the outbreak of the Civil War. Instead of continuing to the Panamints in the heat of summer, they returned to the Sierra Nevada, where Manly spent July hunting deer and grizzly bear.

On July 10, 1862, Manly married Mary Jane Woods of Woodbridge, San Joaquin County. The town was named for her father. Manly rarely makes reference to his wife; they apparently never had children.

In 1877, Manly dictated the first printed account of his overland trip to a reporter (in Woodward 1949b:3–19). Margaret Long (1950:220) was told by Bill Smith who was told by Dyer Geer that Manly returned to the desert east of Death Valley and asked Geer to guide him from Enterprise, Utah, to Fairbanks Spring in Ash Meadows, Nevada. However, Manly said in a letter to Palmer (August 1894) that he never returned to Death Valley.

About 1886, Manly had an accident that prevented him from working, so he wrote "From Vermont to California" during the next three years. About that time he started corresponding with and visiting others who came through Death Valley in '49 to review their memories of the trek.

The Manlys moved to College Park at the corner of Asbury Street and Stockton Avenue in 1892. He wrote a number of articles for publication during the next five years based on his own experiences and his correspondence with others. During this time, and until his death, he kept a scrapbook of pictures, articles, and letters collected from other '49ers. To date this scrapbook has not surfaced. His book *Death Valley in '49* was published in 1894, and the following year he visited Rogers near Merced. In 1898 Manly was quite ill, and in 1901 he fell and broke his hip (Stephens 1902:JA 981), which confined him to a wheelchair for the rest of his life. In July 1902, Mrs. Manly died and was buried in Woodbridge Cemetery. Less than a year later, on February 5, 1903, early in the morning, Manly died at home from a heart attack; he was buried beside his wife at Woodbridge. Treasure hunters tore up his yard and floorboards to look for gold they felt the old miner must have hidden.

John Rogers

The little information we have about John Rogers's life after he reached Los Angeles is in the introduction to part III.

The Bennett Family

The Bennetts mined in the Merced River area and at George-town, where Cuff, their faithful dog, was stolen. They moved to Watsonville and apparently bought a farm at the confluence of the Salinas River and Monterey Bay, although there are no census records or deeds of sale showing their existence there. Another son, John Rogers, was born to them in 1853, and a daughter, Ella Caroline, was born in 1854.

In 1857, Sarah Bennett became very ill. Manly rushed to her bedside after receiving word from her father, Mr. Dilly. She died the day after Manly arrived and was buried in Oak Hill Cemetery, San Jose (Manly 1894:474). Ella Caroline was given into the care of Anna Scott (Mrs. George Edwin Scott) of Scotts Valley, where she remained until her marriage in 1874 to George Gushee.

Bennett sold the farm and bought calico and other supplies to sell in Utah. With two wagon loads he set out with the four older children. He married a Mormon woman and embraced her faith, but because of the heavy tithing and the Mormons' involvement in the Mountain Meadow Massacre, Asabel became dissatisfied with his life there. In 1858, while living in Utah, he led a group of Mormons over part of the '49er trail from Enterprise, Utah, to Dry Lake Valley, Nevada (Stott 1984:119).

He returned with his children to Los Angeles in 1859. Soon afterward he led a small prospecting party that included Charles Alvord into the Death Valley region. Shortly after this trip, Bennett was also in the party that forced Alvord to return to the area to share his gold discovery; when Alvord could not find the lead, they left him to die. Late in 1860, Bennett accompanied Manly and Twitchell to rescue Alvord, only to leave Manly and Alvord stranded in the Panamint Range without provisions when a snowstorm blocked the mountain passes.

George and John Bennett traveled about with their restless father. A George W. Bennett was listed as an officer of the Belmont, Utah, Masonic Lodge in 1881 (Angel 1881:241). When Manly and his wife visited Ella Caroline in Scotts Valley, she said her father was living near Belmont, Nevada. George died March 10, 1884, at his sister Martha's home in Wilmington, California. Martha Ann Bennett, born January 21, 1846 (Woodward 1949b:xi), married William Johnson and had two daughters, Martha (Mrs. W. B. Hewitt) and

Ella (Mrs. Lilly). She died February 27, 1910. Melissa married Judge Rolfe of San Bernardino about 1862. She died a couple of years after the birth of her only child, Agnes (Mrs. Lindner). Asabel Bennett wandered about a great deal until his death in Idaho Falls, April 22, 1891, at 84 years of age (Manly in Woodward 1949b:29, 33). Ages given for the Bennett family in *Index to the 1850 Census of the State of California* (Bowman 1972:145) are: Asael [Asabel], 36; Sarah Ann, 25; George, 8; Melissa, 5; and Martha, 2. These ages are at variance with those given by Manly and Bennett grandchildren. Frank Latta's *Death Valley '49ers* and Woodward's *The Jayhawkers' Oath* have additional information on the Bennetts.

The Arcan (Arcane) Family

The Arcans settled in Santa Cruz. Manly (in Woodward 1949b:28) said the Bennetts and Arcans "both got to the mines and worked in different places." Mrs. Arcan probably did not accompany her husband to the mines since their second child was born in Santa Cruz on July 1, 1850. John established a gunsmith shop in one half of the home he built on the corner of Arcan Street (now Soquel Avenue) and Pacific Avenue early in the 1850s. The Santa Cruz Masonic Lodge met in the hall upstairs, and John was active in many areas of the community. He died at home in 1869 and was buried in Evergreen Cemetery.

Julia S. Arcan, their second child, was born July 1, about four months after their exit from the desert. She lived nineteen days. Julia was the first person to be buried in the newly created Evergreen Cemetery in Santa Cruz. Abigail Harriett Ericsen Arcan bore two more daughters when she was 38. Julia Madeline, retarded, was born at the beginning of the year, and Abigail Carolyn was born at the end of the year. Madeline required Abigail's constant care until her death in 1887 at age 27. Abby was married twice and had two daughters, one of whom survived her. She died in 1918.

Abigail continued to live in the family home with Charlie's family until she died at age 74. Her death on February 24, 1891, was reported in the *Santa Cruz Daily Sentinel*, but there is no record of her burial. Although there is a space between John's tombstone and Julia's, a logical location for Abigail's final resting place, there is no stone. She died as she lived, with scant tribute to her courage and participation in one of the great episodes in our western history.

Little Charlie grew up to become a swimming instructor at Santa Cruz beach and a member of the Hastings Band, which enlivened local social functions and parades. He married at age 19 and fathered five children. After his first wife died, he married Etta Berry Emery, a local beauty. Charlie first worked as a machinist and later owned a bar in Santa Cruz. He died of rheumatism in 1907 at age 59.

More information on the Arcans is found in our book *Julia, Death Valley's Youngest Victim* and in Frank Latta's *Death Valley '49ers*.

The Wade Family

Although the Wades were not part of the Bennett-Arcan party, they were the only other family with young children to head south into Death Valley from Furnace Creek Wash. Instead of crossing the Panamints, they went south to Saratoga Spring before turning west and were the only pioneers to bring a wagon out of Death Valley in 1850. They had an extremely difficult time, but arrived in Los Angeles able to start freighting between there and San Pedro.

After earning enough money from freighting to buy mining supplies, the Wades took the newly opened road past Mission San Fernando, up San Francisquito Canyon, and north to the Tuolumne River, where they mined for gold. When their possessions were stolen by Indians they moved to the valley near Saratoga, where Mary Ann was born on January 2, 1851, in the wagon that carried the Wades out of Death Valley.

Early in 1851, the Wades settled in Alviso, where Harry took up the work he knew best—freighting. As the years went by he expanded his business to include a stagecoach line and an inn called the American House; he also served as justice of the peace and public administrator before he retired in the late 1870s.

Harry Wade was born in Rochester, England, on March 16, 1800. When he married Mary Reynolds Leach on January 24, 1835, he was coachman to the king of England, and Mary, then 21 years old, was governess to the French ambassador's children at the English court. He was probably more experienced than most emigrants in the care and handling of dray animals and wagons. His riding horse and the family milk cow apparently survived at least as far as Death Valley. Although his aloofness appeared to be snobbery, it was probably just common sense to travel behind the others and allow the water holes to fill up and the dust to settle, when there was no danger from attacking Indians. Harry George, the Wades' first child, was born in London, December 18, 1835; within a month of his birth, the family moved to America. They settled first in Pennsylvania, but moved to Joliet, Illinois, after a flood destroyed their lumber mill in 1843. Charles, Almira, and Richard were born during the Wades' sojourn in Illinois before their venture west to California.

Four of the five Wade children traveled through Death Valley. Harry George, who was 15 at that time, first worked with his father, but later bought land and built a deep-water wharf on San Francisco Bay, where goods could be loaded into wagons directly from large ships. In 1869, he married Mary Davis, an Irish lass ten years his junior, at the Santa Clara Mission Parish House. They had three children. Charles Elliot was 11 years old when the family crossed Death Valley. He started in his father's business, but switched to farming after marrying Stefana (Estefana) Alviso in 1863. He had a large dairy as well as crops of strawberries, raspberries, hay, and grain. They had fifteen children, three of whom died in infancy. Almira was 9 when she entered Death Valley. She married John Jacob Ortley and had eleven children. Richard Angus was 5 while in the desert. He established a livery business and ran a passenger stage. James Lick hired Richard as a driver when he built his mountain observatory. Marie Berryessa became Richard's wife; they had no children.

Mary Ann, the Wades' youngest child, was born in California. She took care of her parents until Harry died in 1883 and Mary died in 1889. Mary Ann married at age 35 and had one daughter.

Many descendants of the Wade family still live in the Alviso area. Further information on the Wades is found in *The Wade Story* by Burr Belden, *Death Valley '49ers* by Frank Latta, and *Migration of the Wade Family* by Olaf Hagen.

Appendix A

Dates of Camps on Manly and Rogers's Round-Trip Search for Provisions

Our analysis of the 25 camps (26 days) used by Manly and Rogers on their 1850 rescue trip to the Rancho San Francisco to secure food and horses for the emigrants stranded in Death Valley compared to the 20 camps mentioned in Manly's "From Vermont to California" (1888) and the 22 camps mentioned in his *Death Valley in '49* (1894). Page numbers will direct the reader to camps mentioned in this volume and in Manly's book (first edition).

Night of		Camp	Location	1888 Camp (page)*	1894 Camp (page)
January	15	A (1)	Above Arrastre Spring, Panamint Range	1 (70)	1 (154)
	16	B (2)	Fish Canyon ("Silent Sepulcre"), Slate Range	2 (74)	2 (155)
	17	C (3)	Burro Canyon, Argus Range	3 (77)	3 (157)
	18	D (4)	Indian Wells Spring at Homestead, base of Owens Peak	4 (83)	4 (160)
	19	E (5)	Forlorn Hope Spring, Last Chance Canyon, El Paso Mountains	5 (85)	5 (162)
	20	F (6)	Near California City, Mojave Desert	(**)	6 (165)
	21	G (7)	Rainwater holes between Buckhorn and Rosamond lakes, Edwards AFB	6 (87)	7 (167)
	22	H (8)	Barrel Springs, southeast of Palmdale	7 (89)	8 (168)
	23	I (9)	Babbling brook, Soledad Canyon, 2 miles south of Acton	8 (90)	9 (169)
	24	J (10)	Soledad Canyon (Manly is lame)	9 (**)	10 (171)
	25	K (11)	4 miles east of San Francisco ranch house	10 (92)	11 (174)
	26	L (12)	A mile or two west of the ranch house	11 (94)	12 (177)
	27	M (13)	Mission San Fernando	(**)	13 (182)
	28	N (14)	Ranch house, Rancho San Francisco	(**)	14 (183)
	29	O (15)	Ranch house, Rancho San Francisco	(**)	(**)
	30	P (16)	San Francisquito Canyon (with road builders)	(**)	15 (187)
	31	Q (17)	East of Elizabeth Lake	12 (99)	(**)
February	1	R (18)	Rainwater holes between Buckhorn and Rosamond lakes, Edwards AFB	13 (99)	(**)
	2	S (19)	Desert Spring (willow corral) near Cantil	14 (99)	16 (188)
	3	T (20)	At or east of Indian Wells Spring	15 (99)	17 (188)
	4	U (21)	Paxton Ranch (site), Indian Wells Valley	16 (99)	18 (189)
	5	V (22)	Indian Joe (Providence) Spring, Argus Range	17 (100)	19 (190)
	6	W (23)	Northeast of Manly Pass, Slate Range	18 (101)	20 (191)
	7	X (24)	Redlands Spring in Redlands Canyon, Panamint Range	19 (104)	21 (195)
	8	Y (25)	At or near Mesquite Well, Death Valley	20 (105)	22 (196)
	9	—	*On the 26th day Manly and Rogers arrived at Bennett's Well (long camp), Death Valley.*	—	—

*Page numbers in the present volume.
**Camp not referred to.

Appendix B

Dates of Camps Used by the Families when they Exited from Death Valley

Camps used when the Bennett-Arcan families left Death Valley in 1850, compared to camps mentioned in Manly's "From Vermont to California" (1888) and those mentioned in his *Death Valley in '49* (1894). Page numbers will direct the reader to camps mentioned in this volume and in Manly's book (first edition).

Night of		Camp	Location	1888 Camp (page)*	1894 Camp (page)
February	10	0	Bennetts Well (long camp), Death Valley	0 (110)	0 (200)
	11	1	4 or 5 miles south of Bennetts Well	1 (116)	1 (213)
	12	2	Galena Canyon, Panamint Range	(**)	(**)
	13	3	Arrastre Spring, Panamint Range	2 (118)	2 (215)
	14	4	Redlands Spring, in Redlands Canyon, Panamint Range	3 (119)	3 (219)
	15	5	Fish Canyon ("Silent Sepulcre"), Slate Range	4 (121)	4 (222)
	16	6	Lower Isham Canyon (at dogleg), Slate Range	5 (122)	(**)
	17	7	Indian Joe (Providence) Spring, Argus Range	6 (123)	5 (225)
	18	8	Junction of Sweetwater Creek & Moscow Canyon, Argus Range	7 (126)	6 (227)
	19	9	Paxton Ranch (site), Indian Wells Valley	8 (126)	7 (228)
	20	10	Indian Wells Valley	9 (128)	8 (229)
	21	11	Indian Wells Spring at Homestead, base of Owens Peak	10 (128)	9 (229)
	22	12	Southeast of Freeman Junction	11 (129)	10 (232)
	23	13	Forlorn Hope Spring, Last Chance Canyon, El Paso Mountains	12 (129)	11 (233)
	24	14	Small playa 2 miles southwest of Last Chance Canyon	13 (130)	12 (235)
	25	15	Desert Spring (willow corral) near Cantil	14 (130)	13 (236)
	26	16	Mojave Desert near California City	15 (131)	14 (241)
	27	17	Rainwater holes between Buckhorn and Rosamond lakes, Edwards AFB	16 (131)	15 (241)
	28	18	Northeast of Palmdale	17 (133)	16 (243)
March	1	19	Barrel Springs, southeast of Palmdale	18 (133)	17 (245)
	2	20	North of Soledad Pass (snowline)	19 (133)	18 (245)
	3	21	Babbling brook, Soledad Canyon, 2 miles south of Acton	20 (134)	19 (247)
	4	22	Soledad Canyon	21 (135)	20 (254)
	5	23	Soledad Canyon	22 (135)	21 (256)
	6	24	7 or 8 miles from ranch house	23 (136)	22 (257)
	7	25	Ranch house, Rancho San Francisco	24 (137)	23 (258)

*Page numbers in the present volume.
**Camp not referred to.

Bibliography

Author names are spelled as they appear in the original publication. Thus, there are entries for W. L. Manly and W. L. Manley (the same person), and John Rodgers is spelled with the *d*. We took the liberty of giving names to anonymous articles, enclosed in brackets. When we know the author but the article is not by-lined, we included the author's name in brackets. Only old maps or those difficult to find are listed. Documents in the Huntington Library's Jayhawker Collection are cited by their JA numbers and those in the Palmer Collection by their HM numbers. We have annotated some references and included cross-references where advisable. All references, either original volumes or photocopies of maps or manuscripts, are in our library. Subtitles for most books are not included.

Ackoff, Russell L. *Scientific Method*. New York: John Wiley and Sons, 1962.

[Alameda County]. *History of Alameda County, California*. Oakland: M. W. Wood, Pub., 1883. Pages 953 and 954 give a brief history of Louis Nusbaumer. The ages of Louis's and Elizabeth's children are given as 31, 29, 27, and 21 as of 1883, the publication date of this book. *See also* [San Francisco].

[Arcan]. Obituary for Abigail H. Arcan. *Santa Cruz Daily Sentinel*, Feb. 25, 1891, p. 2, col. 4.

Angel, Myron F., ed. *History of Nevada*. Oakland, CA: Thompson and West, 1881.

Bailey, Gilbert E. *The Saline Deposits of California*. California State Mining Bureau. Bulletin No. 24 (May 1902). Sacramento, CA: Supt. State Printing, 1902.

Bailey, Paul. *Walkara, Hawk of the Mountains*. Los Angeles, CA: Westernlore Press, 1954.

———. "Slaves in the Mojave." In *Brand Book 11*, edited by Russ Leadabrand, pp. 124–141. N.p.: The Westerners, Los Angeles Corral, 1964.

Bailey, Richard C. "Red Rock Canyon." In *Brand Book 11*, edited by Russ Leadabrand, pp. 20–30. N.p.: The Westerners, Los Angeles Corral, 1964.

Beck, John W. Letter to Carl I. Wheat, May 21, 1939. Carl I. Wheat Collection, The Bancroft Library, Berkeley, CA. Beck, in a reply to Wheat's letter of May 17, reveals that Wheat's (1939a) article "Hungry Bill Talks" is fictitious.

———. "Trailing the Jayhawker Route Through the Searles Valley." *Trona Pot-Ash*, March 21, 1940, pp. 1–2. This story was continued in the next issue (March 28) as "Manly and Rogers Trip from Death Valley to Coast." Beck gave the name "Brier Canyon" to the one now called Fish Canyon. He correctly identified the canyon the Brier mess ascended the Slate Range in, but he incorrectly has them descending the western flank in the north (main) fork of Isham Canyon rather than the middle fork.

Belden, L. Burr, ed. *Death Valley Heroine*. San Bernardino, CA: Inland Printing and Engraving Co., 1954.

———. *Goodbye, Death Valley! The Tragic 1849 Jayhawker Trek*. Death Valley '49ers Inc. Pub. No. 4. San Bernardino, CA: Inland Printing and Engraving Co., 1956.

———. *The Wade Story: In and Out of Death Valley*. San Bernardino, CA: Inland Printing and Engraving Co., 1957.

———. Letter to the authors, Nov. 13, 1973. Authors' collection.

———. *The Mississippians and the Georgians of the Death Valley 1849 Party*. Los Angeles, CA: Death Valley Forty-Niners, 1975.

Bell, Major Horace. *Reminiscences of a Ranger*. Santa Barbara, CA: Wallace Hebberd, 1927. Bell (p. 136), citing an unknown source, says, "The first Methodist sermon was preached June, 1850, by

Rev. J. W. Briar [Brier], at the adobe house of J. G. Nichols." According to Brier [1887?], he and his family reached Los Angeles on Saturday, Feb. 12, 1850, and he preached a sermon in Judge Nichols's house the next day.

Bendire, Charles E. "Report of a Scouting Expedition Made in the Region East of Owens Valley, Cal." U.S. Army, May 26, 1867. The report is in the form of a letter from Charles E. Bendire, Lt. 1st U.S. Cavalry, Camp Independence, California, to Brevet Lt. Col. J. D. Devin, Capt. 9th Infantry, Commander, Camp Independence, California. Copies are in Death Valley National Monument Library and the Huntington Library, Palmer Collection (HM 50765). The original has not been located. Dr. T. S. Palmer sent a copy to the National Park Service in 1938, so what is available is a copy of a copy; thus, there could be transcription errors in it.

Benton, Thomas Hart. *Thirty Years' View; or, A History of the Working of the American Government for Thirty Years, from 1820 to 1850.* 2 vols. New York: D. Appleton and Co., 1903.

Bieber, Ralph P., ed. *Southern Trails to California 1849,* vol. 5, The Southwest Historical Series. Glendale, CA: Arthur H. Clark Co., 1937.

Birnie, R., Jr. "Appendix D. Executive Report of Lieutenant R. Birnie, Jr. . . ." In *Annual Report of the Chief of Engineers to the Secretary of War for the Year 1876, Part 3.* 44th Cong., 2nd sess., 1876. H. Ex. Doc. 1, pt. 2, vol. 2:350–355.

Blake, William P. *Report of a Geological Reconnaissance in California.* New York: H. Baillière, 1858.

Blasdel, H. G. "Appendix E, Journal of Explorations in Southern Nevada in the Spring of 1866 by His Excellency Governor Blasdel, of Nevada." In *Annual Report of the State Mineralogist of the State of Nevada for 1866,* edited by R. H. Stretch, pp. 141–147. Carson City, NV: J. E. Eckley, State Printer, 1867.

Bowman, Alan P., comp. *Index to the 1850 Census of the State of California.* Baltimore, MD: Genealogical Pub. Co., 1972.

Boyles, J. C. "He Witnessed the Death Valley Tragedy of '49." *Desert Magazine,* Feb., 1940:3–6.

Brier, Chas. T. Brief Biographical Sketches of James Welch Brier, William Wallace Brier, George Brier, and other members of the family. The Bancroft Library. Berkeley, CA. Manuscript. N.d.

Brier, J[ames] W[elsh]. "Route from Las Vegas de Santa Clara to Walker's Pass, By the Way of Owen's River and Owen's Lake." In Gwinn Harris Heap, *Central Route to the Pacific. . . .* Philadelphia: Lippincott, Grambo, and Co., 1854. Reprinted in Hafen and Hafen (1957:277–281) and Belden (1954:39–41). This fanciful and misleading account was first published in the *Christian Advocate,* a San Francisco religious newspaper. It and

a similar story that appeared in the *San Francisco Daily Herald* on Aug. 25, 1853, are among the first published accounts of the Death Valley '49ers.

———. Letter to Charles B. Mecum, Jan. 17, 1876. Jayhawker Collection, JA 70, Huntington Library, San Marino, CA.

———. Letter to Luther A. Richards & Comrades of the Desert, Jan. 23, 1879. Jayhawker Collection, JA 71, Huntington Library, San Marino, CA.

———. "Death Valley. Its Ghastly Story as Told by an Aged Survivor. A Fearful Experience. A Reminiscence by Rev. J. W. Brier, Who Preached the First Protestant Sermon in Los Angeles." [*Los Angeles Times?*], [1887?]. A copy is in the Jayhawker Collection, J. B. Colton Scrapbook, vol. 1, p. 12.

———. Letter to John B. Colton Esq., Jan. 10, 1893. Jayhawker Collection, JA 69, Huntington Library, San Marino, CA.

———. Letter to Old Comrades, Jan. 16, 1896. Jayhawker Collection, JA 76, Huntington Library, San Marino, CA.

———. Letter to Deacon Richards, Jan. 20, 1898. Jayhawker Collection, JA 73, Huntington Library, San Marino, CA.

Brier, John Wells. "The Death Valley Party of 1849." *Out West Magazine,* March, 1903:326–335; and April, 1903:456–465.

———. Letter to Captain J. B. Colton, May 22, 1908. Jayhawker Collection, JA 87, Huntington Library, San Marino, CA.

———. Letter to Col. John B. Colton, Sept. 4, 1908. Jayhawker Collection, JA 88, Huntington Library, San Marino, CA.

———. "The Argonauts of Death Valley." *Grizzly Bear* 9 (No. 2; Whole No. 50) (June, 1911):1–4, 7.

———. "A Lonely Trail." *Grizzly Bear* 9 (No. 6; Whole No. 54) (Oct., 1911):1–2.

Brier, Juliet. "Our Christmas amid the Terrors of Death Valley." *San Francisco Call,* Dec. 25, 1898, p. 19. Reprinted in Long (1950:197–207) and Belden (1954:21–28).

———. To my Fellow Sufferers. Jan. 23, 1904. Jayhawker Collection, JA 105, Huntington Library, San Marino, CA.

———. Letter to My Respected Friends, Jan., 1905. Jayhawker Collection, JA 106, Huntington Library, San Marino, CA.

———. Letter to Friends and Companions, Jan. 23, 1906. Jayhawker Collection, JA 107, Huntington Library, San Marino, CA.

———. "Mrs. Brier's Last Account." *Carson City [Nevada] News,* June 8, 1913. We have not seen the original of this article but have relied on the reprint in Belden (1954:30–35). This account was first published in the *San Francisco Examiner* on Feb. 24, 1901, after the Jayhawker reunion at L. Dow Stephens's home in San Jose, California.

Briggs, Harry E. Interviews with authors. Southern Homestake Mine, Panamint Valley, CA, Nov., 1972, and Jan., 1973.

Brooks, George R., ed. *The Southwest Expedition of Jedediah S. Smith.* Glendale, CA: Arthur H. Clark Co., 1977.

Brooks, Juanita. *The Mountain Meadow Massacre.* New ed. Norman, OK: Univ. of Oklahoma Press, 1962.

Bunje, Emil T. H. and James C. Kean. *Pre-Marshal Gold in California.* "Vol. 1, Legends and Rumors, 1530–1840," and "Vol. 2, Discoveries and Near-Discoveries, 1840–1848." Produced on a Works Progress Administration Project. Berkeley, CA: Univ. of California, 1938.

Burrell, Mrs. Edward. "Across the Plains in 1849." *Pioneer* [San Jose, CA], Dec. 15, 1894, p. 2, cols. 1–4. The original article appeared in the Plainfield, Illinois, *Enterprise* and is reprinted in Woodward (1949b:157–165). The *Pioneer* article is reprinted in Long (1950:288–293).

California Department of Parks and Recreation. *California Historical Landmarks.* Sacramento, CA: California Office of State Printing, 1971.

[California Pioneers]. *By-Laws and List of Members, California Pioneers of Santa Clara County.* San Jose, CA: n.p., 1907. Charles E. Wade is listed as a living member and W. L. Manley, Mrs. W. L. Manley, and Thomas Shannon are listed as deceased (pp. 24, 29, & 30).

Carter, Harvey L. "William H. Ashley." In *The Mountain Men and the Fur Trade of the Far West,* vol. 7, pp. 23–34. Glendale, CA: Arthur H. Clark Co., 1969.

Caughey, John Walton. "Southwest from Salt Lake in 1849." *Pacific Historical Review* 6(2) (June 1937):143–164.

Chalfant, W. A. *Death Valley, The Facts.* Stanford University, CA: Stanford Univ. Press, 1930.

———. *Death Valley, The Facts.* 3rd ed. Stanford University, CA: Stanford Univ. Press, 1936.

Cleland, Robert Glass, ed. *Constitution of the State of California 1849.* San Marino, CA: Friends of the Huntington Library, 1949.

———. *This Reckless Breed of Men, The Trappers and Fur Traders of the Southwest.* New York: Alfred A. Knopf, 1963.

Clements, Thomas, and Lydia Clements. "Evidence of Pleistocene Man in Death Valley, California." *Bulletin of the Geological Society of America* 64 (Oct., 1953):1189–1203.

Coker, Edward. "The Experiences of Edward Coker." In William L. Manly, *Death Valley in '49.* San Jose, CA: Pacific Tree and Vine Co., 1894. This narrative was not written by Coker; it was "related . . . to the Author [Manly] somewhat as follows" (Manly 1894:373–376).

Colton, John B. "Story of the Jayhawkers." *San Francisco Chronicle,* Feb. 15, 1903, p. 3. This article was not written by Colton but was apparently based on an interview. It has an extensive list of the Jayhawkers and excerpts from Sheldon Young's log starting Oct. 3, 1849, and ending Feb. 5, 1850.

Coolidge, Dane. *Death Valley Prospectors.* New York: E. P. Dutton and Co., 1937. Coolidge (p. 18) relates an uncorroborated story about a Death Valley '49er found dead "who had broken his leg and had been shot through the forehead and body." Carl I. Wheat (1939a) wove this purported mercy killing or suicide into a fictitious story that is too often accepted as true (Beck 1939).

Corle, Edwin. *Death Valley and the Creek Called Furnace.* Los Angeles: Ward Ritchie Press, 1941.

Coulter, Harry. "Escape from Death Valley." *Westways* 41 (Sept. 1949):2–3.

Coville, Frederick Vernon. "Death Valley Expedition Itinerary [Diary]." Personal diary from Jan. 3 through Sept. 1, 1891, handwritten, 113 pages. Smithsonian Institute Botanical Library, Washington, D.C.

———. "The Panamint Indians of California." *American Anthropologist* 5 (Oct. 1892):351–361.

———. "Botany of the Death Valley Expedition." *Contributions from the U.S. National Herbarium,* vol. IV. Washington, D.C.: GPO, 1893.

Cowan, Robert G. *Ranchos of California, A List of Spanish Concessions 1775–1822 and Mexican Grants 1822–1846.* Fresno, CA: Academy Library Guild, 1956.

[Dalton]. Abstract of title of part of Rancho San Francisquito in Los Angeles County, HM 29329. Huntington Library, San Marino, CA.

Delameter, J. A. Manuscript, no title. Jan. 7, 1945. Carl I. Wheat Collection, The Bancroft Library, Berkeley, CA. Delameter's reminiscences begin in 1873. The manuscript sheds little light on the Manly-Rogers routes.

Donley, Michael W., Stuart Allan, Patricia Caro, and Clyde P. Patton. *Atlas of California.* Culver City, CA: Pacific Book Center, 1979.

Dudley, W. W., Jr., and J. D. Larson. *Effects of Irrigation Pumping on Desert Pupfish Habitats in Ash Meadows, Nye County, Nevada.* Geological Survey Professional Paper 927. Washington, D.C.: GPO, 1976.

Dutcher, B. H. "Piñon Gathering among the Panamint Indians." *American Anthropologist* 6 (Oct. 1893):377–380.

Edwards, E. I. *The Valley Whose Name Is Death.* Pasadena, CA: San Pasqual Press, 1940.

———. "The Mystery of Death Valley, How it Was Named." *Branding Iron* [The Westerners, Los Angeles Corral], No. 61 (June 1962a):4–8.

———. *Desert Harvest.* Los Angeles, CA: Westernlore Press, 1962b.

———. *Freeman's, A Stage Stop on the Mojave.* Glendale, CA: La Siesta Press, 1964.

———. "Death Valley's Neglected Hero." In *Brand Book 12*, pp. 59–73. N. p.: The Westerners, Los Angeles Corral, 1966.

———. *The Enduring Desert, A Descriptive Bibliography.* N.p.: Ward Ritchie Press, 1969.

Ellenbecker, John G. *The Jayhawkers of Death Valley.* Marysville, KS: Privately Printed, 1938. Ellenbecker later published a 5-page supplement in which he says the Wade family brought a wagon out of Death Valley.

Evans, George W. B. *Mexican Gold Trail, The Journal of a Forty-Niner.* Edited by Glenn S. Dumke. San Marino, CA: Huntington Library, 1945.

Fairbanks, Ernest E. "Forty-Niners Starved in the Midst of Plenty." *Scientific Americana* 146 (June 1932):348–349.

Farley, Minard H. "Farley's Map of the Newly Discovered Tramontane Silver Mines in Southern California and Western New Mexico [Nevada]." San Francisco, CA: W. Holt, 1861. This is the first published map with "Death Valley" named on it. Long (1950:230) redrew and published the Death Valley and surrounding area. The insert "Map of the Coso Silver Mines" was drawn by Van Dorn, the assistant surveyor of the 1861 U.S. and California Boundary Commission.

Favour, Alpheus H. *Old Bill Williams, Mountain Man.* Chapel Hill, NC: Univ. of North Carolina Press, 1936.

Federal Writers' Project, eds. *Death Valley—A Guide.* Boston, MA: Houghton Mifflin Co., 1939.

Foote, H. S., ed. *Pen Pictures from the Garden of the World or, Santa Clara County, California.* Chicago, IL: Lewis Publishing Co., 1888. Manly's marriage to Mary J. Woods is given as July 10, 1862 (pp. 502–503). A sketch of Charles E. Wade, son of Henry and Mary Wade, is also included (p. 536).

Freeman, Dick. "On Manly's Trail in the Panamints." *Desert Magazine.* 4(5) (March 1941):4–8.

Frémont, John Charles. *The Expeditions of John Charles Frémont.* With map portfolio. Edited by Donald Jackson and Mary Lee Spence. Urbana, IL: Univ. of Illinois Press, 1970.

Gale, Hoyt S. "Salines in the Owens, Searles, and Panamint Basins Southeastern California." *Contributions to Economic Geology*, USGS Bull. 580-L, part L:251–323. Washington, D.C.: GPO, 1914.

George, S. G. [Dr.]. "Our Early History." *Panamint News* I(41) (March 9, 1875): 2; and I(47) (March 23, 1875):1.

Gibbes, Charles Drayton. "A New Map of California." Published by C. D. Gibbes. Stockton, CA: Sherman & Smith, NY, 1852.

Gilbert, Bil. *The Trailblazers.* Alexandria, VA: Time-Life Books, 1973.

Glasscock, C. B. *Here's Death Valley.* New York: Bobbs-Merrill Co., 1940.

Goodwin, T. R. Letter to Carl I. Wheat, June 30, 1936. Carl I. Wheat Collection, The Bancroft Library, Berkeley, CA.

———. Letter to Carl I. Wheat, July 16, 1936. Copy in Death Valley Nat. Mon. Library.

Greene, Linda W. *Historic Resource Study, A History of Mining in Death Valley National Monument*, vol. 1 (of 2), part 1 (of 2). Denver, CO: Nat. Park Service, Historic Preservation Branch, Denver Service Center, Nat. Park Service, USDI, 1981.

Hafen, LeRoy R. and Ann W. Hafen. *Old Spanish Trail, Santa Fe to Los Angeles*, vol. 1 of The Far West and The Rockies Historical Series. Glendale, CA: Arthur H. Clark Co., 1954a.

———, eds. *Journals of Forty-Niners, Salt Lake to Los Angeles*, vol. 2 of The Far West and The Rockies Historical Series. Glendale, CA: Arthur H. Clark Co., 1954b.

———, eds. *Central Route to the Pacific*, vol. 7, The Far West and The Rockies Historical Series. Glendale, CA: Arthur H. Clark Co., 1957.

———. *Fremont's Fourth Expedition*, vol. 11, The Far West and The Rockies Historical Series. Glendale, CA: Arthur H. Clark Co., 1960.

———. *The Far West and Rockies General Analytical Index to the Fifteen Volume Series and Supplement to the Journals of Forty-Niners, Salt Lake to Los Angeles*, vol. 15, The Far West and The Rockies Historical Series. Glendale, CA: Arthur H. Clark Co., 1961.

Hagen, Olaf T. *Migration of the Wade Family.* Palmer Collection, HM 50906, Huntington Library, San Marino, CA. [ca. 1932–35]. Hagen, acting regional historian, National Park Service, prepared this report. A typed carbon copy without the author's name is in the Palmer Collection (HM 50906). Hagen gives Charles E. Wade's birth date as Aug. 12, 1938, whereas Belden (1957:5) gives Aug. 12, 1937—the former is correct.

Hague, Harlan. *The Road to California, The Search for a Southern Overland Route, 1540–1848.* Glendale, CA: Arthur H. Clark Co., 1978.

Hammon, H. B. "Death Valley Report" *U.S. Public Health.* 1933. Parts of this report are cited in the Death Valley National Monument's "Water Source Report" binder, Death Valley National Monument Library. The report is lost; its place of publication and publisher are unknown.

Hanks, Henry G. "An Unexplored Region." *Daily Evening Bulletin.* [San Francisco], Feb. 10, 1869, p. 1. Part of this article is included in Long (1950:312–315).

———. *Third Annual Report of the State Mineralogist.* California State Mining Bureau. Sacramento, CA: Supt. State Printing, 1883. Reprinted in Weight (1955:19–26).

Haynes, Asa. Diary. Jayhawker Collection, JA 1051,

Huntington Library. San Marino, CA. The third copy of the diary and its history are printed in Ellenbecker (1938:124–127).

Heap, Gwinn Harris. In *Central Route to the Pacific*, vol. 7, The Far West and The Rockies Historical Series, edited by LeRoy R. Hafen and Ann W. Hafen, pp. 75–336. Glendale, CA: Arthur H. Clark Co., 1957.

Hillway, Tyrus. *Introduction to Research.* Boston, MA: Houghton Mifflin Co., 1964.

Holland, F. Ross, Jr., and Robert V. Simmonds. *Eagle Borax Works, Harmony Borax Works, Death Valley National Monument California.* National Park Service, Office of History and Historic Architecture. San Francisco, CA: USDI, 1971.

Holt, Warren. "Map of the State of California and Nevada." San Francisco, CA: Warren Holt, 1869 and 1875. The 1869 edition shows "Lost Wagon or Germicle Spr." where McLean Spring is. The 1875 edition shows "Lost Wagon or McCormick Sp" at the same spot. "Hitchings Spr." is on both maps in the approximate area of Emigrant or Jayhawker Spring; the detail is not sufficient to determine whether it is in Emigrant or Jayhawker Canyon.

Hunt, Alice. *Archeology of the Death Valley Salt Pan California.* Anthropological Papers, No. 47. Salt Lake City, UT: Univ. of Utah Press, 1960.

Hunt, Charles B. *Plant Ecology of Death Valley, California.* Geological Survey Professional Paper 509. Washington, D.C.: GPO, 1966.

———. *Death Valley, Geology, Ecology, Archaeology.* Berkeley, CA: Univ. of California Press, 1975.

Hunt, Charles B., T. W. Robinson, Walter A. Bowles, and A. L. Washburn. *Hydrologic Basin, Death Valley, California.* Geological Survey Professional Paper 494-B. Washington, D.C.: GPO, 1966.

Hunt, Rockwell D. *Fifteen Decisive Events of California History.* Los Angeles, CA: Historical Society of Southern California, 1959.

———. *Personal Sketches of California Pioneers I Have Known.* Stockton, CA: Univ. of the Pacific, 1962.

Jackson, Donald and Mary Lee Spence. *The Expeditions of John Charles Frémont*, vol. I, *Travels from 1838 to 1844 and Map Portfolio.* Urbana, IL: Univ. of Illinois Press, 1970.

Jackson, Sheldon G. *A British Ranchero in Old California.* Glendale, CA: Arthur H. Clark Co., 1977.

Jayhawker map. *See* Manly Maps.

Johnson, Harry R. *Water Resources of the Antelope Valley, California.* Water Supply Paper 278. U.S. Geological Survey. Washington, D.C.: GPO, 1911.

Johnson, LeRoy C. *Field Diaries.* Personal diaries of field trips to Death Valley region and southern California, 1971 to present. Authors' collection.

———. Letter to Edwin L. Rothfuss, superintendent, Death Valley Nat. Mon., Jan. 24, 1983. Authors' collection.

Johnson, LeRoy C., and Jean Johnson. *Julia, Death Valley's Youngest Victim.* Roseville, MN: Privately Printed, 1981. This booklet reveals for the first time that Abigail Arcan was 5 months pregnant when she walked from Death Valley to Rancho San Francisco in 1850.

Jones, Gurley. Letter to J. B. Colton, April 6, 1903. Jayhawker Collection, JA 554, Huntington Library, San Marino, CA. Attached to this letter is a map (not in Jones's handwriting) that shows the route the Jayhawkers took over "Townsons pass" (Towne Pass). Wheat (1939b) credits Manly with drawing this map but later says Manly did not draw it (Wheat 1959:104n).

Kelly, Charles. "On Manly's Trail to Death Valley." *Desert Magazine*, Feb., 1939, pp. 6–8, 41 & 43.

Kevil, K. "Death Valley Table-Cloth." *News and Notes from the Santa Clara Historical Society.* Santa Clara Co., CA: Feb., 1960. Reprinted in *California Historian* 6(3) (March, 1960):53–54.

Kirkgaard, Lillie M. Letter to Lawrence Clark Powell, June 10, 1971. Lawrence Clark Powell Collection, The Bancroft Library, Berkeley, CA. Mrs. Kirkgaard granted us permission on August 25, 1975, to quote from this letter.

Koch, Fred W. "Through Death Valley. A Brief Account of a Trip from Daggett to Furnace Creek." *Sierra Club Bulletin* 1(2) (June 1893):40–53.

Koenig, George. "Zeroing in on the Gunsight." *Branding Iron* [The Westerners, Los Angeles Corral], No. 69 (June 1964):6–7.

———, ed. *Valley of Salt, Memories of Wine, A Journal of Death Valley, 1849 by Louis Nusbaumer.* Berkeley, CA: Friends of The Bancroft Library. 1967. This translation of the Nusbaumer journal is not reliable because words and sentences in the original text were not translated. Bertha Whitmore translated the journal Feb. 27, 1933, and part of it was published in Read and Gaines (1944) and Long (1950). Both these authors used her translation—as did Koenig. Original journal in The Bancroft Library.

———. *The Lost Death Valley '49er Journal of Louis Nusbaumer.* Death Valley '49ers, Inc. Bishop, CA: Chalfant Press. 1974. Contrary to the title, the journal was never lost.

———. *Beyond This Place There Be Dragons.* Glendale, CA: Arthur H. Clark Co., 1984. Koenig's major conclusions about the routes taken by the '49ers as they escaped from Death Valley are "iconoclastic," according to the author himself. They are at variance with the '49ers firsthand accounts.

Lastrucci, Carlo L. *The Scientific Approach, Basic Principles of the Scientific Method.* Cambridge, MA: Schenkman Pub. Co., 1963.

Latta, Frank F. *Death Valley '49ers.* Santa Cruz, CA: Bear State Books, 1979.

Leadingham, Grace. "Juliet Wells Brier, Heroine of Death Valley." *Pacific Historian Quarterly Bulletin,* Nov. 1963:171–178; and Feb. 1964:13–20.

Leedy, Paul D. *Practical Research: Planning and Decisions.* 2nd ed. New York: Macmillan Pub. Co., 1980.

Leonard, Zenas. *Narrative of the Adventures of Zenas Leonard.* Clearfield, PA: D. W. Moore, 1839; reprint: New York: Readex Microprint Corp., 1966.

———. *Adventures of Zenas Leonard, Fur Trader.* Edited by John C. Ewers. Norman, OK: Univ. of Oklahoma Press, 1959.

Levy, Benjamin. *Death Valley National Monument Historical Background Study.* Office of Archeological and Historic Preservation. N.p.: Nat. Park Service, USDI, 1969.

Lingenfelter, Richard E. *Death Valley & the Amargosa.* Berkeley, CA: Univ. of California Press, 1986. This book was published too late to be included in the literature review. Its extensive bibliography, endnotes, and index make it a valuable reference book.

Long, Margaret. *The Shadow of the Arrow.* Caldwell, ID: Caxton Printers, 1941.

———. *The Shadow of the Arrow.* 2nd ed., rev. and enl. Caldwell, ID: Caxton Printers, 1950. We feel the first edition is more accurate; the revisions in this edition are mainly based on hearsay and conclusions of others.

Lorton, William B. *Over the Salt Lake Trail in the Fall of '49.* Intro. by John B. Goodman III. Los Angeles, CA: Privately Printed, 1957. This Jan. 30, 1850, letter lists ten of the eleven Pinney-Savage party members. Goodman added Pinney to the list; thus, the eleven members are accounted for.

Lothrop, Gloria. "True Grit and Triumph of Juliette Brier." *Californians,* Nov.–Dec., 1984:31–35.

Lummis, Charles F. "Death Valley in '49 [a review of Manly's book]." *Land of Sunshine, A Southwest Magazine* 6 (Feb., 1897):116.

———. *Some Strange Corners of Our Country.* New York: Century Co., 1911.

Manley, Henry S. *Manley Family: New England and New York, 1650–1950.* N.p.:N.p., 1965. A 42-page genealogy; housed at the California Historical Society, San Francisco.

Manley, W. L. "Title and Deeds, Compiled by Chas. W. Kitts, Att'y at Law, Grass Valley, Nevada Co. Cal. 1800 [for the years 1856–80]." Nevada Co. Office, Grass Valley, CA. W. L. Manley is listed twice as a grantor and once as a grantee in 1858 and 1859. We also found his name mentioned in other Grass Valley documents as late as June 3, 1865.

———. "From Vermont to California." *Santa Clara Valley.* 4(4) (June 1887) to 7(5) (July 1890). The first issue had no by-line, the second had "W. F. [sic] Manley," and the remaining issues were by-lined "W. L. Manley." Thirty-eight issues were apparently printed. The Bancroft Library is missing these issues: 4(11) (Jan. 1888); 6(2) (April 1889); 6(6) (Aug. 1889); 6(10) (Dec. 1889); and 7(5) (July 1890).

———. "Through Death Valley." *San Jose Daily Mercury,* Jan. 9, 1900.

———. "Mr. Manley's Death Valley Experience." *San Jose Daily Mercury,* July 14, 1900.

Manly, W[illiam] L. Marriage License. July 9, 1862. County Recorder, San Joaquin Co., CA, 1862. Manly's age is given as 40 (he was 42) and that of Miss M. J. Woods as 36. They were married on July 10, 1862 (Foote 1888:502–503); not 1861 as in Woodward (1949b:19).

———. "W. L. Manly—How He Crossed the Plains—Description of an Adventurous Journey—Death Valley Experience." *Pioneer* 1(15) (April 21, 1877): 1; and 1(16) (April 28, 1877):1. These sketches were written by a reporter. Woodward (1949b:3–19) reprinted them; he made minor editorial changes and added paragraphs.

———. Letters to various Jayhawkers and unnamed persons between Feb., 1888, and March, 1901, 40 total. Jayhawker Collection, cited by JA numbers. Huntington Library, San Marino, CA.

———. "Charles Alvord." *Pioneer* 10(5) (May 15, 1895):8; and 10(6) (June 15, 1895):1. Reprinted in Woodward (1949b:61–80), where he made minor editorial changes and added paragraphs. The May article begins "In 1862 I [Manly] was requested. . . ." The year was 1860, correctly given in the June article.

———. Maps. There are three extant maps drawn by Manly. For clarity we cite the original maps rather than their reproductions. We arbitrarily named them as follows:

1) Jayhawker map. Housed in Jayhawker Collection, JA 1050, three sheets: 10 7/8 × 8 1/2; 10 7/8 × 8; 10 7/8 × 8 inches, pencil. Huntington Library, San Marino, CA, ca. 1890. References: JA 616; Wheat 1939b; Long 1950:170.

2) Walker map. Housed in Death Valley National Monument Museum, DEVA Catalog 2062, #319, one sheet: 9 1/2 × 11 3/4 inches, pencil. Death Valley National Monument, Death Valley, CA, Aug. 14, 1894. References: Walker 1954 & 1962.

3) Palmer map. Housed in the Palmer Collection, HM 50895, one sheet: 18 1/8 × 22 3/4 inches, pencil. Huntington Library, San Marino, CA, 1890. Lightly penciled on the map, but not in Manly's hand, are: "Enterprise Ut.," "Indian Springs Nev.," "Redlands Canyon," and "Goler Wash." We do not know who added these annotations and we conclude the latter two are on the wrong canyons. The Bennett-Arcan party exited Redlands Canyon, not a

canyon north of it as indicated by the "Redlands Canyon" annotation. References: Wheat 1959:map 628; Walker 1973; Belden 1975; Koenig 1984.

———. Letter to T. S. Palmer, Aug. 1, 1894. Palmer Collection, HM (?) Huntington Library, San Marino, CA.

———. Letter to T. S. Palmer. n.d. Aug. 1894. Palmer Collection, HM 50802, Huntington Library, San Marino, CA.

———. Letter to T. S. Palmer. Dec. 24, 1894. Palmer Collection, HM 50803, Huntington Library, San Marino, CA.

———. *Death Valley in '49*. San Jose, CA: Pacific Tree and Vine Co., 1894. Three editions were printed (see Edwards 1969 for details) and two photographic reproductions issued—Readex Microprint Corp., 1966; and Chalfant Press, 1977. Our page citations are to the 1894 edition.

Mars, Amaury. *Reminiscences of Santa Clara Valley and San Jose*. San Francisco, CA: Mysell-Rollins Co., 1901. W. L. Manley (with the *e*) is listed as a charter member of the Santa Clara County Pioneer Society, founded on May 19, 1894 (p. 268). Charles E. Wade is also listed as a member. *See also* [California Pioneers].

Mecum, C[harles] B. to Honored JayHawkers, [Feb. 4, 1872]. Jayhawker Collection, JA 715, Huntington Library, San Marino, CA.

Mendenhall, Walter C. *Some Desert Watering Places in Southeastern California and Southwestern Nevada*. Water-Supply Paper 224. U.S. Geological Survey. Washington, D.C.: GPO, 1909. Stanley Paher, Nevada Publications, 1983, reissued this as a photographic reproduction under the title *320 Desert Watering Places in Southeastern California and Southwestern Nevada*. Mendenhall's description of Bennetts Well (p. 38) leaves no doubt that he is describing Eagle Borax Spring.

Miller, George. "A Trip to Death Valley." *Annual Publications, Historical Society of Southern California* 11(2) (1919):56–64. A portion of this story is reprinted in Weight and Weight (1959:26–28).

Morgan, Dale L., ed. *The West of William H. Ashley*. Denver, CO: Old West Pub. Co., 1964.

National Park Service, Death Valley National Monument. "Water Source Report." Binder in Death Valley Nat. Mon. Library, n.d. Each spring is given a base map number and is plotted on a USGS quadrangle map. *See also* Hammon (1933).

Newhall, Ruth Waldo. *The Newhall Ranch*. San Marino, CA: Huntington Library, 1958.

Nusbaumer, Louis. *L. Nusbaumer Journal*. Original handwritten journal from March 20, 1849, through March 10, 1850. The Bancroft Library, Berkeley, CA. Louis's daughter, Bertha Nusbaumer Whitmore, translated the journal for her son Welles Whitmore, Jr., on Feb. 27, 1933, and a typed copy is in The Bancroft Library along with

a 1948 typed transcription by Max E. Knight. Portions of the translation have appeared in Read and Gaines (1944), Long (1950), and Koenig (1967 & 1974).

Owen, J. R. N. "Report of J. R. N. Owen to Hon. S. Mowry of a Reconnoisance [*sic*] along the Proposed Boundary Line of the State of California." April 15, 1861. Visalia, Tulare Co., CA. This 34-page handwritten report is housed in California's State Lands Commission Sacramento office. It summarizes the U.S. and California Boundary Commission's reconnaissance route that went through Death Valley in March 1861.

Palmer map. *See* Manly Maps.

Palmer, T. S. *Diary, Death Valley Expedition, 1891*. Personal diary from Dec. 11, 1890, to May 25, 1891, handwritten, 110 pages. Palmer Collection, HM 50827, Huntington Library, San Marino, CA.

———. "List of Locations Visited by the Death Valley Expedition." In *North American Fauna, No. 7*. U.S. Dept of Agriculture, Division of Ornithology and Mammalogy, pp. 361–384. Washington, D.C.: GPO, 1983.

———. Letter to Carl I. Wheat, Dec. 31, 1938. Carl I. Wheat Collection, The Bancroft Library, Berkeley, CA.

———. *Chronology of the Death Valley Region in California, 1849–1949*. Washington, D.C.: Byron S. Adams, 1952.

———, ed. *Place Names of the Death Valley Region in California and Nevada*. [Edited by Daniel Cronkhite.] Morongo Valley, CA: Sage Brush Press, 1980. First editions (1948) of this book are scarce; therefore, Cronkhite reprinted it. An abbreviated version appeared as an appendix in Palmer (1893:361–384).

Parkinson, Wm. P. "Route, Proper Outfit, &c. for California." *Wisconsin Tribune* [Mineral Point, WI], II(19) (Feb. 2, 1849):2.

Perkins, Arthur B. "Rancho San Francisco: A Study of a California Land Grant." *Historical Society of Southern California Quarterly* 39(2) (June, 1957):98–126.

Post, Frederick J. "The Microbial Ecology of the Great Salt Lake." *Microbial Ecology* 3 (1977):143–165.

Powell, J. W. *Exploration of the Colorado River of the West and Its Tributaries*. Smithsonian Inst. Washington, D.C.: GPO, 1875.

———. *Tenth Annual Report of the Bureau of Ethnology*. Smithsonian Inst. Washington, D.C.: GPO, 1893.

Powell, Lawrence Clark. *California Classics*. Los Angeles: Ward Ritchie Press, 1971.

Preston, R. N. *Early California [Maps], Southern Edition*. Portland, OR: Binford and Mort, 1974. The author does not cite the origin of the maps; the dates given on some are incorrect.

Preuss, Charles. *Exploring with Frémont*. Translated and edited by Erwin G. Gudde and Elizabeth K.

Gudde. Norman: Univ. of Oklahoma Press, 1958.

Ramsay, Cynthia Russ. "Death Valley, The Grandeur of Life in a Stark Desert World." In *Exploring America's Backcountry*, pp. 144–177. Washington, D.C.: National Geographic Society, 1979.

Ray, C. Lorin. "Letter Tells of Early Inyo Event." *Inyo Register*, Dec. 29, 1966. Ray reprinted part of S. G. George's (1875) letter titled "Our Early History."

Read, Georgia Willis and Ruth Gaines, eds. *Gold Rush: The Journals, Drawings, and Other Papers of J. Goldsborough Bruff*. 2 vols. New York: Columbia Univ. Press, 1944. Part of Louis Nusbaumer's journal was first published in vol. 2, pp. 1227–1233.

———. *Gold Rush: The Journals, Drawings, and Other Papers of J. Goldsborough Bruff*. New York: Columbia Univ. Press, 1949.

Read, Lena Margaret. "Famous Scouts of the West, 1825 to 1850." Master's thesis, Univ. of California [Berkeley?], 1923.

Reid, John Phillip. *Law of the Elephant, Property and Social Behavior on the Overland Trail*. San Marino, CA: Huntington Library, 1980.

Rodgers, John H. "On the Plains, 1849." *Merced Star*, April 26, 1894. Reprinted in Belden (1954:63–68). The article was by-lined John "H. Rodgers"; Manly consistently spelled his name *Rogers*, without the *d*.

Rothrock, J. T. "Appendix H 5. Report upon the Operations of a Special Natural-History Party and Main Field-Party No. 1, California Section, Field-Season of 1875, Being the Results of Observations upon the Economic Botany and Agriculture of Portions of Southern California." *Annual Report of the Chief of Engineers of the Secretary of War for Year 1876, Part 3*. 44th Cong., 2nd sess., 1876. H. Ex. Doc. 1, pt. 2, vol. 2:422–433 and map.

Rowland, Leon. From an article in "Circuit Rider." *Santa Clara Sentinel* [1942?]. Mrs. Renie Leaman, Santa Cruz, CA, gave us a typed transcription of this undated article.

[San Bernardino County]. *History of San Bernardino County, California*. San Francisco: Wallace W. Elliott, 1883.

[San Francisco]. *The Bay of San Francisco—A History, Vol. II*. Chicago: Lewis Publishing Co., 1892. George Lewis (pp. 347–348) and Emil (pp. 648–650) Nusbaumer are two of the four children of Louis and Elizabeth Nusbaumer and were born on Jan. 5, 1852, and Feb. 13, 1856, respectively. *See also* [Alameda County].

[Santa Clara County]. *Santa Clara County Directory for 1871–72*. Sacramento: H. S. Crocker & Co., 1871.

Schissel, Lillian. *Women's Diaries of the Westward Journey*. New York: Schocken Books, 1982.

Scholl, David W. "Pleistocene Algal Pinnacles at Searles Lake, California." *Journal of Sedimentary Petrology* 30(3) (Sept. 1960):414–431.

Searles, J. W. "Notice of Water Claim. Land, Water, and Mining Claims, Book B," p. 342. Sept. 14, 1878. John Searles "claimed all the fresh water flowing from these springs which are situated at the head of a cañon branching out of grass cañon . . ." This spring is probably Indian Joe Spring, the site of Searles Garden, where John lived.

Shannon, Tom [Thomas]. Letter to Old Jayhawkers, Jan. 11, 1900. Jayhawker Collection, JA 881, Huntington Library, San Marino, CA.

———. "Thomas Shannon's Journey of Peril: With the Jayhawkers in Death Valley Fifty-three Years Ago—A Little Band of Hardy Pioneers." *San Jose Daily Mercury*, Nov. 16, 1903. Reprinted in Belden (1954:57–60). Included in this obituary are Shannon's reminiscences, which were written by a reporter but based on Shannon's notes.

Simpson, Henry I. *The Emigrant's Guide to the Gold Mines. Three Weeks in the Gold Mines, or Adventures with the Gold Diggers of California in August, 1848*. New York: Joyce and Co., 1848. Reprinted in *Magazine of History with Notes and Queries*, Extra Number—No. 176. 44(4) (1932):185–241[?].

Smith, George I. *Subsurface Stratigraphy and Geochemistry of Late Quaternary Evaporites, Searles Lake, California*. Geological Survey Professional Paper 1043. Washington, D.C.: GPO, 1979.

———. Letter to the authors, March 31, 1980. Authors' collection.

Soltz, David L. and Robert J. Naiman, *The Natural History of Native Fishes in the Death Valley System*. Science Series 30 (Nov. 10, 1978). Los Angeles Co., CA: Natural History Museum of Los Angeles Co., 1978.

Southworth, John. *Death Valley in 1849, The Luck of the Gold Rush Emigrants*. Burbank, CA: Pegleg Books, 1978.

———. *Death Valley in 1849, The Luck of the Gold Emigrants*. Burbank, CA: Pegleg Books, 1978 [rev. 1980]. In this revised edition, Southworth replaces "Appendix C: John Lemoigne, Prospector" with "Dr. Wolff and the Manly Trail through the Panamints" and adds "Appendix D: Miscellany."

Spears, John R. *Illustrated Sketches of Death Valley and Other Borax Deserts of the Pacific Coast*. Chicago: Rand McNally & Co., 1892. Photographic reproduction by Sagebrush Press, Morongo Valley, CA, 1977.

———. "Through Death Valley." *California Illustrated Magazine* 3(3) (Feb., 1893):312–321.

Stephens, L. D[ow]. Letter to Sir [J. B. Colton], Mar. 16, 1884. Jayhawker Collection, JA 898, Huntington Library, San Marino, CA.

———. Letter to Comrades, Jan. 20, 1902. Jayhawker

Collection, JA 981, Huntington Library, San Marino, CA.

———. *Life Sketches of a Jayhawker of '49*. N.p., 1916. Stephens wrote this account about sixty-five years after his venture in Death Valley. It is of little value in determining the Bennett-Arcan route in the Death Valley area.

Stevenson, H. J. "Map of the County of Los Angeles, California." Oakland, CA: C. L. Smith & Co. Lith., 1880.

Steward, Julian H. *Basin-Plateau Aboriginal Sociopolitical Groups*. Smithsonian Institution, Bureau of American Ethnology Bulletin 120. Washington, D.C.: GPO, 1938. Reprinted: Salt Lake City, UT: Univ. of Utah Press, 1970.

Stewart, George R., ed. *The Opening of the California Trail*. Berkeley, CA: Univ. of California Press, 1953.

———. *The California Trail*. New York: McGraw-Hill Book Co., 1962.

Stoltenberg, Carl H., Kenneth D. Ware, Robert J. Marty, Robert D. Wray, and J. D. Wellons. *Planning Research for Resource Decisions*. Ames, IA: Iowa State Univ. Press, 1970.

Stott, Clifford L. *Search for Sanctuary, Brigham Young and the White Mountain Expedition*. Salt Lake City, UT: Univ. of Utah Press, 1984.

Stover, Jacob Y. "History of the Sacramento Mining Company of 1849." Edited by John W. Caughey. *Pacific Historical Review* 6(2) (June 1937):165–181. Stover (p. 181), quoting Pinney and Savage, two of the '49ers, said they went to Owens Lake, where the "Indians were catching fish and drying them." This was Owens Little Lake; Owens [Big] Lake was too salty to support fish.

Stretch, R. H. *Annual Report of the State Mineralogist of the State of Nevada for 1866*. Carson City, NV: J. E. Eckley, State Printer, 1867. Portions of Governor Blasdel's 1866 field diary appear in appendix E (pp. 141–147). Stretch also wrote a series of fifteen letters published in the *Virginia City Territorial Enterprise*, March, April, May, and June, 1866, about his trip into southern Nevada and Death Valley. They appeared over the pseudonym "VIATOR."

Teague, George A. and Lynette O. Shenke [with] contributions by Vincent Morgan. *Excavations at Harmony Borax Works*. Western Archeological Center. Publications in Anthropology No. 6. N.p.: USDI Nat. Park Service, 1977.

Thompson, David G. *The Mojave Desert Region, California*. Water Supply Paper 578, USGS. Washington, D.C.: GPO, 1929.

Troxel, Bennie W. and Paul K. Morton. *Mines and Mineral Resources of Kern County, California*. County Report 1. San Francisco, CA: California Division of Mines, 1962.

U.S. Borax. *The Story of Borax*. 3rd ed. Los Angeles, CA: U.S. Borax and Chemical Corp., 1969.

U.S. Geographic Board. *Decisions of the United States Geographic Board. No. 16—Decisions Rendered April 6, 1932*. Washington, D.C.: Library of Congress, 1932.

Unruh, John D., Jr. *The Plains Across, The Overland Emigrants and the Trans-Mississippi West, 1840–1860*. Urbana, IL: Univ. of Illinois Press, 1979.

Uzes, Francois D. *Chaining the Land, A History of Surveying California*. Sacramento, CA: Landmark Enterprises, 1977.

[Van Dorn, Aaron]. "Eastern Boundary Sketches. By One of the Exploring Party of the Late U.S. Boundary Commission." *Sacramento Daily Union* [Sacramento, CA], June 25, 29; July 9, 11, 13, 31; Aug. 7 and 10, 1861. Reprinted in Woodward (1961). These sketches are not by-lined, but we identified the author from Owen's (1861) account.

Viator. *See* Stretch.

Voelker, Fredric E. "William Sherley (Old Bill) Williams." In *The Mountain Men and Fur Trade of the Far West*, vol. 8, pp. 365–394. Glendale, CA: Arthur H. Clark Co., 1971.

Walker map. *See* Manly Maps.

Walker, Ardis M. *The Manly Map and the Manly Story*. Palm Desert, CA: Desert Magazine Press, 1954.

———. *Freeman Junction, The Escape Route of the Mississippians and Georgians from Death Valley in 1849*. San Bernardino, CA: Inland Printing and Engraving Co., 1961.

———. *Death Valley & Manly, Symbols of Destiny*. Death Valley '49ers Pub. No. 8. Palm Desert, CA: Desert Magazine, 1962. The center map (pp. 22–23) is a tracing of Manly's original map that Ardis Walker unselfishly donated to the people of the United States. The original map is now on display in the Death Valley National Monument Museum. Scholars will prefer using the photograph of the original map in Walker (1954:14–15), because the tracing has some omissions.

———. "Walker Pass." *Branding Iron* [The Westerners, Los Angeles Corral], No. 69 (June 1964):2–5.

Walker, Helen. "An Incident of Memory." *Desert Magazine* 36 (11) (Nov., 1973):24–27 & 44.

Wallace, William J. and Edith Wallace. *Ancient Peoples and Cultures of Death Valley National Monument*. Ramona, CA: Acoma Books, 1978.

Wasley, James. "California Letter." *Wisconsin Tribune* [Mineral Point, WI], III(21) (March 1, 1850):2.

Weight, Harold O. *Twenty Mule Team Days in Death Valley*. Twentynine Palms, CA: Calico Press, 1955.

———. "Death Valley's Boldest '49er." *Desert Magazine*. 39(11) (Nov., 1976):28–31 & 38–39.

———, and Lucile Weight, comps. "Death Valley 49er, Arizona Pioneer, Wm. B. Rood . . ." Twentynine Palms, CA: Calico Press, 1959. Portions of Miller (1919) are reprinted. The Weights (p. 27) correctly equate Miller's Grapevine Spring with Emigrant Spring in Emigrant Canyon.

Wheat, Carl I. "Hungry Bill Talks." *Westways* 31 ([May] 1939a):18–19. This fictitious article (Beck 1939) is often cited as true. Reprinted in *Death Valley Tales,* 3rd ed., Pub. No. 3. Death Valley '49ers. San Bernardino, CA: Inland Printing and Engraving Co., 1967.

———. "Trailing the Forty-Niners Through Death Valley." *Sierra Club Bulletin* 24(3) (June 1939b):74–108. Wheat ascribed the map facing page 93 to Manly but later (Wheat 1959:104, n8) said, "Manly's Chart of the Jayhawker Party's Route Leaving Death Valley" was not drawn by Manly. Koenig (1984:80n34) credits the map to Gurley Jones (JA 554), but the map is not in Jones's handwriting. Reprinted as a booklet, San Francisco, CA: Taylor and Taylor, 1939, in which page 3 equals page 74 of the article.

———. "Pioneer Visitors to Death Valley after the Forty-Niners." *Quarterly of the California Historical Society* 18(3) (Sept. 1939c):195–216. Wheat (215, n21) says that James Hitchens apparently wrote a series of articles for the *Alta California* pertaining to the U.S. and California Boundary Commission reconnaissance (see Woodward 1961). But we now know Van Dorn (1861) wrote them. Reprinted as a booklet, San Francisco, CA: Lawton R. Kennedy, 1939, in which page 1 equals page 195 of the article.

———. "The Forty-Niners in Death Valley, (A Tentative List)." *Quarterly of the California Historical Society.* 21(4): (Dec. 1939d):102–117.

———. *Mapping the Transmississippi West,* vol 3. San Francisco, CA: Institute of Historical Cartography, 1959.

Wheeler, George M. *Preliminary Report Concerning Explorations and Surveys Principally in Nevada and Arizona [in] 1871.* Washington, D.C.: GPO, 1872.

———. "Annual Report upon the [U.S.] Geological Surveys West of the One-Hundredth Meridian in the States and Territories of California, Oregon, Nevada, Texas, Arizona, Colorado, Idaho, Mon-tana, New Mexico, Utah, and Wyoming." *Annual Report of the Chief Engineers for 1877, Appendix NN.* Washington, D.C.: GPO, 1877.

Wheeler, George M., and D. W. Lockwood. *Preliminary Report upon a Reconnaissance through Southern and Southeastern Nevada, Made in 1869.* U.S. Engineer Dept., U.S. Army. Washington, D.C.: GPO, 1875. In their chapter "Route Taken by Emigrants Perishing in and near Death Valley," they give an incorrect rendition of the Death Valley '49ers.

Whitney, J. D. *Geology,* vol. I, *Report of Progress and Synopsis of the Field-Work, from 1860 to 1864.* Geological Survey of California. Philadelphia, PA: Caxton Press of Sherman & Co., 1865.

Wolff, John E. *Route of the Manly Party of 1849–50 in Leaving Death Valley for the Coast.* [Santa Barbara, CA: Pacific Coast Publishing Co., 1931].

Woodward, Arthur. "When Manly Returned to Death Valley." *Desert Magazine* 3 (May 1939):24–27.

———. *First Gold Discovery in California.* Leaflet Series, History, No. 5. Los Angeles County Museum. 1949a.

———. *Camels and Surveyors in Death Valley.* Palm Desert, CA: Desert Printers, 1961. Woodward reprinted the eight newspaper articles by Van Dorn (1861) and added an introduction. He cites Wheat (1939b:n21), who says James Hitchens apparently wrote the series. Our research shows Van Dorn wrote them.

———, ed. *The Jayhawkers' Oath and Other Sketches by William Lewis Manly, Author of Death Valley in '49.* Los Angeles, CA: Warren F. Lewis, 1949b. Manly's biographical sketch (written by a *Pioneer* reporter) and his article on Charles Alvord are reproduced (see Manly 1877 & 1895). Also included are articles by John B. Colton and Mrs. Edward Burrell (1894).

Young, Sheldon. Log, 1849–50. Jayhawker Collection, JA 555, Huntington Library, San Marino, CA. This is a typed copy of the log; we do not know where the original is or even if it is extant. Reprinted in Long (1950:257–280).

Index

Subentries dealing with time are listed chronologically. Map pages are indicated in **boldface** and illustrations are indicated in *italics*. Notes are referenced by note number (not by page) and are found on pages 55 through 186. Some information in the bibliography is indexed.

Jayhawkers (continued)
  in Panamint Valley, 173, 182, 185, n160
  approach Searles Valley, 184, n160, n166
  at Indian Wells Spring, **22**, 40, 83–84, 152, n50
  in Last Chance Canyon, 40, 86, n50, n51
  reach Rancho San Francisco, n148
Jayhawkers' Oath and Other Sketches, The, 11, 192
Jayhawkers of Death Valley, 16
Johnson, Barbara, 159
Johnson, Eric, 7, 26, 27, 31, 32, *163*
Johnson, Jean, 8, 26
Johnson, LeRoy, xiii, xiv, 8, 26, 27, 30, 31, *82, 100, 123, 125, 127,* n45, n55
  maps drawn for this volume, 2, 22, 68, 73, 78, 88, 111
Johnson, Mark, 7, 26, 29, 31, 32, *163*
Johnson family, 7–8, 25, 26–32, 37, n21
Jones, Herman, n135
Joshua (cabbage) trees, 87, 89
Julia, Death Valley's Youngest Victim, 193

Kimball, D. D., n74
Kirkgaard, Lillie M., 12
Knight, Max E., 158
Koch, Fred W., n23
Koehn Lake, **88**, n105
Koenig, George, books
  Beyond This Place There Be Dragons, 21
  Valley of Salt, Memories of Wine, 158, n144
Koenig, George, interpretation of routes
  Devils Hole, n1
  Death Valley, n14, n23, n90, n144
  Panamint Range, 24, n35, n75, n153
  Slate vs. Argus Range, n36, n74
  Searles vs. Carricut Lake, n42
  Soledad vs. Bouquet Canyon, 21

La Brea tar pits, n114
Last Chance Canyon (El Paso Mountains), 42, **88**, 129, n51, n52, n105
Latta, Frank, 20
  Death Valley '49ers, 20, 192, 193, 194
Leach, Mary Reynolds, 193
Leach Lake, 165, n146
Life Sketches of a Jayhawker of '49, 15
Lilly, Ella (nee Johnson), 192
Literature review, 9–25. *See also* Manly accounts
  firsthand accounts, 10, 14–16
  secondhand accounts, 17–21

Long, Dr. Margaret
  analysis of the routes, 19
  Shadow of the Arrow, 19
Long camp. *See* Bennett's long camp
Los Angeles (Pueblo de Los Angeles), CA, 141, 168
Lummis, Charles F., 11

Mack, J. A., n74
Manley, xv, 199 *See also* Manly, William Lewis
Manly (Manley), Mary Jane (née Woods), 190, 199
Manly (Manley), William Lewis, 4, 6, *46,* 47–54, 149, 186, n171
  childhood, 47
  in Wisconsin, 48–51
  down Green River, 48
  approaches Death Valley, 53, 56, n1–n4
  in Death Valley, 38, 60–66, 173, n5, n6, n12
  trips out of Death Valley, 39–40, 67–98, 42–43, 116–139, 189–190. *See also* Bennett-Arcan escape route; Manly-Rogers first route out
  in Los Angeles, 143, 188
  life after Death Valley, 15, 20, 48, 188–191, 199, n39, n112, n172
  mining, 188
  return to Death Valley, n96, n109
  marriage, 190, 200, 202
  death, 190
  physical description, 48, 49
  spelling of his name, xv, 203
Manly accounts, xiv, 10–14, 16, 190. *See also Death Valley in 49;* "From Vermont to California"
  contradictions between, 12–13, 16–17, 195–196
  diary, 10
  1877 account, 10, 17
  long letter, 10, 188
  other letters, 10, 11, 13, 21
Manly Fall (Panamint Valley), 18, 20, 24, 29, 30
Manly Lookout (hill 7478, Panamint Range), 24, 28, 37, 39, 118, n32, n33, n122
  Death Valley named from, 42
  Indian camp on, 28
  quarter mile to, n91
  view from, 35, 70–71
Manly maps, 21–24, 202, n34, n42, n54, n56, n72
Manly Pass (Slate Range), 18, 19, 20, 31, 41, 42, 73, 183–184, n36, n42
Manly Peak (Panamint Range), 18, 24, 63, **68**, n25
Manly quoted, 5, 10, 11, 13, 32, 53, 55–143

Manly-Rogers first route out of Death Valley, 39–40, 67–98, **88**, 195, n26–n61
  analyzed by others, 18–23. *See also* Koenig, George, interpretation of routes
  prepare to go, 65–67
  across Panamint Range, 35, 39, 70–72, n27, n31–n33, n35, n36, n91, n122
  across Slate Range, 31, 39, 74–75, n37, n38, n40, n122
  across Searles Valley, 39, 76–77, n41, n42
  across Argus Range, 39, 77–80, n43, n122
  across Indian Wells Valley, 40, 80–84, n44–n47, n50
  across El Paso Mountains, 40, 85–86, n51
  across Mojave Desert, 40, 86–89, n52–n55
  Soledad Canyon, 40, 90–92, n56–n59
  at Rancho San Francisco, 40, 93–98, n61, n65
  meet Mr. French, 40, 96, n63
Manly-Rogers return route to Death Valley, 41, **68**, **73**, **78**, **88**, 99–108, 195, n68–n84
  find Culverwell's body, 41, 105, n79
  approach long camp, 41, 106–107, n80, n82, n83
  number of days gone, 17, n26, n78
Manly-Rogers escape with Bennett-Arcan families, **22**, 42, **68**, **73**, **78**, **88**, **111**, 116–137, *117*, 196, n90–n110. *See also* Bennett-Arcan escape route
  prepare to leave Death Valley, 112–115
  leave Death Valley, 42, 115–118
  over Panamint Range, 42, 116–121
  over Slate Range, 42, 121–122, n150
  over Argus Range, 42, 123–126, n150
  across Indian Wells Valley, 42, 127–129
  across the Mojave Desert, 43, 129–133
  at Barrel Spring, 43, 133
  down Soledad Canyon, 43, 134–137
  at Rancho San Francisco, 43, 138–140
  at Los Angeles, 141–143
  number of days, 17
Manly's writing assistant, 12–13, n53, n57, n59, n65, n82, n90, n91, n102
Maps, 21–24, 202. *See also* Farley, Minard H.; Frémont, John C.; Holt, Warren; Jayhawker map; Johnson, LeRoy; Manly maps; Mitchell's map; Palmer map; U.S. and California Boundary Com-